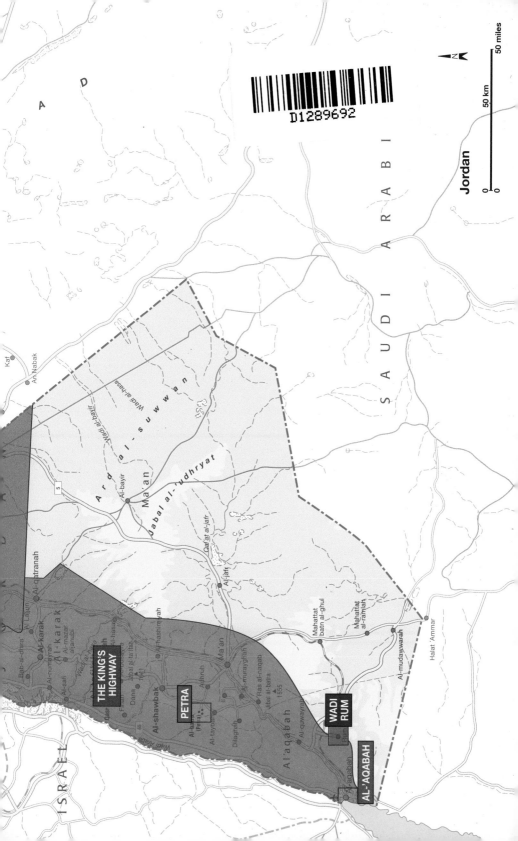

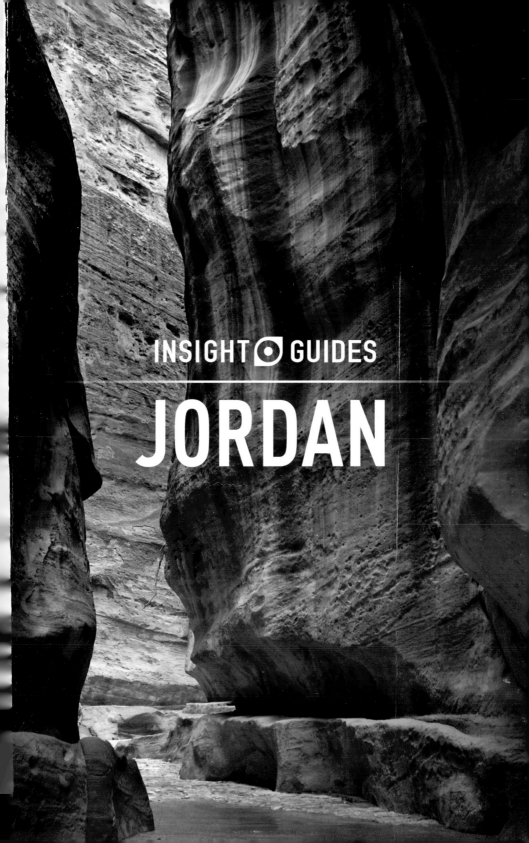

INSIGHT ⊙ GUIDES

JORDAN

Walking Eye App

YOUR FREE DESTINATION CONTENT AND EBOOK AVAILABLE THROUGH THE WALKING EYE APP

Your guide now includes a free eBook and destination content for your chosen destination, all for the same great price as before. Simply download the Walking Eye App from the App Store or Google Play to access your free eBook and destination content.

HOW THE WALKING EYE APP WORKS

Through the Walking Eye App, you can purchase a range of eBooks and destination content. However, when you buy this book, you can download the corresponding eBook and destination content for free. Just see below in the grey panels where to find your free content and then scan the QR code at the bottom of this page.

Destinations: Download your corresponding essential destination content from here, featuring recommended sights and attractions, restaurants, hotels and an A–Z of practical information, all for free. Other destinations are available for purchase.

Ships: Interested in ship reviews? Find independent reviews of river and ocean ships in this section, all available for purchase.

eBooks: You can download your free accompanying digital version of this guide here. You will also find a whole range of other eBooks, all available for purchase.

Free access to travel-related blog articles about different destinations, updated on a daily basis.

CONTENTS

HOW THE DESTINATION CONTENT WORKS

Each destination includes a short introduction, an A–Z of practical information and recommended points of interest, split into 4 different categories:
- Highlights
- Accommodation
- Eating out
- What to do

You can view the location of every point of interest and save it by adding it to your Favourites. In the 'Around Me' section you can view all the points of interest within 5km.

HOW THE EBOOKS WORK

The eBooks are provided in EPUB file format. Please note that you will need an eBook reader installed on your device to open the file. Many devices come with this as standard, but you may still need to install one manually from Google Play.

The eBook content is identical to the content in the printed guide.

HOW TO DOWNLOAD THE WALKING EYE APP

1. Download the Walking Eye App from the App Store or Google Play.
2. Open the app and select the scanning function from the main menu.
3. Scan the QR code on this page – you will then be asked a security question to verify ownership of the book.
4. Once this has been verified, you will see your eBook and destination content in the purchased ebook and destination sections, where you will be able to download them.

Other destination apps and eBooks are available for purchase separately or are free with the purchase of the Insight Guide book.

LEGEND
♀ Insight on
◎ Photo Story

THE BEST OF JORDAN: TOP ATTRACTIONS

△ **The Dead Sea**. Bobbing like a cork in the viscous waters of the Dead Sea is a must-do activity. Round the experience off with a massage or beauty treatment using Dead Sea mud in one of the luxury spa hotels. See page 198.

△ **Wadi Rum**. Lying a few kilometres south off the Desert Highway (Al-tariq al-sahrawi), this stunning landscape of soaring cliffs, pinnacles and desert dunes has inspired many travellers, including Lawrence of Arabia who made it famous. See page 245.

▽ **Jarash**. Jarash in northern Jordan is one of the best-preserved and most evocative Roman towns in the world. See page 173.

▽ **The Desert Castles**. East of Amman lies a string of Ummayad strongholds that served as pleasure palaces and hunting lodges. Don't miss the stunning frescoes at the Unesco World Heritage Site of Qusayr 'amrah. See page 272.

△ **Ma'daba**. Attractive and tranquil, Ma'daba contains one of the great treasures of the early Christian period: the Ma'daba Map. The earliest-known map of the Holy Land, it's just one of myriad ancient mosaics that litter the town. See page 208.

△ **Petra**. The famous rose-red, rock-cut city of the Nabataeans, hidden in a valley in southern Jordan, is a Unesco World Heritage Site and one of the Middle East's must-sees. See page 227.

△ **Dana Biosphere Reserve**. Lying in western-central Jordan, Dana is Jordan's largest, most diverse nature reserve. Hiking one of the beautiful trails makes a great break from the cities or Roman ruin trail. See page 219.

▽ **Al-'aqabah**. Jordan's only outlet to the sea is a springboard for diving and snorkelling among the Red Sea coral reefs. See page 259.

△ **Umm qays**. In Jordan's far north lie the impressive and atmospheric Roman ruins of Umm qays. See page 183.

▽ **Al-karak Castle**. As impressive for its vast walls and sturdy defences as its colourful and bloody history, Al-karak is one of the most fascinating crusader castles along the King's Highway. See page 213.

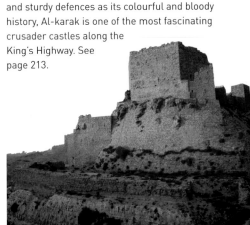

THE BEST OF JORDAN: EDITOR'S CHOICE

The road from Little Petra to Wadi Araba.

BEST BIBLICAL SITES

Jabal nibu (Mount Nebo). Identified as the site where Moses died and ascended to Heaven, Jabal nibu is marked by a Byzantine basilica. Also here is Ain Moussa, the so-called Spring of Moses. See page 207.

Sanctuary of Lot. A cave in the side of a hill near the Lisan Peninsula is where Lot and his daughters reputedly took refuge after the destruction of Sodom. See page 217.

Lot's Sanctuary.

The River Jordan. Bithani-beyond-the-Jordan, just north of the Dead Sea, is now widely regarded as the site of the baptism of Jesus. See page 196.

Mukawir. The wind-swept and haunting ruins of Mukawir are said to be the site where Salome performed her dance in exchange for the head of John the Baptist. See page 211.

Tel Mar Ilias. According to the Bible, this was where the Prophet Elijah was taken up to heaven in a chariot driven by horses of fire. See page 197.

Umm qays. This was Roman Gadara, overlooking the Sea of Galilee, where Jesus is reputed to have performed the miracle of the Gadarene swine. See page 183.

BEST LANDSCAPES

Wadi Rum. For sheer scale and spectacle, it's hard to beat the extraordinary Wadi Rum, described by T. E. Lawrence as "vast, echoing and godlike". See page 245.

Dana Biosphere Reserve. The 15th-century stone village of Dana is a springboard for treks through beautiful valleys and rocky desert. Look out for the ibex around Rummana Campsite. See page 219.

'Ajlun Forest Reserve. North of 'Ajlun Castle is a rolling landscape of juniper, oak, pistachio and strawberry tree forests, and, in spring, carpets of wild flowers. See page 181.

Wadi al-mujib. For spectacular vistas, drive along this valley as it plunges down some 900 metres (3,000ft). Better still, walk amid waterfalls and gorges in the Wadi al-mujib Nature Reserve. See page 212.

Petra. Take the Petra By Night Tour and see the tombs, monuments and cliffs lit up by the moon from above and thousands of candles from below. It's magical. See page 228.

View over Wadi al-mujib from the King's Highway.

TOP ARCHAEOLOGICAL SITES

Petra. The 1st-century, rock-cut tombs and temples of the Nabataeans are beautifully crafted and remarkably well preserved. See page 227.

Jarash. This once prosperous and powerful Roman city formed one of the principle cities of the Decapolis. Its highlights include mighty temples and the column-lined Cardo (Shari' kardu or main street). See page 173.

Pella. Nestling in the verdant Jordan Valley, Pella boasts not just Byzantine churches and early Islamic structures, but Bronze and Iron Age settlements and dolmens too. See page 193.

Umm qays. Less visited than Jarash but just as impressive, Umm qays has remarkable Roman ruins and a well-restored Ottoman village. See page 183.

'Abilah. Remote and little visited, the site boasts scattered churches, tombs and the remains of a theatre. See page 182.

BEST EXPERIENCES

Camp under the stars at Wadi Rum. Spend the night on desert dunes around a campfire in a Bedouin encampment. See page 246.

Dead Sea. Float in the salty waters, or smear thick, mineral-rich mud on yourself on the shoreline. See page 198.

Jarash Festival. Attend the arts festival held in the classical ruins in July. At other times of the year catch one of the regular displays of live chariot races and gladiatorial combat. See page 178.

Birdwatching. Jordan has several areas that are good for birdwatching, particularly the Azraq Wetlands and Dana Biosphere Reserve. See pages 103 and 219.

Biblical panorama. Spot the Sea of Galilee or the Golan Heights from Biblical Gadara (Umm qays), or do as Moses did and survey the Promised Land from the heights of Jabal nibu (Mount Nebo). See pages 183 and 207.

Follow in the footsteps of T. E. Lawrence. Visit the castle at Qasr al-azraq and ride by camel in the magical landscape of Wadi Rum. See pages 277 and 246.

Azraq Wetland Reserve.

BEST ADVENTURES

Dive off Al-'aqabah. Al-'aqabah's Red Sea dive sites are unspoilt, easily accessible and diverse, offering wrecks, coral gardens and unusual fauna such as sea horses. Snorkel, scuba or take a glass-bottomed boat. See page 266.

Horse riding. Much the best way to take in the magisterial landscapes of Wadi Rum or Petra. See page 246.

Camel safaris. Join a one-day, three-day or week-long safari through Wadi Rum. Tours can be booked at the Visitor Centre in Rum. See page 246.

Canyoning in Wadi al-mujib. This river valley provides an exciting playground of torrents, pools and waterfalls. See page 112.

Rock climbing in Wadi Rum. Permitted in several areas of Wadi Rum, it is best organised through one of the specialised local guides in advance, or through Rum's Visitor Centre. See page 246.

Hiking to Petra. For an experience never forgotten, consider arranging or joining an organised trek from Shawbak, a distance of around 80km (50 miles), staying in Bedouin tents en route. See page 220.

Camel riding in Wadi Rum.

Sunset over the Dead Sea.

Al-Husseni mosque, downtown Amman.

Bedouin camp near Little Petra.

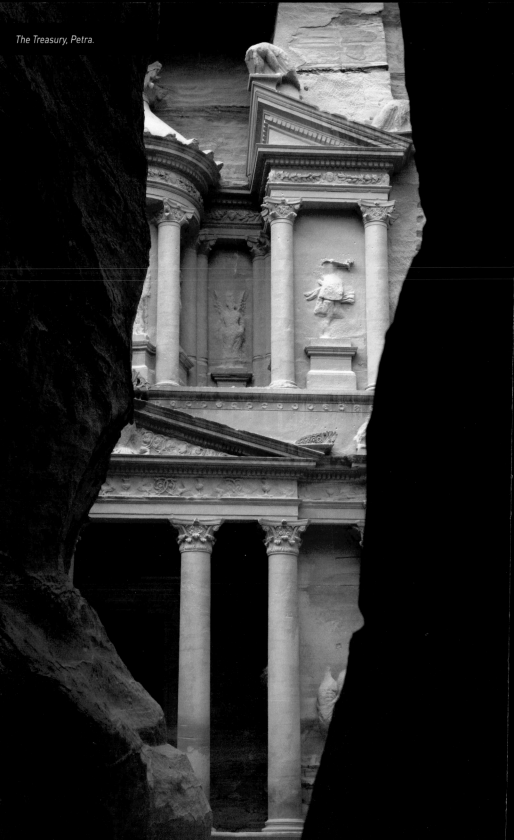

The Treasury, Petra.

WELCOME TO JORDAN

Jordan combines the best qualities of the region – legendary hospitality, breathtaking desert landscapes – with unique attractions of its own, from unspoilt Red Sea reefs to stunning monuments of ancient civilisations.

Bedouins and their camp fire in Wadi Rum.

Petra, Jordan's most famous attraction and a Unesco World Heritage Site, is quite simply one of the world's "must sees". Even if you've visited before, Petra never fails to awe, due in part to the wonderful sense of arrival after the walk along the narrow corridor-like *siq*. Visitors suddenly emerge face to face with one of the world's most magical buildings: the Treasury, rose-pink, carved straight out of the rock.

Hot on the heels of Petra's masters, the Nabataeans, and eyeing the trade routes which made them prosperous, were the Romans. They came, saw and conquered, but also left a legacy of their own: wealthy cities that can still be walked around today. Their metropolises comprise not just the monumental gates and temples that can be seen in other parts of the world, but baths, shops and theatres too. Few places in the world conjure up daily Roman life so evocatively as they do at the Jordanian sites of Jarash, Umm qays and others.

South Theatre at Jarash.

Amman, Jordan's lively capital, boasts its own Roman treasures – a remarkable and well-preserved Citadel, Odeon and theatre – where visitors would linger much longer if they weren't lured away by attractions outside the city.

The Jordan Valley, part of the famous "Fertile Crescent", the cradle of all civilisations, has long seen peoples come and go. Stone tools found at the ancient site of Pella testify to settlement over 800,000 years ago. Since then, merchants, conquerors and occupiers have passed through, including names familiar from the Bible: the Canaanites, Hittites and Amorites, and later, Egyptians, Assyrians, Babylonians, Persians, Macedonians, Romans, Byzantines, Crusaders, Arabs and Ottomans... Of this litany of peoples, many have left visible marks, including the dramatic crusader castles of Al-karak and Shawbak, or the more recreational Ummayad desert castles in Jordan's east.

In contrast to the "cultural concentration" found in the fertile Jordan Valley, is the vast and sparsely populated desert hinterland spreading eastwards and southwards. Distinct geographically, it is also different historically and ethnically too. Largely ignored by the merchants and powers of the past who fought for control of the cities, settled areas and lucrative trade routes, the Bedouin tribes of the desert were left to get on with what they did best: eking out a living from the desert – and war.

Hoping to harness the fearsome reputation of these Arab tribes during World War I was a British soldier: Lawrence of Arabia. Today, slightly ironically, it is largely due to T.E. Lawrence's writings that Wadi Rum is one of the most visited sites in Jordan.

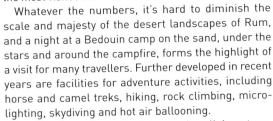

Whatever the numbers, it's hard to diminish the scale and majesty of the desert landscapes of Rum, and a night at a Bedouin camp on the sand, under the stars and around the campfire, forms the highlight of a visit for many travellers. Further developed in recent years are facilities for adventure activities, including horse and camel treks, hiking, rock climbing, microlighting, skydiving and hot air ballooning.

With a momentum all of its own is religious tourism, boosted by the quite recent, international consensus that Bithani-beyond-the-Jordan is indeed the site of Jesus's baptism and Pope John Paul II's visit

Azraq Wetland Reserve.

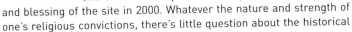

and blessing of the site in 2000. Whatever the nature and strength of one's religious convictions, there's little question about the historical and emotional significance of some of Jordan's extraordinary biblical sites. You can gaze over the Holy Land as Moses did at Jabal nibu (Mount Nebo), dance in Herod's palace as Salome dared do at Mukawir, and even be baptised in the River Jordan as Jesus was.

Under further development too are Jordan's remarkable conservation plans. With seven nature reserves already established and seven more in the making, it's now possible to overnight in delightful eco-lodges and camps around the country. Thanks to successful programmes of captive breeding, beautiful native animals such as the oryx are now on the increase again and will soon be reintroduced into the wild.

Sayadiya, a local speciality of fish and rice.

It's not all good news, however. Jordan is beset by high unemployment and price rises, an under-developed and stagnant economy, water-supply issues and slow political reform. Almost completely surrounded by the Middle East Crisis, Jordan has escaped the fate of its conflict-ridden neighbours, but problems in the region – the Syrian Civil War, the presence of ISIL, Israeli-Palestinian unrest and the refugee crisis – continue to threaten Jordan's stability, and tourist figures have dropped dramatically since 2011.

Meanwhile, the reaction of the ordinary Jordanian is a shrug of the shoulders, a resigned "It's God's will" with a wry smile and the offer to visitors of a mint-infused cup of tea. In this region, after all, "a guest is a gift from God". *Bismillah* – enjoy.

Gazing out over the Dead Sea.

THE JORDANIANS

Jordan is a conservative country where ancient pride runs deep, old allegiances matter and fortunes are forged by fate.

Take a pinch of Bedouin from the desert wadis, combine with the country folk and villagers of the Jordan Valley, add a dash of shrewd city merchants and traders, a sprinkling of Armenian artisans, Druze mountain men, Circassian farmers, Kurdish settlers and Bahai gentlemen, then mix in at least 2 million Palestinian refugees, over 500,000 Iraqis, 656,000 Syrian refugees (with some sources placing the figure much higher) and thousands of Egyptians, Libyans and other Arabs, and you begin to have some idea of Jordan's rich ethnic mix.

Meanwhile, many "original" Jordanians live outside the country. For years, Jordan received most of its financial capital through remittances from expatriates working in the wealthy Gulf states or in developing Arab countries such as Yemen, Oman and Sudan.

Jordan's extraordinary cultural and ethnic multiplicity, as well as its relatively flexible political, cultural and legal infrastructure, have made it unique in the region. In few other countries have Muslim revisionists and Westernised Arabs lived side by side so peacefully. Lying east of the biblical river that gave the country its name, Jordan is home to the full spectrum of Muslim and Christian sects, though the vast majority of people (around 95 percent) belong to the Sunni branch of Islam – which goes some way to explaining why Jordan hasn't suffered the same religious tensions as other nations in the region. Jordan's population is also relatively educated: the country boasts the highest number of university graduates per capita in the Arab world.

CONSERVATIVE SOCIETY

Land locked and isolated from the sea – bar a single outlet in the form of Al-'aqabah in the far

Bedouin tea comprises special blends made with desert plants.

southwestern tip – Jordan's people are conservative both by nature and tradition. Even within the Arab world, Jordanians are known for their introverted character. Reserved they can be, at least when first meeting strangers, but like their neighbours in the Middle East, they are also known for their extraordinary hospitality: *marhaba* and *ahlan wa-sahlan*, variations on "welcome", are refrains that the visitor will hear constantly. Hardly a day passes without an invitation to drink tea, coffee or eat at someone's shop or home. If ever in need of help, such as when seeking directions, Jordanians will compete with one another to offer help and advice. Instead of just giving directions, they'll take you there in person.

BEDOUIN HERITAGE

Amman, the largest and most populated city in Jordan, containing over 2.5 million people, is one of the most vibrant, liberal and culturally diverse cities in the Arab world. But scratch the surface of this modern city and you will soon find ancient Bedouin pride and old allegiances.

Even people born in Amman are likely to identify with the town from which their families come, and when asked will claim they are from, say, Al-salt, Jerusalem or Nablus rather than from Amman.

Musicians in Amman's upmarket neighbourhood Jabal Amman.

People also identify with the relationship that their forefathers had to the land, and will continue to refer to themselves as *fellahin*, meaning farmers or villagers; *Bedu*, meaning Bedouin; or *madanieen*, meaning city folk, depending on their origin and irrespective of their present circumstances.

The same regard for heritage is found in the reverence still paid to Jordan's Bedouin population, the country's indigenous inhabitants. Clan and family ties carry weight not only regionally but also in Amman. Many parties and organisations are still based on clan allegiance or identification, and six of the 80 seats in Parliament (Al-barlman) are reserved for Bedouin leaders, in fact making them over-represented.

The Bedouin warrior and warmongering past sometimes manifests itself in a querulous, fractious nature. In 2012, two Jordanian politicians famously came to blows during a live TV interview, when one pulled a gun on the other.

REGIONAL DIFFERENCES

Although Jordan is relatively small in area (about the size of Portugal), it has marked regional differences. Amman's neighbour Al-salt, for example, lying just 45 minutes to the west is, in contrast to the capital, traditionally hostile to outsiders, and its conservative, closed character is mirrored by its enclosing mountains, which protect the Al-saltis and bar the stranger.

THE NORTH

Northerners – including the residents of Jarash, the industrial town of Al-zarqa' and the university city of Irbid – have a different history from the people of the south. Influenced by Damascene culture and outlook, northerners are considered shrewder and more business-oriented than their southern compatriots. There are physical and psychological differences too: they are frequently fairer and taller, betraying Syrian origins, and are known for their cool heads and sharp tongues as well as the beauty of their women. Their cultural affiliation with Syria since the 19th century has also influenced their social and political outlook.

Irbid and Jarash have also witnessed a large influx of Palestinians, who play a major role in the political and cultural life of the north.

THE SOUTH

The most significant town in southern Jordan is Al-karak, whose people claim descent from migrants from the West Bank town of Hebron up to 400 years ago. Like the Hebronites, many Al-karakis are light-skinned and fair-haired, reflecting their Crusader ancestors. The majority are Muslims, but the town is also home to one of the most prominent Christian populations in Jordan. Almost exclusively of Arab origin, the Al-karaki Christians are believed to make up one of the oldest Christian communities in the world.

Ma'an, for centuries an important commercial centre on the north–south trade route, retains its links with transport to this day. Over 90 percent of its male population work in the transport sector. Traditionally conservative and independent-minded, Ma'an has been the scene of anti-government riots in the past (such as following the economic downturn in 1989), which is believed to have led indirectly to a nationwide demand for political and economic reform.

WORK AND WAGES

Around 50 percent of Jordan's workforce is government-employed. Salaries are low: a newly qualified graduate teacher or a less-educated civil servant with 10–15 years' experience would both earn about US$350 a month, while an assistant professor at the University of Jordan may receive a salary in the region of US$700, although this would come with a raft of benefits, such as cheap health care, subsidised shopping facilities and a social-security system including a pension plan.

Meanwhile, with a nationwide surfeit of professional labour, an influx of often well-educated refugees from many countries of the Arab world, and a major downturn in the economy (see page 72), unemployment is high at around 15 percent. All over Jordan, visitors will see men of all ages sitting unoccupied outside cafés.

Meanwhile, the cost of living in Jordan is not cheap. In an attempt to introduce long-overdue economic reform, the government ended subsidies, and this, combined with other national and international economic factors, sent the cost of basic goods and services, including fuel, sharply rising. Accommodation is also expensive. Rent on even a small flat in a cheap area outside Amman (which is much dearer) is at least US$200 a month. As a consequence, many people, especially civil servants, have two jobs. Typical moonlighting takes the form of supermarket work, estate agency work or driving taxis.

Portrait of a girl from Al-karak.

⊘ JORDANIAN MUSIC

Music has been played around Bedouin campfires for millennia, often in the form of poetry accompanied by a stringed instrument such as the ancient *rababah* that praised God or nature, rallied warriors to battle, celebrated victories or served to flatter a leader. The tradition continues today in the songs of flattery sung at weddings, or patriotic songs to mark national ceremonies or occasions. Verses are often improvised on the spot and musicians win kudos for their ingenuity and quick wit. Other traditional instruments include the oud, *arghul*, *tablah* and reed pipe. A popular Bedouin singer is Omar al Abdallat. Other famous composers and musicians include Khalid Asad, Sameer Baghdadi and Hani Mitwasi.

Meanwhile, Jordan's modern music scene is vibrant and ever-changing. Amman is the hub of modern music and boasts a thriving alternative music scene as well as rock, heavy metal, jazz, indie, hip hop and, current favourite in bars and nightclubs, house. Private raves and underground techno events are organised in and around Amman. Different genres of music are also often fused. Big pop names currently include Dania Karazon, a Jordanian-Palestinian singer and winner of *Superstar* (the Arabic version of *Pop Idol*) and Zade Dirani, who has performed around the world. Among the most successful bands currently is the New Age group RUM, with an impressive national and international following.

VALUES AND MORAL CODES

In traditional Bedouin culture, family and family values were paramount. This is still the case in Jordanian society today and underlies an unspoken but strict moral code. Over the years, consecutive waves of political refugees, used to a more liberal climate in Palestine, Lebanon and more recently Iraq, Egypt, Syria and Libya, have had to adapt: prostitution rings have been closed down, public drunkenness is not tolerated and gambling is against the law – a jurisdiction that has in fact won widespread popular support. Even belly-dancing is confined to the large hotels.

Reflecting the strict moral climate, Jordan's crime rate is low. Murder is, in around 25 percent of cases, a so-called "crime of honour", especially in cities, and is usually to do with women allegedly flouting sexual taboos.

SUPERSTITIONS

Though Islam plays a prominent role in the lives of the great majority of Jordan's Muslims, superstition and belief in the supernatural is still rife, leftovers from pre-Islamic, pre-Christian paganism.

When a person falls ill or has an accident, it is believed to be a result of *rire* (jealousy) and *hassad* (envy) on the part of another. To dispel the malevolence or "evil eye", incense is burned, a lamb is sometimes offered to the poor, or a blue medallion (often bearing an evil eye – deflecting like with like) is worn or hung in the home or car.

If a person is believed to be afflicted by the evil eye, it is common to send them incense or readings from the Holy Qur'an or Bible. Silver plaques with verses from holy books promising fertility, luck, health and a long life also commonly guard the bedside of many a Jordanian child. Jordanian women often consult *fattaha* (openers) who read their fortune in the residue of a cup of coffee.

Schoolchildren board a bus in Amman.

⊘ JORDAN'S REFUGEES

Jordan has long provided a sanctuary for displaced peoples. Some say the refugees, numbering now in the millions, explain the Jordanian coolness towards newcomers. Though the Palestinians on the whole have received sympathy for their plight (though political tensions are increasingly bubbling), there has been some resentment at others. The civil war in Syria has brought the most recent influx of refugees to test Jordan's infrastructure. As of 2017, Jordan hosted over 656,000 Syrian refugees, although authorities effectively closed the Syrian-Jordanian border to new entries in 2016, leaving thousands of Syrian refugees stranded in remote border regions with little access to aid.

A WOMAN'S PLACE

In common with the rest of the Middle East, Jordan is still very much a patriarchal society and public life is still very male-dominated. While women have tentatively started to have a role in political life, with a 2015 cabinet reshuffle including a record five female ministers, in 2016 the figure was reduced to only two – a decision viewed as extremely disappointing by female activists. In the minds of most Jordanians however, a woman's role is as a wife and mother. Those who do have jobs are employed mainly in teaching, which comprises 38 percent of the labour force, and nursing, which forms approximately 16 percent. Statistics reveal that about seven out of 10 women in Jordan do not enter the labour force – or are not given the opportunity – in spite of the fact that 84 percent of women are well educated. A

> *Male circumcision is an important Muslim ritual. In the past, it took place at the age of 13, usually at the hand of the local barber, and was followed by a big celebration. Today almost all baby boys are circumcised in hospital soon after birth.*

recent, more encouraging phenomenon – and one supported and often backed by the government – is the mushrooming of co-operatives around the country, in which communities of (often disadvantaged) women come together to make and sell good-quality traditional crafts (see page 89).

According to the Jordanian Constitution, men and women have "equal rights". However, civil law and ingrained prejudice against women often undermines this. It wasn't until 1998, for example, that women finally gained the right to carry their own passports without the permission of husbands or male "guardians", and they are still unable to pass Jordanian citizenship down to their children. Meanwhile, a much darker tradition still survives in Jordan, despite attempts to eradicate it. Jordan's law still absolves from due punishment a husband or close male relative who kills a woman caught in adultery, or commits a crime – even murder – in a "fit of rage". According to official statistics, on average around 15–20 of these so-called honour killings occur every year (campaigns against the practice claim the number is far higher and on the rise), and are catalysed not just by acts of adultery, but by young women refusing an arranged marriage, fleeing or leaving a husband, having sex outside marriage or just bringing shame upon the family. Even victims of sexual violence, including rape, have been killed in the past.

While women remain inadequately protected against sexual and other forms of violence, pressure is mounting on Jordan to address issues of women's rights and the problem of honour killings. A small step was taken in 2017 when parliament abolished a law that allowed rapists to avoid punishment by marrying their victims.

The great majority of Jordan's Muslim women wear a hijab (veil). If you see non-veil-wearing women, in wealthy areas of Amman such as 'Abdun, for example, or in the city of Ma'daba, most likely they'll be Christian. Westerners often equate the veil with male dominance and female submission. In fact, the decision to don the headwear can carry far more subtle nuances, and can have as much to do with personal fulfilment as politics and a rejection of Western imperialism. In the aftermath of the war in neighbouring Lebanon, for example, and the eight-year Iran–Iraq War, people often looked to religion in search of meaning, peace

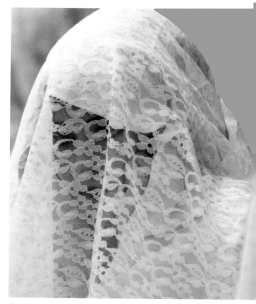

Ready for the big day.

⊘ HOME AND FAMILY

Homes are traditionally constructed so that floors can be added when the sons of the family marry, resulting in three- or four-storey homes accommodating extended families, who dine and socialise together.

As well as making good economic sense, this system of family cohabitation helps with the division of labour. Grandparents act as babysitters and daughters-in-law nurse ageing parents. Daughters-in-laws' roles tend to be confined to the house, where they do most of the cooking, although all female family members normally participate in kitchen-related duties.

Jordan used to have one of the highest birth rates in the world, and families still have five or six children.

of mind and direction. Many women turned away from their former ostentatious Arab style of dress to a more modest garb.

MARRIAGE AND DIVORCE

As in other Arab countries, getting married in Jordan is the most important event in life. In terms of cost, it is second only to buying a home, and today, men from the middle- and lower-income groups often do not marry until their thirties because they cannot afford to.

Many marriages are still the result of family introductions, if not outright matches made by female members of the future bride's and/or groom's family. Increasingly, upper-middle-class Jordanians and well-heeled city dwellers usually court one another in a Western fashion and marriage is rarely forced upon an unwilling couple. An eligible groom should typically have a respected family lineage, wealth, education, be of the same religion as the bride and should be marrying for the first time. The same applies for the bride, but she must also be virtuous. The dowry required for meeting such conditions can be vast; traditionally, the dowry for the bride's family consisted of presents equivalent to the bride's weight in gold.

About one in five marriages currently ends in divorce, though in half of these cases, separation occurs during the period between the signing of the legal contract and consummation, the time when the couple are "preparing to live together". Though legally married, couples don't usually consummate their marriage until the night of the "wedding party", often as much as a year later.

Like most Islamic countries, Jordan's legal system used to allow only men to file for divorce, but women now have the same right.

Divorce for women still carries a stigma and until recently – and still in most rural areas – many divorcees did not remarry, instead returning to their parental homes or to that of their nearest living male relative, on whom they then depend for their economic survival. Women rarely live alone.

Teenagers wearing hijabs in Ma'daba.

⊙ BIRTH AND DEATH

Once married, a woman's primary role is to produce children. The birth of a child is considered the happiest of all occasions and money and time are invested in preparing for the new arrival. Guests stop by with gifts and food before the due date, and once baby has arrived safe and well, there will often be a big feast with the traditional grilled lamb. The mother's family is responsible for providing the child's first wardrobe and furniture. A male is almost always preferred as a first child and a woman with many sons is considered more powerful than a woman with daughters. Jordanian mothers spoil sons; girls tend to be independent at an earlier age. But children of both sexes are treasured, and their education is highly valued.

When a death occurs, the *aza* (condolence period) is another important ritual during which respects are paid to the immediate family of the deceased. It is considered a social obligation to attend the *aza* of a neighbour or colleague, and even relations of neighbours, colleagues, business contacts and in-laws. It takes place in the home of the deceased or that of a relative. Men and women sit in separate rooms – sexual segregation is practised at both Muslim and Christian *azas* – and black, unsweetened Arabic coffee is served. For 40 days after a death, an *aza* is reopened every Monday and Thursday. The traditional colour of mourning in Jordan is black with a white headscarf.

THE ROYAL FAMILY

Jordan's royal family have always played a key role in the national and international affairs of the country.

When the young King Husayn assumed his constitutional duties on 2 May 1953, his love of flying, motorcycling, water sports and racing-car driving generated a rather adventurous and daring image in the Western press. He was frequently portrayed as the dashing young Arab monarch, who bridged the ways of the Orient and the Occident, and was as comfortable talking to presidents of NATO member states as to Bedouin tribal leaders at home.

King Husayn recognised early on that despite the sentimental and political appeal of mid-20th-century pan-Arab ideology, the key to the survival of Jordan and its royal family was the improvement of people's daily living conditions, establishing a sense of national and political identity, and creating hope and security for the future.

The king was also careful to continue the great Bedouin tradition of the *majlis*: remaining accessible to one's people and receiving their complaints, suggestions and personal requests through both formal gatherings and more informal encounters. In theory, every Jordanian is entitled to take his grievance to the king; in practice, requests for a meeting with the king will be granted occasionally.

Personal charisma was an important element of King Husayn's success, and his son, King Abdullah II, is credited with having at least some of the same quality. He continues to be seen to play the traditional paternal role of looking after his subjects' welfare, in going up in a helicopter after a bad snowstorm or rainfall to check on hard-hit areas, or paying personal condolences at the homes of Jordanians who have died in the line of duty.

Born in Amman in 1962 to Princess Muna (aka Toni Gardiner, Husayn's English-born second wife), Abdullah II trained at Sandhurst military academy in England. He is married to Queen Rania, a Palestinian from a prominent family with roots in the West Bank town of Tulkarm; the couple have four children.

Along with the king, some two dozen princes and princesses carry out public duties. Several, meanwhile, pursue careers in private business or the armed forces, and many provide patronage for, or actively participate in, charitable activities.

Whilst still a princess, Queen Rania created the Jordan River Foundation (JRF) (see page 89), which focuses on children's welfare and youth issues as well as women's needs, the arts, rural development and the environment. Today, royal family members are quite often seen leading charity walks or participating in sports and cultural activities, mixing easily and casually with what they always refer to as "the Jordanian family". This was epitomised by the marriage in 2012

King Abdullah II and Queen Rania of Jordan in London.

of Prince Hamzah, Abdullah's half-brother, to a commoner, subsequently Princess Basmah, whom he met through their common interest in flying. The couple now have three children.

Before his death, King Husayn spoke of fulfilling the goals of the Great Arab Revolt by transforming Jordan into a credible example of an Arab/Islamic state based on democratic pluralism and respect for human rights.

Respect for elders and leaders has always formed an integral part of traditional Bedouin culture and this is reflected today in the respect and affection Jordanians genuinely hold for their royal family. However, in light of recent challenges (see page 72), it is clear that the monarchy can't rely any more on personal charm, autocracy, the support of the military or foreign aid and loans: the future stability and welfare of both Jordan and the royal family lie in dramatic economic and political reform.

DECISIVE DATES

9000 BC
First inhabitants settle on the West Bank of the Jordan River near modern Jericho.

3000–1550 BC
Early Bronze Age; Amorites and Canaanites arrive in modern-day Jordan.

c.1280 BC
Moses leads Israelites out of Egypt; 40 years later they settle east of the Jordan River.

c.1225 BC
Joshua captures Jericho; Palestine is divided among the 12 tribes of Israel.

c.1000 BC
David is proclaimed King of the Israelites; he conquers Jerusalem and makes it his capital.

960–922 BC
Reign of Solomon; he expands kingdom through treaties and marriages, and builds the first Temple in Jerusalem. The kingdom is divided on his death into Judah in the south and Israel to the north.

722 BC
Assyrians, led by Sargon II, destroy the Kingdom of Israel, replacing the inhabitants with settlers from Syria and Babylonia.

612 BC
Babylonian Army under Medes captures Nineveh, the Assyrian capital.

597–587 BC
Jerusalem, Palestine and Jordan fall to the Babylonian King Nebuchadnezzar.

538 BC
Nabataeans establish a kingdom based at Petra in southern Jordan.

332–1 BC
Alexander the Great conquers Syria, Palestine and Egypt.

323 BC
Alexander dies and his Middle Eastern domain is divided between his top generals. Ptolemy I is given Egypt and parts of Syria, and Seleucus is granted Babylon.

198 BC
The Seleucid Army under Antiochus III defeats the Ptolemies' Army; both states are consolidated under Seleucid control.

64 BC
Damascus falls to Pompey.

63 BC
Palestine falls to Pompey's Roman Army and is renamed Judaea.

63 BC–AD 106
The Decapolis, or the League of 10 Cities, is formed in the area.

40 BC
Parthian kings of Persia and Mesopotamia invade the Decapolis; Roman Mark Antony leads the army which repels them.

106
Nabataean Kingdom incorporated into the Roman Empire.

325
Roman emperor Constantine converts to Christianity.

525–565
The reign of Justinian. Churches are built at Christian holy sites.

629
Christians and Muslims battle for the first time near Al-karak; Muhammad takes Mecca.

638
Jerusalem falls to Muslim Arabs.

The Dead Sea scrolls at the Jordan Museum in Amman.

Mosaic dating from AD 597 in the museum at Mount Nebo.

642
Arabs conquer Egypt.

658
Omayyad Dynasty founded in Damascus. A brilliant period in arts and architecture ensues.

750
Omayyads are overthrown by the Abbasids, who move the caliphate to Baghdad.

1095
Pope Urban II launches the first Crusade to retake Jerusalem from the Muslims.

1099
Crusaders establish a kingdom in Jerusalem, and build fortresses in Jordan and Syria.

1250
Mamlukes take power in Cairo. They eventually rule over an area from Egypt to Syria.

1516
Syria and Palestine are absorbed into the Ottoman Empire.

1909
Revolt by the Young Turks in Istanbul encourages nationalism among populations under Ottoman rule.

1914–18
World War I; Ottoman Empire sides with Germany.

1916
The Arab Revolt. The Arab Pan-nationalist Movement, under Emir Feisal's leadership, joins forces with the British to drive out Ottoman Turks.

1917
British troops occupy Jerusalem and Al-'aqabah.

1920
The Conference of San Remo reconfirms the 1916 Sykes-Picot agreement, denying the Arabs an independent state and giving Britain a mandate to rule Palestine, and France authority over Syria and Lebanon.

1923
Britain recognises Transjordan's independence under its protection, with Abdullah, Feisal's brother, as its king. The Arab Legion is formed under a British officer, J.B. Glubb (Glubb Pasha).

Depiction of Crusaders bombarding Nicaea in 1097.

1939–45
World War II; Jordan offers its Arab Legion to fight with the Allies.

1946
Britain gives up mandate. Transjordan becomes an independent monarchy.

1947
United Nations vote to partition Palestine; Hashemite Kingdom of Jordan is created.

1948
Britain's mandate over Palestine expires; State of Israel proclaimed; the first Arab–Israeli war begins as the last British troops depart.

1950
King Abdullah I formally annexes the West Bank and East Jerusalem into his kingdom.

1951
Abdullah is assassinated at Al-Aqsa Mosque in Jerusalem.

1952
Husayn becomes king at 17 after his father, Abdullah's son Talal, is declared mentally unstable.

1955
Jordan becomes a member of the United Nations; Egypt nationalises the Suez Canal.

1960
Iraqi Government overthrown; Palestinians, with Egypt's backing, try to depose King Husayn, who offers citizenship to all Palestinian refugees.

1964
The Palestine Liberation Organisation (PLO) and its more militant cousin, Al-Fatah, are formed.

Allied Arab Legion soldiers fire at Jewish fighters in Jerusalem, 1948, during the first Arab-Israeli conflict.

1967
The Six-Day War between Israel and the Arab armies leaves Jordan devastated. Jerusalem and the West Bank are lost.

1969
Yasser Arafat is elected chairman of the PLO.

1970
King Husayn clamps down on the PLO's growing power, culminating in Black September. The civil war between local Palestinians and the government routs the PLO.

1974
King Husayn recognises the PLO as the sole representative of the Palestinian people.

1988
King Husayn gives up legal and administrative claims to Jerusalem and the West Bank.

1989
Prices rise for basic staples, as dictated by the IMF as part of an economic recovery package for Jordan. Bread riots ensue. In Ma'an, 11 die.

1990
Iraq invades Kuwait, backed by large sections of Jordan's population. Around 300,000 Palestinian refugees arrive in Jordan.

1992
Israeli–Palestinian peace talks begin in Madrid. Law passed legalising all political parties.

1993
Jordan's first multi-party democratic elections are held.

1994
Jordan and Israel sign a peace treaty.

1998
A peace deal is struck between Yasser Arafat and Israeli prime minister, Binyamin Netanyahu.

1999
King Husayn dies of cancer, having nominated his eldest son, Abdullah, as his successor in place of his brother Hassan, Crown Prince for 33 years.

2000
Camp David peace talks with Israel breakdown; Palestinian intifada erupts in the West Bank.

2002
Jordan and Israel agree a joint plan to pipe water from the Red Sea to the Dead Sea.

2005
Amman returns its ambassador to Tel Aviv after more than four years of suspended diplomacy during the intifada. In November, Al Qaeda suicide bombers attack three hotels in Amman, killing 60 people and wounding 115 others. It's the first terrorist attack on Jordanian soil.

2008
State subsidies on petrol and other consumer goods end, causing prices to spiral (by up to 76 percent for fuel).

2009
Pope Benedict XVI visits the Holy Land and controversially calls for the creation of two states, Israel and Palestine. In November, the king dissolves

The Jordanian prime minister, Hani Al-Mulki (3rd from left) at the Jerash Festival in 2017.

Parliament and appoints a new government to push through economic reform.

2010
November elections are boycotted by the Islamist opposition in protest at "unfair electoral laws". Nearly a dozen seats are won by women.

2011
Street protests demanding reform lead King Abdullah to sack his government. Clashes between government supporters and opponents in Amman mark the "Arab Spring". Fresh waves of immigrants arrive from Libya and Egypt.

2012
Jordan braces itself for further waves of immigration from Syria. King Abdullah recalls parliament to amend electoral law. The IMF promises a US$2bn credit package to Amman over the next three years, a move thought to reflect Western

concerns about stability in the region.

2014
Growing regional instability due to the emergence of the Islamic State of Iraq and Levant (ISIL), with approximately 2,000 Jordanian fighters. Jordan executes 11 murder convicts, ending its 2006 moratorium on capital punishment.

2016
Ten people killed in terrorist attack, later claimed by ISIL, in the town of Al-karak. Proportional representation reintroduced to parliament in the general election; King Abdullah appoints Hani Al-Mulki as prime minister. Jordan effectively closes its borders to Syrian refugees.

2017
Jordan hangs 15 people, including 10 convicted of terror charges. Parliament repeals law that allows rapists to escape punishment by marrying their victims.

Ma'daba's 6th-century mosaic map of the Holy Land.

AN ANCIENT LAND

The early history of Jordan is one of migration and trade, cities founded and fought over and the creation of no fewer than three world religions.

Abraham had departed for Egypt to escape the tribal anarchy and famine that had plagued the region. Not long after, people began to settle in the Jordan Valley. Egypt was on the point of building an empire, and as the imperial frontier pushed towards Mesopotamia, the area it encompassed benefited from unprecedented, if less than perfect, law and order. Bedouin tribes remained a law unto themselves, but urban development took root at Ma'daba in the plain of Moab and at Jarash in the mountains of Gilead.

> "A frightful desert, almost wholly without vegetation," was late 18th-century Swiss explorer Johann Burckhardt's summation of Moses' wilderness. Burckhardt went on to rediscover Petra.

Sixth-century manuscript showing the flight of Lot and the destruction of Sodom.

Under the umbrella of Egyptian security, it was a natural step for nomads to exchange their peripatetic existence for permanent homes, and for a host of petty kingdoms to emerge, including Edom (of which today's Petra lies at the heart) and Moab, of which modern-day Al-karak formed part.

SODOM AND GOMORRAH

The whereabouts of Sodom and Gomorrah is more problematic. By tradition, these proverbial cities of sin were consumed in Abraham's lifetime by a storm of fire and brimstone whose ashes were deposited at the bottom of the Dead Sea. Old maps invariably showed them under fathoms of water but still engulfed in flames. In recent years, divers laden with extra weights to counter the excessive buoyancy of the water have scoured the sea bed without success, but various academic theories have put the site of the cities on the Plain of Jordan and the shores of the Dead Sea, including Bab ad Dhraa (Bab al-dhira'). Scholars favouring the Lisan Peninsula, which juts into the sea below the mountains of Moab in the east, have been encouraged by the fairly recent discovery of a necropolis containing some 20,000 tombs, many apparently untouched since 2500 BC.

THE EXODUS

By 1280 BC, the Israelites had outstayed their welcome in Egypt and embarked on the Exodus under Moses. The direct route lay through Edom, but in spite of Moses' promise not to veer left or right from the beaten track of the King's Highway, the Edomites refused to allow him and his party through their territory. The detour amounted to 40 years in the wilderness before the weary refugees were able to climb Jabal nibu (Mount Nebo) in Moab and survey the Promised Land. Moses died in Moab without ever crossing to the west bank of the Jordan. He was buried in a valley "over against Bethpeor: but no man knoweth of his sepulchre unto this day." While the location of his grave remains a mystery, there is general agree-

Moses surveying the Promised Land from Mount Nebo.

ment among experts today that Jabal nibu is one of three possible peaks, about 10km (6 miles) west of Ma'daba, where Moses could have been buried.

THE PROMISED LAND

The Israelites had to fight their fellow Semites for a place in the Promised Land. Battles took place everywhere; the most interesting on Jordanian territory was probably fought at Rabbath Ammon (now Amman), the Ammonite capital. King David of Israel approached Rabbath Ammon on the pretext of consoling the Ammonite king on the recent death of his father. The king was not taken in. Instead, the messengers were seized and had their beards shorn off, followed by a crude re-tailoring of their clothes which left their bottoms exposed.

This insult in itself was cause enough for war, but David had another reason for ordering battle to commence. The lovely Bathsheba, on whom he had his eye, was inconveniently married to Uriah the Hittite. David made a point of ordering the luckless husband into the thickest part of the action with the happy thought that he could not possibly survive. Uriah duly perished, David was free to marry Bathsheba, and the son she subsequently bore him was the future King Solomon. David may have delighted in his coup, but was not inclined to show magnanimity towards the conquered population, who were apparently roasted alive in a kiln.

REGIONAL CONFLICT

For all its candour about the human foibles of the Israelite kings, the Old Testament seems to give a rather partisan account of the wars, with the Israelites appearing to enjoy a surprising rate of success. A different version is imparted by the Mesha or Moabite stone, a block of basalt inscribed with 34 lines of writing in a script that falls somewhere between ancient Phoenician and Hebrew, which was discovered just north of Jordan's Wadi almujib in 1868, in Moab (see page 212). This is the voice of King Mesha of Moab, boasting about liberating the land from the yoke of the Israelites in the 9th century BC, and in particular a battle in which he managed to kill 7,000 Israelites (though sparing the women). "Israel is laid waste for ever", he declares. Not the case. The state eventually carved out by David and Solomon became the leading power in the region. Eventually, Urusalim (Jerusalem) was captured in around 1000 BC and replaced Hebron as the capital of the Israelite kingdom.

On the death of Solomon in 922 BC, the kingdom divided into two: Israel in the north and Judah in the south, the respective capitals being Samaria and Jerusalem. Both kingdoms were overwhelmed, however, by the Assyrian invasion of 722 BC. Though the Israelites were carried away to captivity in Mesopotamia, Judah was left intact, albeit as a vassal state, after agreeing to pay tribute. There was no second reprieve, however, when Nebuchadnezzar II of Babylon conquered the empire in 587 BC: Jerusalem was sacked, Solomon's Temple on Mount Moriah was completely destroyed and the population was taken to captivity in Babylon.

Cyrus I of Persia conquered Babylon 50 years later, whereupon the men of Judah were allowed to return to Jerusalem. They rebuilt the temple and cultivated special treatment at the hands of the Persians by remaining aloof from local rebellions against Persian rule. Deir Alla in the Jordan Valley (where Jacob recuperated after wrestling with an angel) was evidently a Persian settlement.

ALEXANDER THE GREAT

Alexander the Great, conqueror of Persia and its possessions in 332 BC, was responsible for drawing the Near East into the orbit of Hellenistic civilisation in the 4th century BC. Trading posts and

The first major staging post was Mecca. Its future role at the centre of Islam was not unconnected with its traditional pre-eminence in trade and commerce. Another of the staging posts was Palmyra in Syria, and between the two, caravans were serviced and taxed at Petra.

PETRA AND THE NABATAEANS

Very little is known about Petra in the early days of ancient Edom. Biblical references to the Edomite capital of Sela probably refer to the area of the western wall of the canyon. The

Part of the Isaiah Scroll, one of the Dead Sea scrolls.

settlement followed in the wake of the triumphant Macedonian Army, and although the Greeks were not inclined to stray very far from the coast, their influence reached well into the Jordan Valley. Rabbath Ammon, for instance, acquired a Greek name, Philadelphia. As always, the desert tribes of the remote interior remained unaffected by the profound cultural transformation on all sides.

Although Alexander did not live long enough to consolidate his colossal empire, he managed to revitalise trade between east and west, and for Jordan, straddling a historic trade route, this proved immensely lucrative. The key stretch was the overland camel caravan route from Aden and Yemen up the east coast of the Red Sea to Damascus and points beyond.

Nabataeans, a tribe of nomads originating in western Arabia, seem to have settled around Petra in the 6th century BC.

Making the most of Petra's strategic position, they prospered and grew. Inevitably, they attracted covetous enemies, none more so than Antigonus, one of Alexander the Great's Seleucid heirs. His energies were divided between several unsuccessful attacks on Petra itself and attempts to take a larger slice of Alexander's legacy from the other principal heirs, the Ptolemies of Egypt. The latter had a foothold in Jordan at Gadara (later named Umm qays), which, like Petra, served as an important trade and staging post. The Seleucids eventually seized Gadara from the Ptolemies in 218 BC, but were in turn dispossessed of Gadara by the Jews in 100 BC.

Petra could afford to maintain forces capable of seeing off enemies like Antigonus. It could even afford to buy Roman recognition of its independence when the Roman legions in 63 BC seized Syria and Palestine. Having reached an agreement with Rome, the Nabataeans then undid it by taking the side of the Parthians in a dispute against Rome.

The agreement was revoked and Rome took over. As the new masters of Petra, the Romans began their customary re-modelling to suit

arguments for arbitration to the new Roman master of Damascus, Pompey. He lost patience with all sides, besieged the walls of Jerusalem himself and marched into the temple. He also subjugated the Nabataeans, hoping to replace their efficient trading tentacles with a kind of common market of 10 semi-independent cities, which he called the Decapolis (see page 171).

HEROD THE GREAT

As there were rarely enough Roman-born citizens to administer the rapidly expanding

Looking down the colonnaded street to Temenos gate and Qasr al-Bint, Petra.

their own needs and tastes. If the remnants are impressive today, the impact at the time must have been startling.

THE MACCABEES AND THE ROMANS

West of the Jordan, in the meantime, the Seleucid Antiochus Epiphanus caused shockwaves in the region when he took Jerusalem by storm in 170 BC, slaughtering most of the inhabitants and selling the rest into slavery. The temple was re-dedicated to Jupiter, an outrage which Daniel called "the Abomination of Desolation". The Jewish backlash was led by the Maccabees, a strait-laced sect who caused consternation among the Edomites by insisting on their circumcision. The Maccabees took their

empire, top positions were often delegated to local men, among them, Herod the Great. Herod joined the imperial service as governor of Galilee and in 31 BC was nominated King of Judaea, in which capacity he effectively ruled the Jordan Valley. His mind was apparently unsettled by something of an identity crisis. He was, it was said, "by birth an Idumaean (ie Edomite), by profession a Jew, by necessity a Roman, by culture and by choice a Greek." Soaking in the hot springs at Al-zarqa' Ma'in ("Callirhoe" in the Bible and hot springs to this day), he concocted various architectural schemes which were designed either to intimidate or placate his restless subjects. Machaerus, now known as Mukawir, was one of a string of fortresses serving the first purpose (it can be visited today, see page 211); the Western Wall at the temple in Jerusalem was built to please the Jews. As Cleopatra had evidently lost interest in Jericho, he stepped in with an offer to lease it.

> *It is said that Cleopatra requested Petra as a gift from Caesar. He baulked at the idea, but offered her Jericho instead, which the queen graciously accepted.*

Herod's dispute with John the Baptist began and ended at the Machaerus (or Mukawir) Fortress. The origin of his animosity was, according to some historians, John's opposition to his incestuous marriage, which went against Old Testament teaching. For this, John was himself thrown into Mukawir and later beheaded, famously at the request of Salome, Herod's stepdaughter.

Herod's vindictiveness towards John presaged the acute paranoia which characterised his rule and led him to massacre any segment of society he distrusted, including allegedly the famous Massacre of the Innocents in Bethlehem, which saw Mary, Joseph and the baby Jesus take flight to Egypt.

Herod's successors could be equally uncongenial, including his grandson Herod Agrippa, Caligula's great friend. Emperor Claudius at once demoted the kingdom to the status of a province under a Roman governor. Pontius Pilate (AD 26–37) then alienated the Jews still further by milking their Sacred Fund to pay for a new aqueduct. As far as Christians are concerned, Pontius Pilate earned lasting condemnation through his role in the Crucifixion.

JESUS CHRIST

Tracing Christ's movements in Jordan through biblical references is complicated above all by changes in place-names. The region east of the Jordan River was administered by the Romans as Peraea, one of four divisions of Palestine, but this name does not appear at all in the New Testament. On the two occasions when Jesus visited the quarter, it is referred to as "the country of the Gadarene", in other words the area around Gadara,

or Umm qays. Seized by the Jews from the Seleucids in 100 BC, the former trading city is only a ruined shadow of its former self in the 7th century. During one of the more notable of Jesus's visits to Gadarene country, he is said to have met two tomb-dwellers possessed by evil spirits and cast their demons into a herd of pigs (Matthew 8: 28–34; see page 186).

While Christ's own preaching was mainly an appeal to Jews to reform their own religion, St Paul of Tarsus introduced the idea of aiming the Christian message at heathens like the

The triclinium of Herod's Mukawir Fortress.

⊘ THE PROPHET MUHAMMAD

Born in around AD 570, Muhammad's early life was difficult. Adopted by his uncle when his father, mother and grandfather all died successively, he was forced to work as a caravan trader. However, his efficiency, integrity and honesty soon impressed a wealthy widow who made him her agent, and later her husband. Meanwhile, Muhammad became increasingly disillusioned with the lax morality of Meccan society. Following an ancient Middle Eastern custom, he withdrew in order to contemplate. In a small cave near Mecca, Muhammad, at around the age of 40, began to have the famous revelations that formed the basis of the Qur'an, itself the basis of a new religion: Islam.

population of Gadara. This new objective was considerably helped by the Jews being preoccupied by rebellion against Rome, which reached a gory climax in the destruction of Jerusalem by Titus in AD 70, a massacre in which Jewish converts to Christianity were equal victims.

THE ARRIVAL OF CHRISTIANITY

Christianity readily fitted into the Greek intellectual traditions which had prevailed in the Near East since Alexander the Great's conquest. Compared with the struggle for survival in Rome itself, Eastern Christians could indulge in a debate over the extra iota which turned the Greek word Homoousios into Homoiousis. The former meant that Father and Son were "of the same essence"; the latter that they were merely "of like essence". The distinction dug a chasm between the so-called Monophysitic and Orthodox schools of thought. While Constantine's edict of toleration in 324 made life easier for Christians in the Roman Empire as a whole, the debate over the extra iota resulted in Christians killing Christians in what had been their original sanctuary. The conflict continued unabated in the region for centuries to come.

Fully occupied by the skirmishes endemic in desert life, the tribes were totally indifferent to both religious schism and the titanic wars between Byzantium and Persia that characterised the 6th and 7th centuries. Their religion remained rooted in the worship of sacred objects and heavenly bodies. The parallel streams of their ritual were bridged by a "holy of holies", a large meteorite preserved in a cubicle temple in Mecca, the Ka'aba. The same black stone is the focal point of Muslim pilgrimage to Mecca today, but was no less revered by pagans long before the birth of the Prophet Muhammad.

JORDAN'S BIBLICAL SITES

Modern-day Jordan is littered with sites that are directly linked with both the Old and New Testaments. Among the many biblical figures connected to the land are Abraham, Job, Moses, Jacob, Lot, Ruth, Elijah, John the Baptist, King Herod the Great, Christ himself and the Apostle Paul. Most of Jordan's biblical events occurred in the area known as the "Plains of Moab" in

the Old Testament and as "Peraea" in the New, which extend east of the River Jordan, and west along the Dead Sea coast. Among Jordan's most significant biblical sites are Bithani-beyond-the-Jordan (see page 196), where Jesus was baptised by John the Baptist and met at least four of his apostles (Andrew, Peter, Philip and Bartholomew/Nathanial). It is also where Jesus began his mission and the New Testament and Christianity started.

Nearby, at Tel Mar Elias, Elijah is believed to have ascended to heaven. Ma'daba (Medaba

Church of St John the Baptist, Bithani-beyond-the-Jordan.

in the Old Testament; see page 208) is linked to Moses and the Exodus, King David's war with the Moabites and King Mesha's victories over the Israelites. The town is also the site of some of the earliest, finest and historically most important Christian mosaics, including the earliest surviving religious map of the Holy Land. Nearby, Jabal nibu (see page 207) was where Moses surveyed the Promised Land of Canaan during his flight from Egypt, and which became a place of pilgrimage to very early Christians. Herod the Great imprisoned and beheaded John the Baptist at Mukawir (see page 211). Near Safi on the King's Highway, Lot is said to have taken refuge in a cave (see page) as he and his family fled the destruction of Sodom and Gomorrah, itself sometimes said to have taken place on the site of the ancient cities of Bab ad Dhraa (Bab al-dhira') and Al-numayrah (see page 216). At Umm qays (see page 183), the site of the ancient city of Gadara, Jesus is said to have performed his miracle of the Gadarene swine.

CHRISTIAN RELICS

Christianity's equivalent of the Black Stone was the True Cross, long housed in the Church of the Holy Sepulchre in Jerusalem. When the Persians captured Jerusalem in 614, they burned down the church and carried off the cross. Heraclius, the dashing young emperor of Byzantium, avenged the outrage by defeating the Persians 13 years later and personally carrying the recaptured True Cross along Via Dolorosa to its rebuilt home. Heraclius hoped that in his hour of triumph he could effect a reconciliation between Orthodox and Monophysite leaders. Alas not, but his victory over Persia was tantamount to redrawing the map of the Near East, an achievement celebrated by the contemporary mosaic map still to be seen, on the floor, in the Orthodox Church of St George at Ma'daba (see page 209).

Otherwise, the fruits of Heraclius's victory were short-lived: disturbing reports were received of armies advancing on three fronts, and the possibility of the Persians returning could not be ruled out.

THE ARRIVAL OF ISLAM

The invaders were in fact Muslim Arabs, devotees of the Prophet Muhammad, who had died three years before in Medina. To begin with, Muhammad's call to arms against unbelievers was aimed not at Jews or Christians, but at the population of Mecca, who had driven him out of their city and monopolised the proceeds of pilgrimages to the Black Stone. Eight years after Muhammad's flight to Medina (the Hegira), Mecca was captured, and the Black Stone was at once absorbed into the religious ritual of the victorious Muslims.

Most of the tribes of Arabia had submitted to Islam before Muhammad's death in 632, a miraculous show of unity given their history of perpetual anarchy. It is not known whether

Muhammad intended to carry his revolution beyond the Arabian Peninsula, and more significantly he left no instructions about a successor. Abu Bakr, one of his earliest adherents, was proclaimed Caliph, but there were already hints of rival claims, which later were to spark protracted successor conflicts and create a chasm between Sunni and Shi'ite sects.

Early in 633, Abu Bakr organised three columns to invade Byzantine territory. One followed the coastal route to reach the plains

Miniature from the Siyer-i-Nebi, the Turkish epic about the life of Muhammad.

of Beersheba; the others skirted the edge of the desert as they advanced north. In early encounters with Byzantine troops, the desert Arabs demonstrated a degree of mobility that made them formidable opponents in open country and, although they had little knowledge of siege warfare, they were able to capture a number of fortified positions.

After decades locked in combat with Byzantine Greeks over the infamous extra iota, Monophysite Christian defenders were not averse to throwing open their gates to fellow Arabs whose commitment to one God, however recent, seemed initially at least compatible with their own.

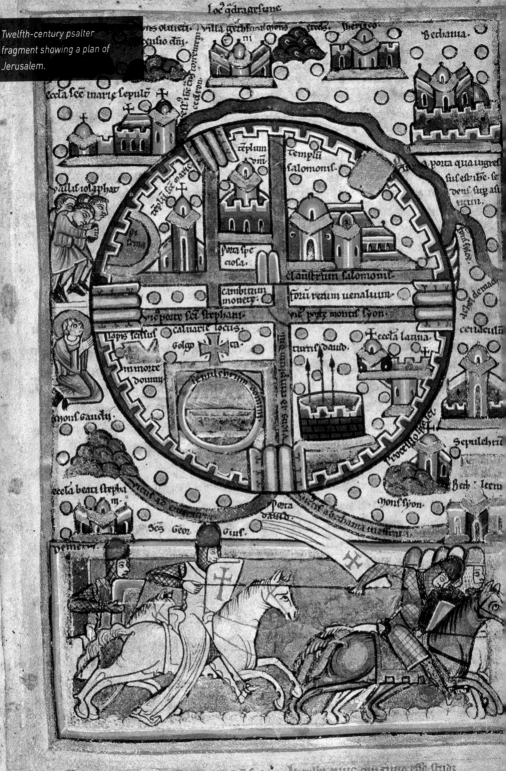

Twelfth-century psalter fragment showing a plan of Jerusalem.

THE CRUSADES

In the 11th century, the Byzantine emperor Alexius Comnenus called for the first Crusade; at stake for the Byzantines was the survival of Christianity in the Holy Land.

All through the summer of 636 (the Prophet Muhammad had been dead for three years), Muslim Arab and Christian Byzantine armies glared at one another along the banks of the Yarmouk River, the boundary between modern Jordan and Syria. The afternoon of 20 August then produced a fierce sandstorm. Keeping the driving sand behind them, the Arab horsemen scythed through the blinded Byzantines, and with this swift dispatch ended 1,000 years of Graeco-Roman-Byzantine domination in the region. Within a year, the Arabs controlled most of the Near East, including Jerusalem.

ARAB DYNASTIES

The Arabs were magnanimous victors, assimilating the unfamiliar skills of their subject peoples and tolerating both Jews and Christians (whom they respectfully called the "peoples of the book"), as long as they paid their taxes.

There appears to have been some reciprocity: Byzantines lent a hand in 691 to help build the Dome of the Rock in Jerusalem on the spot where Muhammad is believed to have ascended into heaven.

Byzantines helped to build Jerusalem's Dome of the Rock.

When the Abbasid Caliph Mehedi made the pilgrimage to Mecca, he made sure the camels carried special containers for snow so that his drinks could be served cold.

Ruling from Damascus, the Omayyad Dynasty indulged their nostalgia for life in the desert by building, east of Amman, a string of castles and hunting lodges where they stayed for a few weeks each year. Those at Azraq (see page 277) and Hallabat (see page 275) were built on the remains of Roman forts, and can be visited today.

When the Abbasids overthrew the Omayyads in 750 and moved their capital to Baghdad, Jordan was reduced to a backwater whose population reverted to Bedouin ways. As the Abbasids did not retain the Omayyads' fondness for desert life, the castles fell into disuse.

The Abbasids reached unprecedented levels of artistic and intellectual achievement under Harun ar-Rashid, immortalised in the tales of *Arabian Nights*. Not for the first time, however, did the death of a dazzling leader lead to the partition of his empire among spiteful sons, and its rapid subsequent disintegration.

Jordan was swept along in a shift of power from the waning Abbasids in Baghdad to the militant Shi'ite Fatimists in Egypt. Under the Fatimid Caliph al-Hakim at the beginning of the 11th century, the long tradition of Arab religious toleration broke down. He made Christians wear black and hang wooden crosses from their necks. Jews, too, were ordered into distinctive dress: in the public baths, they had to wear bells.

Word on the street had it that al-Hakim was going mad, the more so when he officially banned the game of chess and the sale of female footwear; the latter, so he thought, an ingenious way of ridding the streets of prostitution. In 1009, however, he went one step too far in ordering the destruction of the Church of the Holy Sepulchre in Jerusalem.

Christians everywhere were up in arms, but the danger of war receded unexpectedly when al-Hakim set off one night on one of his customary donkey rides and mysteriously failed to return. Christians rebuilt the Holy Sepulchre and, for a while, pilgrims once again made their way to Jerusalem unmolested.

THE FIRST CRUSADE

Not long after, Christians again found the way barred, but this time by the Seljuk Turks, who captured Baghdad in the course of conquering most of Asia Minor. Hordes of undisciplined troops made the pilgrim trail impassable. In 1069, the Byzantine emperor Alexius Comnenus warned that Christianity in the east was in peril; his call for a Crusade was later further endorsed by Pope Urban II.

The First Crusade consisted of four separate feudal armies. They met up in Constantinople, captured Nicaea in June 1097 after a siege of six weeks and Antioch a year later. But nothing in Europe had prepared the troops for conditions in the desert, where suits of armour were infernos in the heat and wholly impractical for the bouts of chronic dysentery that struck down the soldiers.

It was not until June 1099 that the Crusaders finally reached Jerusalem. However, the daunting defences of the ancient city seemed to shrink next to the exhilaration of at last being there. "When they heard the name of Jerusalem called," William of Tyre recorded, "they began to weep and fell on their knees, giving thanks to our Lord... Then they raised their hands in prayer to Heaven and, taking off their shoes, bowed down to the ground and kissed the earth."

The thoughts of the engineers, though, were elsewhere: on the absence of timber for siege machines, without which the city walls looked impregnable. The solution to this problem came by accident rather than design, through a certain Tancred, a Norman knight whose dysentery and modesty forced him constantly "to dismount, go away from the group and

Seal of the Knights Templar on a cross.

⊘ THE KNIGHTS TEMPLAR

On his return to Jerusalem from the Idumaean country, Baldwin I set himself to work administering his kingdom. In 1119, he founded a new Military Order, drawn from a community of monks whose duties since 1070 had been to look after poor and sick pilgrims visiting Jerusalem. Although still owing allegiance first and foremost to the Pope, they now provided the kingdom with a much-needed regular army of trained soldiers. The monks, based in a wing of the royal palace (the former Al-Aqsa Mosque in the temple area), soon adopted a distinctive red cross on a white tunic as the insignia of their new order: the Knights Templar.

find a hiding-place". Having withdrawn into a deep recess beneath a hollow rock, Tancred spotted a large quantity of sawn timber. This windfall became the raw material for the siege machines that eventually breached the walls of Jerusalem on 15 July 1099.

CONTROLLING JERUSALEM

After the fall of the city, Godfrey de Bouillon, Duke of Lorraine, was put onto the throne of the proudly proclaimed "Latin Kingdom of Jerusalem". With famous modesty, he declined to wear a crown in a place where Jesus had worn thorns. He was succeeded by his brother Baldwin I, whose strategic priority was to secure an adequate coastline and build a line of inland fortresses which would give him mastery over Arab caravan routes. But the frenzy of activity in construction warned Toghetekin of Damascus, who also coveted the revenue from the routes.

In 1108, Toghetekin attacked a recently completed fortress east of Lake Tiberias. Its custodian, Gervase of Basoches, was put to death and his scalp, a shock of wavy white hair, paraded on a pole. But Baldwin decided to overlook this act and agreed with Toghetekin to share their assets to mutual benefit rather than turning the trade routes into a battleground. They drew up a truce in northern Transjordan designed to last 10 years.

It was characteristic of the times that a truce in northern Transjordan in no way prevented Baldwin and Toghetekin from battling elsewhere. The land between the Dead Sea and the Gulf of Al-'aqabah was important to them both. For Toghetekin, it was a base from which to raid Judaea; for Baldwin, it provided a buffer against Egyptian designs to join with the eastern Muslim world against the Christian kingdom of Jerusalem.

While the sympathies of the Bedouin population lay with Muslim Damascus, the Christians had the support of the Greek monasteries in the Idumaean wilderness. Crusaders and Damascenes soon clashed in Wadi musa, near Petra, but again they agreed on a tactical disengagement. The Damascenes withdrew, leaving Baldwin to smoke their Bedouin allies out of their caverns and steal their flocks.

FRANKISH FORTIFICATIONS

Baldwin decided in 1115 that, in the interest of security, the Idumaean country would have to be permanently occupied. The necessary first step was to build a great castle at one of the few fertile spots, Shawbak. He named the castle Montreal (Royal Mountain) before pushing further south to the Red Sea at Al-'aqabah. While the Crusaders bathed their horses, the local inhabitants took to their boats and fled. Baldwin fortified the town with one citadel and built a second on the little island of Jezirat Far'un, which the Franks called

Illustrated manuscript showing the Knights Templar before Jerusalem.

Le Graye, just offshore. With garrisons in both strongholds, the Franks dominated the roads to Arabia and Egypt, enabling them to raid caravans at their ease and effectively separating Egypt from the heartland of Islam.

Meanwhile, Baldwin had another concern: that the influx of Westerners was diluting the warrior and clerical ethos of the kingdom with bourgeois attitudes receptive to the indolent habits of the East. The creation of a regular army (see page 44) went some way towards relieving his fears. Matters such as the imperfect truce with Toghetekin in Transjordan also required constant vigilance, as did the demarcation of the frontier.

THE FORTRESS OF AL-KARAK

Baldwin's eventual death symbolised a sea change: the supplanting of the pioneer Crusaders by a second generation from the West. The latter wished to exercise more systematic control of the country east and south of the Dead Sea as Muslim caravans found ways of circumventing Montreal, Baldwin's castle. An increasing number of desert raiders were also managing to slip past to attack the coastal plain. It was thus with a view to tightening control along the Dead Sea that the great fortress of

Al-karak fortress.

Al-karak was built. Nevertheless, there was still no serious Frankish colonisation of the area and the Bedouin tribes continued their nomadic life.

Al-karak was built on the crest of a hill, a twilight world of stone-vaulted chambers, halls, stables and corridors behind deep moated walls. To Western pilgrims, a glimpse of *Outremer* (Crusader state) life in castles such as Al-karak was shocking because of its luxury and licence. "We who had been occidentals have become orientals," Fulcher of Chartres bemoaned. An Arab traveller noted approvingly that on being invited to dinner at the home of an elderly Outremer knight, he was assured that all meals were prepared by Egyptian women and pork never crossed the threshold.

REYNALD DE CHATILLON

From 1150 onwards, Jerusalem sent increasingly urgent messages to the West with reports of Muslim encroachment and predicting that another Crusade would soon be necessary. It was at this point that an ambitious young knight named Reynald de Chatillon entered the scene. More than any other person, Reynald proved fatal to Christian Jerusalem.

In 1160, Reynald set off north of Jerusalem to plunder the seasonal movement of grazing herds from the mountains to the plain. Slowed down by the huge number of cattle, camels and horses that he had stolen, he was himself captured and carried away, bound on a camel, to a gaol in Aleppo.

During his 16-year absence, the Franks were confronted by their most formidable Muslim adversary to date: Saladin, a Kurdish mercenary who had risen to become vizier of Egypt. In the course of harassing the Crusader states, he managed to capture most of Syria. Aleppo remained independent, but only because a Frankish army came to its assistance and lifted Saladin's siege. Gumushtekin, the ruler of Aleppo, showed his gratitude by releasing all Christian prisoners, among them Reynald de Chatillon.

Back in his domain, Reynald resumed his thievery, and in 1181 fell on a caravan on its way to Mecca and made off with its goods. Saladin retaliated by taking hostage 1,500 Christian pilgrims forced to land in Egypt because of bad weather. Reynald still refused to return the goods and war became inevitable.

Undeterred by news that Saladin was marching north, Reynald launched a fleet (built with timber from the forests of Moab and tested on the Dead Sea) to raid sea-caravans on the Red Sea and to attack Mecca itself. He succeeded in capturing Al-'aqabah, which had been in Muslim hands since 1170, and sent his fleet down the Red Sea. They caused havoc by plundering richly laden merchantmen from Aden and India, sinking a pilgrim ship heading for Jedda, setting fire to shipping in almost every port on the Arabian coast and even sending a landing party ashore to pillage an undefended caravan that had crossed the desert from the Nile. The Muslim world was outraged, and even the Frankish princes were appalled at the actions of their compatriot.

> *While rocks were hurled at the walls of Al-karak, the bridegroom's mother personally prepared a selection of tasty dishes which were sent to Saladin with her compliments.*

SALADIN'S REVENGE

Saladin left Damascus in September 1183 with Reynald in his sights. Reynald, never a man to allow the plans of others to get in the way of his own, did not allow Saladin's reported advance to interfere with his plans for a gala wedding between his 17-year-old stepson, Humphrey of Toron, and Princess Isabella, aged 11. Many distinguished guests, jugglers, dancers and musicians from all over the Christian East arrived at Al-karak throughout November. And on 20 November, so too did Saladin.

The Muslim army went to work straight away. They attacked the lower town and managed to force an entrance. Reynald was able to escape back into the castle only because one of his knights held the bridge over the moat until it could be destroyed behind him.

The walls of Al-karak held out against the pounding of Saladin's nine mangonels, and on 4 December, reports of a Crusader force approaching past Jabal nibu (Mount Nebo) persuaded him to lift the siege and return to Damascus. Saladin tried to besiege Al-karak again the following year, but the result was the same. Under pressure of other business elsewhere, both Franks and Saladin declared a truce.

Peace meant that Muslim caravans could again travel through Frankish lands. However, once again the sight of riches passing by from Egypt was more than Reynald could resist. The merchants were forcibly diverted into the castle at Al-karak, Saladin lost patience, and war resumed.

Assembling the largest army he had ever commanded, Saladin crossed the Jordan at Sennabra on 1 July 1187. Taking Tiberias in less than an hour, he then led his army on to Hattin, a village with pastures and plenty of water, where the road descended towards the lake. The Frankish army, including Reynald, approached Saladin's position along a road with no water. On the afternoon of 3 July, they gained the plateau above Hattin, but heat and thirst had taken a grievous toll.

THE END OF THE CRUSADES

The Christians spent a miserable night, racked by thirst and the sound of song and prayers from the Muslim camp below. Worse, the Muslims set fire to the scrub covering the hillside, sending up gusts of choking hot smoke.

The attack began at first light. Many of the knights and infantry were slaughtered at once, but those that remained fought with desperate courage. Jerusalem fell to Saladin on 2 October 1187, but he chose to spare most of the survivors.

Engraving of Saladin raising his arms in victory after killing a Christian during the Crusades.

A series of equally misguided Crusades then ensued. The Outremer Franks failed to regain Jerusalem or Transjordan, but they held on to coastal cities for most of the 13th century. They were sustained by the export of sugar, taxes on transit trade and dissension among Saladin's descendants. In 1291, however, Al-Mansur Qalawun, a Mamluke, positioned a huge siege train against the walls of Acre, the main Christian stronghold on the coast, and took it after a fight which saw every last defender killed.

Europe was now preoccupied by the Hundred Years War. Religious warfare was far from over, but the saga of Crusaders in the Holy Land died in the dust of Acre after 194 years.

Mamlukes, the Circassian military caste.

MAMLUKES AND OTTOMANS

As the Crusades drew to a close, the Mamlukes ushered in a remarkable age of military might and cultural flowering. Hot on their heels came the Ottomans.

With the expulsion of the Crusaders at the end of the 13th century, the area that comprises modern-day Jordan was absorbed by a new power: the ever-expanding Mamluke Empire.

THE MAMLUKES

The term Mamluke was first applied in Saladin's day (the 12th century) to young boys who were bought or captured abroad in order to be trained for the professional corps of the army. Over time, a preference developed for children who originated from the tough Circassian and Caucasian nomadic tribes. This led to the Mamlukes generally being white ("Caucasian"), even if they adopted Islam and grew up speaking Arabic. Far removed from family and tribal ties, the Mamlukes could be relied upon to give their masters undivided loyalty.

The word "Mamluke" means "belonging to", since Mamlukes were slaves. Unlike domestic slaves, however, Mamlukes could not be sold on.

'Ajlun castle.

A distinguished Mamluke in Cairo once had a terrible desire for Lebanese cherries and sent an order by pigeon. Three days later, 600 birds arrived, each carrying a single cherry in a silk purse.

Servitude was exclusive to the original purchaser, and when he died, his Mamlukes were at liberty to market their services either as individual mercenaries or, in cooperation with other Mamlukes, as a private army. These private armies proliferated as the Mamlukes grew rich on military plunder and bought their own Mamluke slaves; non-Mamlukes were thus turned into subjects of the former slaves. Over time, the system became a kind of self-perpetuating, oligarchical meritocracy.

The Mamluke Empire lasted for nearly three centuries before the Mamlukes were reduced to a military caste in Egypt. As such, they were still around to fight Napoleon on the banks of the Nile, although the last of their number were massacred soon afterwards, in 1811.

The Mamluke legacy in Jordan, though modest, does not always get the credit it deserves. 'Ajlun Castle (Qala'at al-Rabad) at 'Ajlun (see page 180), for example, is a fine piece of Mamluke military architecture, and the Montreal Crusader castle at Shawbak (see page 220) is, as it stands, a Mamluke 14th-century restoration of the 12th-century Crusader original.

'Ajlun Castle was a link in the typically ingenious communications network by which the Mamlukes ran their empire from Cairo. Lofts in the castle contained pigeons ready to relay messages attached under their wings, and at times they even carried air freight.

THE OTTOMAN TAKEOVER

The end of Mamluke rule in Jordan drew closer with the Ottoman victory over the Persians at Chaldiran in 1514. Ironically, Ottoman success owed much to its famous Janissaries who – with

Engraving of Sultan Abdul Hamid.

an infantry composed of boys taken from their families to be trained – bore a similarity to the Mamlukes. Salim the Grim, whose grandfather Mehmed II captured Constantinople in 1453, occupied Jordan on behalf of the Ottomans in 1516.

Whereas the Mamlukes had ruled Jordan from Cairo and Damascus, the Ottomans attempted to do so from Constantinople, several weeks' travel away. Additionally, they saw waging war on Christendom as their main concern, and this was best discharged by going west into Europe. Although the likes of Suleiman the Magnificent built superb monuments in other parts of his empire, the area east of the Jordan River was as good as ignored. Ottoman administration in Jordan was from the northwesterly trading town of Al-salt (see page

163), where very well-preserved Ottoman houses and administrative buildings can be seen today.

In the desert meanwhile, the real rulers were still the Bedouin, who lived on the proceeds of inter-tribal plunder and tolls exacted from travelling merchants. As T. E. Lawrence observed: "...Camel-raiding parties, self-contained like ships, might cruise confidently along the enemy's cultivation-frontier, sure of unhindered retreat into their desert-element which the Turks could not explore." In the 1880s, the Ottomans hoped to collect taxes from the tribes, but were unable ever to put such plans into action.

On the international stage, relations east and west were also mercurial. Britain, Turkey's ally against Napoleon, immediately afterwards supported a Mamluke revolt against Turkish suzerainty in Egypt. The British Navy also sank the Turkish fleet in the interest of Greek independence in 1826, but Britain and Turkey were allies again in the next year against Russia.

From Catherine the Great onwards, Russian designs on Turkey's Balkan possessions were presented as a latter-day Crusade: Christians liberating Christians from the Muslim yoke. Suffering themselves at the hands of Russian expansion and aggression, and also useful to the Ottomans for service in the imperial army, were Circassian Muslims. These refugees were encouraged to settle in Amman by the Ottomans (see page 142).

In 1900, the Sultan Abdul Hamid embarked on a huge project: the building of the Hejaz railway line to Medina. This was designed above all to improve communications between Damascus and the Arabian provinces. The railway followed the old pilgrim trail to Mecca and thus cut through the heart of Jordan. While it had previously suited Turkey to keep inter-tribal warfare festering, stability in the area was now essential to protect the safety and prestige of the railway.

However, in 1910, a Turkish governor appointed to Al-karak in the interests of security was confronted by a tribal rebellion. This was partly the result of Arab resentment of Ottoman suzerainty, and partly an echo of political convulsions in Istanbul. Following the Young Turk Revolution in 1909, nationalism among the subjects of the Ottoman Empire was on the rise. The empire's lines of communication were long and fragile, and along it, its peoples were increasingly restless – especially the Arabs.

Doorway of Beit Mismar, a grand old Ottoman house in Al-salt.

Husayn bin Ali, Sherif of Mecca
and King of Hejaz, leaving his
palace in Amman, 1924.

THE ARAB REVOLT

First mooted by Husayn, Sherif of Mecca, the Arab Revolt was intended to free the Arab world from the yoke of the Ottoman Empire and create a unified Arabian state.

Since the beginning of the 20th century, the Ottoman Empire had been dubbed the "Sick Man of Europe". Inspired by its apparently terminal condition, Husayn, Sherif of Mecca, spotted an opportunity. He dreamed of reviving the past glory of the Abbasid Empire by creating a vast Arab confederacy. Husayn envisaged himself and his sons ruling this reawakened kingdom, and in so doing, establishing a powerful role for the Hashemite descendants of the Prophet Muhammad.

In February 1914, Husayn's second son, Emir Abdullah, was dispatched to Cairo to speak to Lord Kitchener, the British Agent and Minister of War. The object of Abdullah's visit was to find out if Britain would support a campaign against Turkey. Kitchener was interested in the potential of such a campaign, but was much more preoccupied with the possibility of war with Germany and remained non-committal.

Later that year, the Sultan of Turkey, in response to the threatening posturing of the British, Russians and French, evoked his authority as Caliph, the spiritual head of the Islamic faith. He declared a *jihad* (holy war) on the European powers. In theory, this made it incumbent upon Muslims everywhere to take up arms against the Europeans. The jihad was not taken lightly by Britain, France and Russia; each of these powers had huge numbers of Muslim subjects – Britain alone ruled 70 million Muslims in British India.

Emir Abdullah's suggestion of a campaign was revisited by the Europeans, and suddenly seemed more attractive. If Turkey's Arab subjects were in a rebellious mood, their Islamic loyalty to the Turkish Caliph might be compromised by a countermand from the Sherif

Emir Abdullah with Lord Allenby and T.E. Lawrence during the Arab Revolt, c.1917.

of Mecca, even though he occupied a lesser rung on the ladder of spiritual hierarchy than the Caliph.

THE ARAB REVOLT BEGINS

Husayn now procrastinated, cannily holding out for guarantees of his Abbasid dream in return for military support. Meanwhile, British forces suffered a humiliating evacuation from Gallipoli at the hands of the Ottomans, and increased their pressure on Husayn for action.

On 5 June 1916, Ali and Feisal, the Sherif's first and third sons, duly raised the crimson banner outside Medina to signal the start of the Arab Revolt. Some 30,000 Arabs assembled in response to Husayn's call, volunteers that ranged in age between 12 to 60 or more.

But a siege of Medina, the terminus of the Hejaz railway from Damascus, was deliberately not pressed, or at least not pressed with any great conviction.

"The Turk was harmless there," a British advisor later explained. "We wanted him to stay at Medina, and every other distant place, in the largest numbers. Our ideal was to keep his railway just working, but only just, with the maximum of loss and discomfort."

The adviser was a certain second-lieutenant Lawrence, later known as the legendary "Lawrence of Arabia" (see page 57). In 1916, Lawrence was given the responsibility by British Army Intelligence of estimating the leadership qualities of Husayn's sons. He concluded that Feisal was the most promising.

Subsequently, large numbers of Turkish troops were successfully tied down in Medina. This allowed the Arab irregulars to dictate the pace of the battle as they fought their way up the Red Sea to Al-ʿaqabah. Al-ʿaqabah, with

T.E. Lawrence surveys the results of a train-wrecking mission, c.1918.

⊘ FIGHTING AND INFIGHTING

While the Arab forces under Feisal's command began to resemble a regular army (joined later by Arab deserters from the trained Turkish Army and Ottoman prisoners of war), Lawrence's guerrilla strike force of tribal irregulars revelled in its unorthodoxy. "The men were a mad lot," Lawrence wrote, "sharpened to distraction by hope or success." As every fourth or fifth man was a sheikh who would recognise no other sheikh, Lawrence often had to act as referee. In the course of one operation lasting six days, he had to adjudicate on "twelve cases of assault with weapons, four camel-liftings, one marriage, two thefts, a divorce, 14 feuds, two evil eyes, and a bewitchment."

its port on the Red Sea, was ideally placed to receive British arms shipments from Egypt.

THE TAKING OF AL-ʿAQABAH

The positioning of Ottoman defences at Al-ʿaqabah was based upon the presumption that an attack would come from the sea. Instead, Lawrence plotted an attack via a looping course through the Nefud desert, which many believed to be impassable. This would enable a small number of Arabs to take the Turks by surprise from the landward side.

The Ottoman blockhouse, Abu al-Lissal, had to be taken en route, a test of the fighting qualities of the Howeitat tribesmen and in particular Auda Ibu Tayi, their warrior chief. In 30 years of incessant warfare, he was reputed to have killed 75 men with his own hand.

Surveying the Turkish positions in Abu al-Lissal, Lawrence remarked, rather mischievously, that from what he had seen of the Howeitat so far, they had fired a lot of shots to hit very little. In *The Seven Pillars of Wisdom*, Lawrence described Auda's dramatic response to such an insulting accusation.

"Almost pale with rage, and trembling, he tore his head-cloth off and threw it on the ground beside me. Then he ran back up the hill like a madman, shouting to the men in his dreadful strained and rustling voice."

Lawrence ran after him but Auda's response was simply: "Get your camel if you want to see the old man's work." Within no time, they were in the midst of a furious downhill camel charge, with Auda's men firing from the saddle. Lawrence, up front on his racing camel, fell out of the saddle when his mount tripped, and had to sit out the action. By the time he had recovered his senses, the battle was over. Some 300 Turks had been killed and 160 taken prisoner – all for the loss of just two Howeitat.

Donning the uniforms of the defeated Turks, the Arabs rode down the Naqab Pass and across the Quweira Plateau towards the port of Al-'aqabah. The surprise assault from the landward side worked to perfection. Turkish outposts were thrown into panic and quickly surrendered. The Arab force raced on through a sandstorm to capture Al-'aqabah and triumphantly splash in the sea.

Victory at Al-'aqabah wrapped up the Hejaz phase of the war. General Allenby now led the British advance from Sinai to Syria with the Arab troops making up his right wing.

THE BIRTH OF TRANSJORDAN

In the meantime, the Arab army pushed up through the corn belt east of the Dead Sea, taking Shawbak, Al-tafulah, Al-karak and Ma'daba. Numbers swelled as more and more tribes joined the rebellion. Meanwhile, the mounted army's military might was strengthened by the addition of British-supplied artillery.

After the capture of Amman, the Arab force began their advance along the gorge of the Yarmouk River. The Arabs then linked up with

the British Army, took Dir'a, and made ready for their triumphant entry into Damascus.

By this time it was becoming evident, however, that Husayn's dream of a new Arab empire and his reward for his support might not be realised. In an attempt to force it, an Arab government was proclaimed in September 1918 under Feisal. The Western powers meanwhile, busy carving up the Ottoman Empire, had other plans for the region. In an attempt to placate and compensate Feisal, they offered him Iraq.

General Allenby enters Jerusalem in 1917.

Lawrence usually adopted an Arab mode of dress when dealing with the Bedouin. "If you can wear Arab kit when with the tribes," he advised his British colleagues, "you will acquire their trust and intimacy to a degree impossible in uniform."

Out of the wreckage of the defeated Ottoman Empire arose Transjordan. Abdullah, who had first explored with Lord Kitchener the idea of an Arab revolt five years earlier, would rule the new country, albeit under British tutelage, not an Arab one. For the Arabs, this represented a terrible betrayal (see page 58).

T.E. Lawrence in Arab dress.

LAWRENCE OF ARABIA

The complex contribution – and character – of T.E. Lawrence continues to fascinate and inspire. Whatever his legacy, his role in Jordanian history was an important one and his legend lives on.

Lawrence of Arabia – "T.E." (Thomas Edward) to his friends – was a legend before he was 30. In Arab dress, a golden dagger at his side, Lawrence could mount a moving camel from the ground using its tail. He was an expert shot with either hand, as useful with a pistol as he was with the Lewis machine gun packed in a basket on his camel. For the war-weary British public, the figure of Lawrence, particularly seen against a backdrop of desert dunes, was an irresistible antidote to the terrible tales of trench warfare issuing from the Western Front.

Inevitably, the legend attracted iconoclasts, notably Richard Aldington, whose biography painted Lawrence largely as a posturing, melodramatic homosexual. Nonetheless, Lawrence's image – in part the consequence of Peter O'Toole's mesmeric performance in David Lean's 1962 film *Lawrence of Arabia* – remains largely heroic and romantic. However, with the gradual unpicking of official British military secrets, it now seems that Lawrence was more closely tied up with British Intelligence and interests than had hitherto been suspected. His cause was less Arab independence than anti-French imperial expansion.

EARLY LIFE

Lawrence was born in 1888 in Wales, the son of an Anglo-Irish landowner called Chapman, who had left his wife and four daughters to elope with the girls' governess, Sarah Maden. Both changed their names to Lawrence but never married. Thomas Edward was the second of their four sons, a boy with an unusually brisk step and an unwavering gaze. A dose of mumps in adolescence probably stunted his growth: his 1.65 metres (5ft 5ins) looked less because of his disproportionately large head.

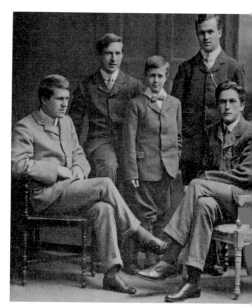

Lawrence (on the left), aged 22, and his four brothers, 1910.

Young Lawrence apparently had some kind of premonition about his future. He toughened himself by sleeping on bare floorboards, bicycling till he dropped and going days without food. An interest in medieval castles led to the study of famous battles. Reflecting on his brilliant military career in the desert, Lawrence liked to say breezily that "of course" he had had no army training and had only read "the usual schoolboy stuff". In reality, there was probably not an army general in Britain, let alone a schoolboy, who had trawled through all 25 volumes of Napoleon's dispatches, along with the historical military strategy of everyone from the Roman Procopius to Clausewitz and Foch.

ARCHAEOLOGIST AND AGENT

Whilst at Oxford University, Lawrence caught the eye of D.G. Hogarth, an archaeologist and – on the quiet – a British Intelligence expert on the Middle East. Interest in the region at the time focused on the tottering Ottoman Empire, a tantalising target for European imperial powers, not least because of the oil reserves located in Ottoman provinces. Germany initially stole a march on rivals by arranging to build a rail link between Berlin and Baghdad with an oil concession extending 17km (12 miles) on either side of the line.

Lawrence with D.G. Hogarth.

London saw this scheme as a threat to British India, the Suez Canal and its own oil interests. It was therefore not pure coincidence that, at Oxford, Hogarth made preparations for an archaeological expedition to a Hittite site at Carchemish, which happened to overlook construction of the Berlin–Baghdad railway. Among Hogarth's recruits was Lawrence, who, at Hogarth's insistence, took crash courses in Arabic and photography.

When the Carchemish dig closed for the hot summer months, Lawrence roamed further afield with a young Arab who was known as Dahoum. It was on one of these excursions that Lawrence was first arrested, and held prisoner at Azraq as a suspected deserter from the Turkish Army. A bribe to one of the guards eventually secured his release.

ARAB GUERRILLA

It is for his participation in the Arab Revolt that Lawrence is most famous. Fighting under Sherif Husayn's son Feisal and his irregular band of Arab troops, Lawrence planned and participated in many guerrilla attacks against the Ottomans, most famously employing hit-and-run tactics on the supply line of the Hejaz railway. The continual assaults along the line occupied precious Ottoman manpower and resources, held up troop transportation and provisions and helped increase the success rate of attacks elsewhere.

On 6 July 1917, Lawrence helped plan and organise a successful attack on the strategically important town of Al-'aqabah (see page 54).

BETRAYAL OF THE ARABS

Lawrence was later much haunted by accusations that he had misled the Arabs (and Feisal in particular), and that he had led them to believe that they were fighting for a single independent Arab state. Modern scholarship strongly suggests that Lawrence knew all along about the Anglo-French Sykes-Picot plan to partition the Arab world into British and French spheres of influence (see page 61). Lawrence tried to console himself, however, with the thought that a deception which helped to defeat Germany and Turkey was better than losing the war altogether.

Later, Lawrence tried to withdraw from the celebrity status he himself had partly created, by enrolling under a pseudonym in the ranks of first the Royal Air Force (as "John Hume Ross") and afterwards the Royal Tank Corps (as "Private T.E. Shaw"). Not long afterwards, on 13 May 1935, Lawrence set out from his cottage on his beloved motorcycle. In swerving to avoid a cyclist, Lawrence crashed and fractured his skull. He died six days later at the age of just 46.

LEGACY

Though a controversial figure in his own lifetime, and unquestionably polemical today, Lawrence's legend lives on. In Jordan itself, where he is held in much lesser regard than in the West, it's possible to visit many of the places Lawrence visited and later wrote about. Proving a useful and lucrative draw for today's tourism industry, particularly in Wadi Rum, it seems that Lawrence's legacy may be worth something after all, and that Jordan's Bedouins may just be having the last laugh.

Portrait of Emir Abdullah, who later became King of Jordan.

ENTER THE HASHEMITES

Hashemite dreams of a pan-Arab nation were thwarted by complex post-war deals concocted by Western powers.

When Emir Abdullah, heir apparent to the Hashemite dynasty, arrived in Ma'an by train from Hejaz in 1920, Transjordan was teetering on the edge of chaos. The order that had been established by the Ottomans during the second half of the 19th century had broken down with the demise of their empire and the outbreak of World War I. Meanwhile, the efforts of the Emir's brother Feisal to extend his authority from Damascus had been unsuccessful (see page 55). In July 1920, Feisal's fledgling kingdom fell apart when he was driven out of Syria by the French, who now controlled the country following secret wartime agreements struck with Britain.

The British, still unsure of what to do with Transjordan, had recognised three separate governments, in Irbid, Al-salt and Al-karak, and sent British advisers to each one. The government based in Al-salt was moderately successful. The local Christians and Circassians continued to pay their taxes, and officials appointed by Feisal's short-lived kingdom in Damascus were able to maintain order. But the authority of the administrations in Irbid and Al-karak was partial, and the country consisted of a patchwork of local sheikhdoms. The Bedouin had begun to raid again and the line between desert and *ghor* fluctuated from day to day. As the Lebanese historian Kamal Salibi described it, "a state of utter lawlessness" prevailed in the countryside.

Yet within a very short time, Emir Abdullah had managed to restore order and created a new state where one had never before existed. That state was Transjordan.

A GRAND PLAN

Transjordan was not Emir Abdullah's initial objective and it was never his final one. When he alighted

Emir Abdullah in Cairo, c.1921, for a meeting with the British High Commissioner in Egypt.

from the train in Ma'an, he immediately announced his intention of marching on Syria to regain it for the Hashemites. From his point of view, the Arab Revolt had been fought to establish a pan-Arab kingdom in the area under his family, which was uniquely qualified to rule on account of its direct descent from the Prophet Muhammad. Britain had promised to lend its support to this scenario in return for Hashemite backing in World War I.

However, Britain had made conflicting promises during the war, and under the Sykes-Picot agreement – a secret pact between France and Britain with Russia's assent – the area known as modern-day Jordan was to come under British control. This abject carve-up of the Middle East was further complicated by Britain's commitment to the idea of a Jewish national home in Palestine, established in the Balfour Declaration. Though undoubtedly underhand, and against assurances and promises made to other parties, the deal between France and Britain was ratified by the League of Nations in 1920.

So, while Emir Abdullah's announcement at the railway station in Ma'an accurately reflected his Arab Nationalist convictions, he must have known that the British would not support him against the French. The bitter experience of his brother Feisal in Syria had made that clear. The Emir's immediate and most pressing aim was to salvage something from the broken promises made by Britain in World War I.

Transjordan, poor, undeveloped and lawless, had thus far avoided allocation in the Great Power land-grab and increasingly it must have seemed like a good starting point for the Emir's wider ambitions. However, he had little financing to back his ambitions and his army was small. His initial objectives, therefore, were to secure both material and moral support from Britain.

Members of the Arab Legion.

ESTABLISHING THE EMIRATE

Wary at first, the British quickly recognised that it was in their own interests to back Emir Abdullah. The local administrations that had been established by Feisal from Damascus were largely incompetent and discredited. Emir Abdullah, with British help, would restore order in a territory for which they felt some responsibility but had no firm plans. Support for the Emir, it was hoped, would also help to assuage the broken promises Britain had made to the Hashemites after the Arab Revolt.

On 15 May 1923, therefore, the Emirate of Transjordan came into existence, albeit on the understanding that the new country would be closely supervised by Britain while it proceeded on the road to full independence.

Meanwhile, the Emir and his plans were well received by many of Transjordan's inhabitants. His Hashemite heritage stood him in good stead and he quickly developed links with local Bedouin tribes. Settled communities like the Christians and the Circassians, whose lives were disrupted by persistent lawlessness, also welcomed him. Emir Abdullah consolidated these links by staying with Christian families, such as the Abu Jabers and Sukkars of Al-salt and with the Circassian Muslim al-Mufti family in Amman. He also lived and held court in Bedouin-style encampments on the outskirts of Amman and in Shuneh in the Jordan Valley. The Emir's strongest card, however, was the control of the only military force in the country.

THE RUMBLE OF DISCONTENT

Though determined to establish his authority and restore law and order, the Emir's task was not an easy one. As early as 1921, at Kura, near Irbid, a sheikh named Kulayb al-Shurayda led villagers in a revolt against the Emir's tax collectors. Over the following two years, a more serious threat was presented by the Adwan Bedouin tribe, who were also joined by educated town dwellers from Irbid, Al-salt and Al-karak.

While the Adwan protested against the alleged favouritism shown to the Beni Sakhr tribe, the townsmen demanded a more democratic form of government. Both also raised the slogans "Transjordan for the Transjordanians" and "foreigners out", reflecting their anger about the way in which they felt power was being monopolised by Syrians, Hejazis and other Arabs employed by Emir Abdullah in line with his pan-Arab convictions.

In order to survive and forge a state from Transjordan, the Emir felt he had no alternative but to turn to the British. A new military force, which later became the Transjordanian army (known as the Arab Legion), was subsequently created under the command of a British army captain, Peake Pasha (see page 65). Typically, Emir Abdullah tried to solve his rebellions peacefully by personal

intervention, and only when all else failed did he order his army into action. It was also to become a Hashemite hallmark that the leaders of the recent revolts were later pardoned.

In 1928, partly in response to widespread street demonstrations, a constitution was promulgated and a part-elected, part-appointed Parliament was introduced. Its function was largely advisory, but it served the Emir's purpose of bringing his Transjordanian inhabitants into the system. The Emir was also careful to ensure that it reflected the diverse demographic make-up of the country.

Emir Abdullah reviews a unit of the Arab Legion with Glubb Pasha, 1941.

By the mid-1930s, Emir Abdullah was able to claim: "We entered Transjordan to find four governments, each one separate from the other... Our first aim was to put the country together and secure its need to achieve unity. And here it is today... enjoying the complete unity to which sister countries in its neighbourhood still aspire."

A STATE OF INDEPENDENCE

On 22 March 1946, Transjordan finally secured full independence from Britain. Two months later, the title Emir was changed to king, and the country was renamed Jordan. Four years later, Jordan absorbed the West Bank. Both king and country had come a long way since 1920. But at what cost?

To this day, King Abdullah I remains a controversial figure in the Arab world. The king's detractors have accused him of serving British interests in the region to secure his own survival and aggrandisement. During World War II, Transjordan remained loyal to Britain while helping crush Arab nationalists in Iraq.

Admirers of King Abdullah, on the other hand, have portrayed him as a pragmatic politician who was years ahead of his time. For them, he correctly evaluated the balance of power in the region from the beginning. Working within the constraints it

themselves, at a time when their leadership was in a state of complete disarray.

THE TAINT OF COLONIALISM

King Abdullah's detractors formed the majority and were most outspoken during the late 1940s and the 1950s. Colonial rule was coming to an end all over the region and any government tainted by association with colonial powers came under wide popular attack. Increasingly, the call was for independence and Arab strength through unity.

King Abdullah I with his youngest son, Prince Naif bin Abdullah, 1949.

imposed, he managed to carve out the state of Jordan as a first step towards a larger Arab kingdom. As a Hashemite, it is argued, he had more claim to Arab leadership than any other individual or any other ideology.

Foiled in Syria, the king had turned his attentions towards Palestine, where he recommended a conciliatory course rather than the "all or nothing" approach advocated by the Palestinian leader of the time, Haj Amin al-Husayni, the Mufti of Jerusalem. King Abdullah's admirers point out that had it not been for the Jordanian Army in the 1948 war, all of Palestine would have been lost to Israel. They also argue that the union of the East Bank and West Bank was carried out at the request of the Palestinians

The perceived failure of the Arab states to prevent the loss of Palestine, the creation of Israel and the exodus of 700,000 Palestinians from their homeland in 1948 finally proved one shock wave too many for the region. After 1948, several successive governments were overthrown in Syria, and in 1951 the Prime Minister of Lebanon was assassinated. The next year, King Farouk of Egypt was removed from power by a group of army officers, among them Gamal Abdel Nasser.

It was against this turbulent background that King Abdullah took his regular trip to Al Aqsa Mosque in Jerusalem for Friday prayer on 20 July 1951. As he entered the mosque, he was shot dead by a Palestinian gunman, watched by his shocked grandson and eventual successor, Husayn.

GLUBB OF ARABIA

The British officer, Glubb Pasha, not only set up Jordan's Desert Patrol, he turned it into a crack fighting force that survives to this day.

Born John Bagot Glubb in 1897, he was raised in a military family in an atmosphere of loyalty to the British Empire and confidence in the colonial future. He came to serve on the Western Front in World War I, and in 1917 was badly wounded by shrapnel when part of his chin was blown off.

For 10 years after the war, Glubb served in Iraq, where his particular mandate was to pacify the desert, and guard Iraq's southern borders against Bedouin incursions. To this end, he developed the revolutionary idea of employing Bedouin to police themselves. Glubb developed his links with and love of the Bedouin during this time, and it was then that his Arab moniker, Abu Hunaik ("father of the little jaw"), was coined.

Glubb's next mission was to serve in the Emirate of Transjordan, where he was charged with the setting up of the Desert Patrol of the Arab Legion, as the Transjordanian army was known. Composed of Bedouin, the soldiers of the Desert Patrol had their own distinctive uniforms: a long khaki coat modelled on traditional Arab garb, a red belt and a red and white Arab headdress (shamagh). The soldiers and their distinct uniform can be seen by visitors today, particularly around Wadi Rum (see page 251), where the Desert Patrol are based and operate.

Within two years, Glubb had brought raiding to an end. The Desert Patrol had also begun to evolve into the elite striking force of the Transjordanian Army, loyal unquestioningly to its commander and the Emir Abdullah. Soon, because of increasing trouble in Palestine and the outbreak of World War II, the army was expanded and more Bedouin were recruited.

In recognition of his achievement, Glubb replaced Peake Pasha as commander of the Arab Legion in 1939, assuming the mantle of "Pasha", an honorary title awarded to senior Jordanian officials.

Under Glubb's command, the Arab Legion served with distinction both in Iraq and Syria during World War

General Sir John Bagot Glubb, 1950s.

II. During the 1948 war against Israel, the Jordanian Army's successes far outnumbered those of any other Arab fighting force. However, during these particularly troubled times, Glubb's dual loyalties to Britain (blamed by Arabs for the creation of Israel) and to Jordan came under strain.

Winds of change were also blowing through the region. The cause of Arab nationalism, led by Gamal Abdel Nasser in Egypt, was sweeping through the area. Increasingly, Glubb was ostracised as British imperialism's chief agent in the Arab world.

When King Husayn came to the throne in 1953, he was barely 18 years old, and found it difficult to deal with Glubb's old-fashioned thinking and ways. The king also wished to rule without British interference, and was sympathetic to calls for the Arabisation of the army, which was still dominated by British officers.

Sadly, Glubb failed to recognise that his time had passed, and in 1956 was dismissed from the king's service after spending 26 years in Jordan. He retired to the English countryside.

King Husayn paid a final and just tribute to Glubb at his funeral at Westminster Abbey in 1986. The king described a man of "impeccable integrity, who performed quietly and unassumingly the duties entrusted to him by his second country, Jordan, at a crucial moment in its development."

Within the Arab world today, Glubb Pasha is both better known and better regarded than Lawrence of Arabia. And unlike Lawrence, Glubb was a genuinely modest and self-effacing man.

MODERN JORDAN

Jordan's modern history is nearly as turbulent as its ancient one. At the helm since the beginning of the 20th century, the country's Hashemite kings continue to navigate the troubled waters.

Following the assassination of Abdullah, his son, Talal, was the designated successor. But in a secret Parliamentary session in 1952, Talal was deposed in favour of his eldest son, Husayn, on the grounds of mental illness. As Crown Prince Husayn was not yet 18, a regency council was appointed until he reached the legal age of accession, which he did in May 1953.

While King Abdullah had created Jordan, it was his grandson's task to consolidate this achievement. Like Abdullah before him, the new king quickly came under attack from Arab nationalist forces, which were particularly active during the 1940s and 1950s. Many of his own Transjordan citizens were also swept up in the radical politics of the day.

A POLITICAL U-TURN

The first few years of the young king's reign were characterised by riots, demonstrations and general unrest throughout the country. The crowds were protesting in particular against the special relationship that Transjordan still enjoyed with Britain. Matters came to a head in December 1955 as the king leaned towards joining the Baghdad Pact, a British-inspired bloc of countries designed to check the spread of Communism in the Middle East.

For most Arabs, Israel and the imperialist powers were their real enemies, not Communism. A policy of "non-alignment" seemed to hold out the promise of real independence for the Arab states. In September 1955, the President of Egypt, Gamal Abdel Nasser, signed an arms deal with Czechoslovakia, signalling that his country would no longer be dependent on military supplies from the West.

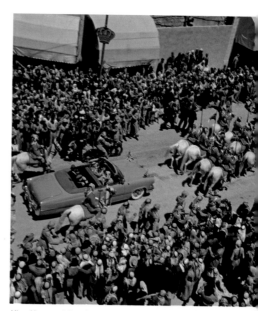

King Husayn drives by crowds at his coronation, May 1953.

Local and regional pressure forced King Husayn to recognise that Jordan was swimming against the historical tide. Following the anti-Baghdad Pact riots of December 1955, he promised the country free elections within a few months, and in March 1956 he dismissed Glubb Pasha, the British commander of the Jordanian Army (see page 65) and replaced him with a promising young Jordanian officer, Ali Abu Nuwar. Despite these moves, the king was to face the greatest threat to his throne so far in April of the following year.

DOMESTIC TROUBLES

An incendiary combination of local and regional developments formed the background to the crisis of April 1957. The Jordanian elections of

1956 resulted in the voting in of a radical Parliament and government under the leadership of Suleiman Nabulsi. At the end of the same year, Britain, France and Israel launched the Suez War against Egypt. The tripartite aggression, as it is known in the Arab world, ended with the ignominious withdrawal of the three powers under American pressure. Arabs saw the war as a victory for Nasser, Egypt's leader. Increasing support for him was coupled with a fresh surge of anger against the old colonial powers, Britain and France, and the new enemy, Israel.

King Husayn reviewing Bedouin troops loyal to him, 1957.

UNREST MOUNTS

Differences between the Nabulsi cabinet and the king came to a head with the resignation of the government on 10 April 1957. When the king attempted to form a new cabinet, the new army Chief of Staff, Ali Abu Nuwar, attempted a military *coup d'état*. However Bedouin units loyal to the king nipped the coup in the bud.

On 24 April, Nabulsi supporters met in Nablus in the West Bank (part of Jordan at that time) and called for a general strike and street demonstrations against the regime. The king took immediate and dramatic action. He formed a new government under Ibrahim Hashem, and using Bedouin and other loyal troops imposed martial law and a countrywide curfew. All

political parties were immediately dissolved and leading opposition figures were arrested.

These moves were welcomed by the United States as a necessary step against encroaching Communism. The American press carried articles about "the plucky little king". However, Egypt and Syria vociferously attacked Jordan, and regional trends seemed to be in their favour.

In 1958, Syria and Egypt announced the formation of the United Arab Republic. Feeling hemmed in and threatened by hostile neighbours, King Husayn responded by allying himself with his Hashemite cousins in Iraq. But in July 1958, there was a bloody coup in Baghdad and Iraq's royal family was massacred.

The next few months and years proved a bumpy ride for the king. In October 1958, the Syrian Air Force tried to bring down a plane piloted by the king. In February 1959, General Sadeq al-Shara'a led another coup attempt. In August of the following year, one of the most promising of a new generation of politicians, Prime Minister Haza al-Majali, was assassinated.

STABILITY RESTORED

The king stood fast, however, and through an unusual combination of tough security measures and enlightened policy, both he and the country survived. Democracy was temporarily laid to one side for the sake of stability and Jordan was ruled by a government appointed by and responsible to the king. The army was placed under the command of Habes al-Majali, an ultra-loyal supporter of the king, and the intelligence and internal security services were developed. At the same time, a booming economy and relatively free elections held in 1961 encouraged many Jordanians to develop a stake in the country and the regime.

When Gamal Abdel Nasser called for an Arab summit to discuss these and other issues, King Husayn responded with alacrity. The meeting in Cairo in 1964 proved to be the beginning of a slippery political slope that would eventually lead to the disastrous 1967 war with Israel.

WAR WITH ISRAEL

At the 1964 summit meeting, it was felt that the Palestinian question was being forgotten by the world and that the Palestinians needed a focal point for preserving their identity. The PLO (Palestine Liberation Organisation) was therefore set up, which promised to work closely with Jordan. The summit also made a decision to avoid offensive action against Israel until the Arab states were ready for war. But there were other Palestinian organisations on the scene, among them Yasser Arafat's Fatah. Their strategy was to take the war to Israel and provoke a conflict which they believed the Arab states would inevitably win. Increasingly, the PLO was pushed to take a similar stand as the Fatah.

Jordan clamped down on the operation of the PLO and Fatah within its borders, but towards the end of 1966, a number of raids against Israel managed to get through. As the king had anticipated, Israel's response was ferocious. Eighteen people were killed in a punitive attack against the Jordanian West Bank town of Samu'a on 13 November 1966.

Arab summit resolutions were forgotten in the ensuing wave of anger. Jordan was widely blamed for not arming villagers along the ceasefire line, meaning they were unable to defend themselves against the Israeli attack. Riots flared up in all of Jordan's major towns in frustration and anger.

SIX DAY WAR

The response of the Arab states was to descend into a destructive spiral of one-upmanship in action against Israel. The latter responded in kind. In April 1967, six Syrian warplanes were shot down by Israel.

In May, partly in response to Jordanian accusations of cowardice, President Nasser of Egypt requested a withdrawal of the UN forces that had been based on the Sinai Peninsula since the 1956 war. He also closed the Straits of Tiran to Israeli shipping, effectively shutting off access between the Israeli port of Eilat and the Red Sea. The actions of Egypt were provocation enough for a country already fired up for war; Israeli forces attacked the Arab states in June 1967.

Despite warnings of certain defeat from respected figures such as ex-Prime Minister Wasfi at-Tell, the Jordanian king felt compelled to join the Arab side. Within six days, the war was over; the Arabs resoundingly defeated. Jordan was the biggest loser, with Israeli forces now occupying the West Bank. At a stroke, Jordan had lost a large part of its population and the source of 40 percent of its gross national product. The defeat

also created the conditions for what was perhaps the greatest threat yet to the Kingdom of Jordan.

BLACK SEPTEMBER

The Jordanian Army had been badly mauled in the 1967 war, and the king's authority was openly questioned in its wake. Economically, the country was also in dire straits and additionally had to provide for about 350,000 Palestinian refugees from the West Bank.

Palestinian guerrilla organisations (referred to collectively as the Palestinian Resistance)

King Husayn speaks to crowds after surviving his flight over Syria in 1958.

began to operate above ground, but their undisciplined behaviour in Jordan's towns and villages alienated many of their Jordanian supporters. The radical leftist politics of the Popular Front for the Liberation of Palestine (PFLP) and the Democratic Front (DFLP) frightened the Palestinian and Jordanian middle class. Jordanians were particularly upset by the chauvinistic behaviour of most of the Palestinian organisations, and increasingly sought refuge in a new Jordanian nationalism.

By 1970, the Palestinian guerrillas had developed into "a state within a state" and were seen as posing an unacceptable challenge to the king's authority. In September 1970 – which Palestinians call "Black September" – Jordan's army moved against the Resistance. After 10 days of fighting, more than 3,000 people were killed according to Palestinian estimates. By then, the army had the upper hand, and by July 1971, the Resistance had been forced out of Jordan.

ECONOMIC AND POLITICAL PROGRESS

After 1970, the country finally entered a phase that was more stable politically and economically. The 1970s and early 1980s in fact proved a boom time for Jordan, with the country benefit-

Palestinian fighters in Amman in 1970, during the events of Black September.

ing in particular from the collapse of Lebanon and the oil boom in the Gulf. By the mid-1970s, more than 28 percent of the population was working abroad. By 1980, Jordan had a 9 percent growth rate and zero unemployment. Palestinians started to invest in real estate in Jordan, signalling their commitment.

However, the relationship between the PLO (which now represented all Palestinian organisations) and the Jordanian Government continued to grate. The two sides finally got together again towards the end of the 1970s, but efforts to reach a joint position on common problems broke up in 1986. While the king claimed the West Bank, the PLO argued that it represented all Palestinians, even those in the East Bank, and a stalemate ensued.

Meanwhile, the king was coming under pressure to democratise politics in Jordan. He was accused of using the West Bank crisis as an excuse for not holding elections.

In the meantime, the *Intifada* (uprising), which had begun in 1987, made it clear that the Palestinians of the West Bank looked to the PLO for leadership. King Husayn responded calmly but resolutely to these pressures. In July 1988 he renounced claims to the West Bank. In return the PLO promised to keep out of Jordanian politics. This paved the way for a greater degree of democracy.

On 8 November 1989, Jordanians went to the polls in the first free elections since the 1950s. It was also a first for Jordanian women, who had been given the right to vote in 1974. A national charter was later drawn up by a special commission, which stressed national unity and equality of citizenship. A new law was also passed which legalised all political parties.

ISLAMIC FUNDAMENTALISM

It was not all plain sailing in the years ahead, however. The 1990–91 Gulf War presented several of its own difficulties. The rising influence of Islamists was another thorny problem, and when, shortly before the 1993 elections, the king changed the electoral law, most observers agreed that this step was aimed at reducing the power of Islamic activists. The changes were initially criticised for reinforcing tribal and conservative voting patterns. Later, the king was accused of manipulating the outcome of the elections to ensure the passage of Jordan's controversial peace deal with Israel, and to push through other legislation disagreeable to the public.

The changes also inspired fear that the elections would be cancelled because of the unexpected Palestinian–Israeli peace accord of September 1993, but in the event, 800,000 people went to the polls in November to vote for candidates from some 20 parties. It was widely agreed that the composition of the new Parliament reflected the country's respect for the king, and was an endorsement of his call for moderation. But the change to the election law remains a point of contention to this day; it was a factor leading to a boycott by nine opposition parties, led by the Islamists, during the election of 1997.

In 1994, following Israeli withdrawal from parts of the Occupied Territories, Jordan signed a historic peace treaty with Israel. The agreement was greeted with hope for increased prosperity for the whole region. Before long, Israelis were visiting Petra as tourists.

THE END OF AN ERA

But dark clouds were gathering on another front. In the early 1990s, the king developed cancer of the lymphatic system. His ailing health began to raise uncomfortable questions about

United States in 1992 with a clean bill of health, most of the country came out on the streets to welcome him home, a testament to the people's genuine love and respect for their king. Following a relapse in 1998, when the king addressed his subjects via satellite from the Mayo Clinic in the US, not a car could be seen driving in Amman. When he returned home, apparently given the all clear, he was again greeted by an ecstatic welcome.

During Husayn's absence, the country was governed by his brother, Prince Hassan, his designated successor since 1965. However, in

Female voter casting her ballot.

the future, including who would succeed him, and even whether the country had the stability to survive without his unifying presence.

But the king mounted a valiant fight against cancer, and when he returned from treatment in the

Jordan's political parties have existed since the 1950s and include the Popular Unity Party, the Jordanian National Alliance, the Democratic Party of the Left, the Baathist and Communist parties, the Unionist Arab Democratic Party, the Future Party and the Islamic Action Front.

January 1999, the King suddenly made his eldest son, Abdullah, Crown Prince in place of Hassan. Shortly afterwards, the King was forced to return to the US for emergency medical treatment. Boarding his plane to the States, he looked ill and frail. A week later he was on the way home again, but this time on a life-support machine. Within days he was proclaimed dead.

King Husayn's funeral drew not just enormous crowds into the streets, but a dazzling array of world leaders, including four American presidents past and present, President Yeltsin of Russia, himself very ill, and a few sworn enemies of the past such as the late President Hafez Assad of Syria and Binyamin Netanyahu, the former Prime Minister of Israel.

KING ABDULLAH II

Stepping into his father's shoes hasn't proved easy for King Abdullah II. Though Jordan is more united than it has been at any time in its history, both domestic and regional developments are, as usual, testing the strength of its social fabric.

Over recent years, vocal discontent has increased amid a high unemployment rate, spectacular corruption scandals (involving appointees of the king), grindingly slow economic and political reform and high food prices. In response – as well as being influenced by

that erupted in the neighbouring West Bank and Gaza Strip pulled Jordan back into political uncertainty. Since then, relations have remained volatile and tense. Meanwhile, progress was made in June 2012 when the World Bank approved the feasibility study for the Israeli-Jordanian Red Sea–Dead Sea Canal (see page 201), which is due to begin construction in 2018.

Though the war in Iraq, Jordan's easterly neighbour, proved less destabilising than some commentators predicted, the fallout included considerable loss of revenue and an Al Qaeda

King Husayn's funeral procession.

the "Arab Spring" and intense instability in surrounding areas – Abdullah II has accelerated his long programme of reform, reviewing the laws governing politics and public freedoms. The general election in 2016 saw proportional representation reintroduced in Parliament, and in the same year Jordan launched its Comprehensive National Plan for Human Rights. Despite these improvements, for many, Jordan's political system remains pro-royalist and dominated by "East bankers" – Jordanians who predate the arrival of the Palestinian Jordanians in 1948.

The country's fortunes have always been directly linked to its neighbours', including the success or failure of the peace process and events across the Jordan River. In late 2000, the Palestinian *Intifada*

suicide bomb attack in 2005, resulting in some 60 deaths. While relations between Jordan and Iraq have traditionally been strong, with an emphasis on trade, land routes between the two countries have been greatly impacted by ISIL taking over swathes of Iraq's Anbar province in 2014.

On the country's economic front, fortunes are little better. Following the debt crisis of 1988–89, Jordan introduced a long-term economic and social reform plan known as the National Agenda. However, while developments have been made in reforming education and expanding privatisation and liberalisation, major regional and international events over the past couple of decades have severely hindered progress. The 1991 and 2003 wars in Iraq; the global economic crisis of 2008; the Syria and Iraq crises and the unprecedented influx of refugees; disrupted trade routes; plummeting tourist numbers; and high employment have all conspired against this largely peaceful nation.

On the social front, King Abdullah has sought to improve the rights of women in Jordan – women may now file for divorce, for example, and in 2017 a law allowing rapists to evade punishment if they married their victims was thankfully repealed. Female representation has also increased in Parliament (women MPs won 20 of 130 seats in the

hoped. In 2016, the IMF agreed to a Jordanian request for a three-year extended fund facility of around US$723 million to support the country's economic reform strategy; the sum will also help to manage the impact of Syrian refugees.

In spite of the challenges posed by the surrounding Middle East Crisis, Jordan remains a largely peaceable country, with a wealth of history and stunning landscapes to explore. And with tourist figures down, perhaps this is the perfect time to go – to help boost the local economy and visit mesmerising sights without the crowds.

King Abdullah II and Queen Rania with their eldest son and King Abdullah's uncle, former Crown Prince Hassan.

2016 elections, although their representation in the cabinet actually decreased).

JORDAN TODAY

Despite the turbulence in the region and some unrest at home, Jordan has avoided the instability and violence still experienced by many of its neighbours. Loyal armed forces, a powerful security service and lack of serious opposition (bar the Islamic Action Front, itself divided by in-fighting) will keep King Abdullah secure at least for the immediate future. Though the economy's poor performance has threatened to stir up social unrest, foreign aid, such as the IMF US$2bn handout in 2012, has helped maintain stability, as Jordan's Western allies fervently

⊘ THE REFUGEE CRISIS

The ongoing Syrian Civil War, as well as ongoing crises in Iraq, have caused instability in Jordan as well as spillover violence and waves of refugees. In 2017, an estimated 656,000 (registered) Syrian refugees lived in Jordan, contributing to Jordan's total refugee count of around 2.7 million people – a staggering figure for a small country with a population of under 10 million.

In 2016, Jordan effectively closed its borders to Syrian refugees following an attack on a Jordanian army post on the Syrian border near Rukban. The car bomb, claimed by ISIL, killed six soldiers. Sealing the border left thousands of refugees stranded in remote border areas beyond the reach of humanitarian aid.

A Bedouin man surveys Petra.

Bedouin men in Petra.

THE BEDOUIN WAY OF LIFE

Few Jordanians may lead a Bedouin way of life today, but a scratch below the surface reveals how much of Bedouin culture, tradition and thinking remains, and the importance of good etiquette.

BEDOUIN NOMADS

Only an estimated 7.5 percent of the country's population can still be regarded as nomadic (though 98 percent of Jordanians claim Bedouin ancestry). The massive settlement of the Bedouin over the past decades is a reflection both of well-meaning governmental policy and a desire for a more comfortable lifestyle on the part of the Bedouin themselves.

Though there are 15 major tribes in Jordan, the number of families who still move about in tents is a tiny fraction of the whole population. Yet wherever one goes, the Bedouins' long, narrow tents can be spotted from afar, pitched on remote mountainsides or on the outskirts of cities, from the Sirhan tribe in the northeast, and the Beni Sakhr in central Jordan, to the Howeitat in the south and the Palestinian tribes from the Bir Sheba area in Wadi 'arabah.

A Bedouin woman near Petra.

> The long black dress worn by Bedouin women is called a thaub or a madraga. They cover their heads with a band called a usaba.

The Bedouin nomad, by definition, keeps moving from one place to the other, following grazing and water sources. Semi-nomadic Bedouin, by contrast, raise crops as well as livestock, and their settlement in villages is seasonal. After spending the winter in villages, they return in spring and summer to their nomadic lifestyle. As more Bedouin settle to take advantage of the schools and clinics and electricity and water provided by the government in villages, towns and cities, the lines between city, village and nomadic life are blurred. Today, it is individual families who move from place to place, not the tribe.

THE BEDOUIN TODAY

Today fewer than 50,000 of Jordan's Bedouin are thought to be truly nomadic (around 1.5 percent of the total population), and around 6 percent semi-nomadic. Though scattered pockets are found throughout the country, including on the outskirts of Amman, the majority are found in the desert plains of the Badia in the east of Jordan, and in the desert dunes to the south. Look out for the unmistakable black and white goat hair tents set up a safe distance from the road. Only today, the camp furnishings may well include large 4WDs, TVs attached to long cables and lots of mobile phones recharging.

Though most Jordanians you meet are likely to be settled, well-educated urbanites, it doesn't take much digging to reveal the Bedouin beneath the surface: even young men recall life spent herding goats, or have parents or grandparents who recount tales of their lives as wandering nomads.

The Bedouin heritage also runs deep, and its traditions and culture pervade many aspects of

name", "What is your nationality", takes the place of "What is your tribe?".

The Bedouin respect, loyalty and deference shown to elders and their leaders also still shows itself in the reluctance (albeit much less in recent months) to criticise their king and royal family. Honesty is still considered a cardinal Bedouin virtue, and huge anger is expressed towards corruption. Clan and tribal ties also remain paramount. Even among today's politicians in Jordan's Parliament, family ties come before all, including party and political allegiance. Jordan's main opposition

Pouring Bedouin tea, made using the dried leaves of desert plants.

Bedouin girls' names are often poetic, or have religious significance.

Jordanian society. On a superficial level, most Jordanians retain a deep passion for the desert, camping, picnics and camels, and will find any excuse to indulge it.

Deeper traits include the tremendous tradition of hospitality, once accorded to strangers passing through tribal territory in the potentially deadly terrain of the desert. The idea is built around reciprocity: you look after me in your territory; I'll look after you in mine and we'll all have a better chance of survival. The old Bedouin need to quickly identify friend or foe is reflected in the barrage of questions that visitors sometimes find tiring and intrusive: "Where are you from?", "What is your

consists of an Islamic party bound together by religion not politics.

Many Bedouin still manage to live fully or partly from the desert. Generous hospitality is still offered to strangers, but this time the travellers are tourists and there is a charge for it. Safe passage across the desert is also still offered – by camel and horse in the old manner as well as by 4WD – as is desert guiding, but to tourist attractions in Wadi Rum rather than wells or villages. Pride in hospitality is still key, but word of mouth is digital as well as physical, as Bedouin camps in places such as Wadi Rum advertise themselves. See page 254 for more on the Bedouin.

BEDOUIN ETIQUETTE

Many ancient rules of etiquette persist to this day. If invited to a Bedouin tent, it is polite to approach from behind and pause before entering. A guest is considered welcome for three and a third days; during that time the host doesn't even have the right to ask the guest's name. However, to outstay a visit is a big social no-no; there is even a saying that "the serpent is more acceptable than the guest who overstays his visit".

Inside the tent, strict etiquette also applies. Perfect conduct is expected on the part of the guest, who must guard above all against looking at the host's wife or daughters. When leaving, the host for their part must "see the guest off like a minister", but not too well in case it looks as if the host is glad to see the back of the guest!

When more than one guest visits, coffee, poured traditionally from an elegant pot called a *dalleh*, is first offered to the main guest, while tea is offered from the right. If a guest wants more coffee, the tiny porcelain cup is held out to be served again. To indicate that enough has been drunk, the cup is wiggled from side to side.

When eating, only the right hand is used. The left hand, reserved for ablutions, is kept firmly to one side or behind the back. Utensils are not used and food is shared from a large communal plate. When eating rice such as the Jordanian national dish (of Bedouin origin), *mansaf* (lamb on top of a bed of rice), fingers are used to shape a mouth-sized ball of rice, meat and sauce.

It's considered good etiquette to eat only from the food directly before one – not that in front of a neighbour. The head of the sheep, often placed in the centre of the *mansaf*, is traditionally left untouched since it symbolises the welcome accorded the guest. Hogging all the meat, rice or sauce is thought to show greed; finishing all the bread suggests the host wasn't as generous as he should have been.

BEDOUIN WEDDINGS

When travelling around Jordan, look out for the large marquees erected close to the road. Many will host Bedouin weddings and you may well be invited to join in the celebrations. Bedouin marriage as a ritual has changed very little over the years and is governed by strict protocol.

The *jaha*, the asking of a bride's hand, follows a set procedure. Before visiting the bride's family, the groom's family enlists the support of the most respected members of the community.

At the bride's house, the father of the bride or the head of her tribe welcomes the visitors. One cup of coffee only is poured for the main guest. Identifying this important person forms part of an elaborate ritual: the cup is passed around

Bedouin boy.

☉ WHAT'S IN A NAME?

Girls in Bedouin society are often given names that reflect the community's life spent outdoors, close to nature. These may be poetic names, evocative of the environment in which the Bedouin exist, or of natural phenomena: "Ishbeh", for example (meaning blade of grass), "Shatwa" (spring shower) or "Sharqiya" (the east wind that was blowing on the day the girl was born). Many names are believed to date to pre-Islamic time. Some girls' names are rather more prosaic: for example "Kifaya" (meaning "that's enough [girls]"!); others, such as Aisha and Fatma, have religious significance (in this case they are the names of the wife and daughter of the Prophet Mohammed).

until someone accepts it. As it is passed among the group, each demurs in turn, saying "No, it should be so-and-so, not me". The one who finally accepts the 'cup of the *jaha*' doesn't drink it but begins instead a speech: "In the name of God the all-merciful and compassionate, we are the *jaha*. We would like to be your in-laws. We want your daughter for our son..." The petitioner must never mention the name of the girl during the speech. Then the girl's tribe is praised and a declaration of friendship between the two clans is made.

Traditionally, a group of women would fetch the bride from her tribe on a Thursday afternoon. In the past, they would go on 100 to 200 horses. When the bride saw them coming, she was obliged to run away so that the women couldn't accuse her of being eager to be married. When they eventually caught the bride, the women first bathed her and painted red henna on the palms and soles of her feet before carrying her back to their village.

The official ceremonial lunch was then held on the Friday, the day after the marriage of the

Inside a goat-hair tent, Wadi Rum.

⊘ FAMILY FIRST

In the past, if a man wanted to get engaged to a woman from outside his tribe, the girl's male cousins had priority over him, even if her parents had agreed to the match. This rule applied right up to the wedding day. The practice caused much trouble among the tribes, often leading to bloody feuds, and the tradition was eventually outlawed. However, marriage between cousins is still common and even encouraged among the Bedouin, and is not unusual in Jordanian society as a whole. In the past, it was a way of maintaining tight clan ties and loyalty in a dangerous and warring world.

couple. The women guests sat separate from the men, who lay under a black goat-hair tent. Guests would bring a gift (*nuqout*) which was often a sheep, some rice or money. Today, it's more likely to be a TV, silver or a piece of crystal. Praise-singing is traditional in which the virtues of the bride and groom are extolled, and the father of the groom is recognised as a distinguished leader who comes from a good, strong tribe. Celebrations before the wedding can still last for up to three nights, during which there is much singing and firing of guns, building to a frenzy the night they bring the bride. A week later, the bride traditionally pays a visit to her parents, traditionally taking with her a sheep, rice, sugar and a pot of clarified butter.

View over the Golan Heights and Sea of Galilee from Umm qays.

THE PALESTINIANS

Though first arriving over half a century ago and for the most part successfully establishing themselves, the status and future of Jordan's Palestinians remain uncertain.

At Umm qays in the north of Jordan, the site of an impressive Greco-Roman town (see page 183), there is a magnificent view over the Sea of Galilee and Israel. Cars from many different Arab states – Saudi Arabia, Syria, Iraq and the Gulf – park here nearly every day; many belong to the diaspora of Palestinians returning to glimpse what was once their homeland. Most tourists who come here to pick over the ruins, eat at the excellent Umm qays restaurant and admire the lovely views are unaware of the deep nostalgia and sombreness of the place.

THE DIASPORA

In 1947, there were about 1.3 million Palestinian Arabs living under the British Mandate in Palestine. Two years later, more than 700,000 of them had dispersed throughout the Middle East, driven from their homes by Israeli forces. In 1967, when Israel occupied the West Bank – the last remaining part of historical Palestine – 150,000 existing refugees moved on again, and a further 300,000 became refugees for the first time.

Palestinian wearing a keffiyeh, the traditional Arab headdress.

Most of these Palestinians settled in Jordan, where they have been granted Jordanian citizenship. Some are allowed to visit their homeland – with the permission of the Israeli authorities (Israel still controls the Palestinian Authority's borders) – but only a small fraction have been given leave by Israel to return to live in their former homeland.

HISTORY OF THE JORDANIAN PALESTINIANS

Under the Ottomans, who ruled modern-day Jordan from the 15th century onwards, there was unrestricted movement throughout an empire that stretched from North Africa to modern Iraq and from Turkey to the Yemen. Links between the east and west banks of the Jordan River were particularly important for trade and connections even between individual towns were close: Al-salt with Nablus, Nazareth and Jerusalem; Al-karak with Hebron; and, in the north, Irbid with Beisan, Tiberias and Galilee.

This close association survived the British Mandate. Indeed, many Palestinians west of the Jordan had better access to education than those east of the Jordan River, and many subsequently found jobs in Emir Abdullah's administration. Palestinian peasants on both sides of the river continued to cross back and forth in pursuit of seasonal labour.

However, the carving up of the Middle East into spheres of influence by Britain and France, and the creation of the Emirate of Transjordan along with Britain's commitment to establishing a Jewish national home in Palestine, turned everything on its head.

The new factions began to compete. The primary purpose of Emir Abdullah, Transjordan's new head of state, was to sustain and develop his Emirate. The main objective of the Palestinian leader, Haj Amin al-Husayni, the Mufti of Jerusalem, was to foil British plans to turn Palestine into a Jewish national home. The Mufti consequently adopted a firm anti-Zionist, anti-British stand, while Emir Abdullah favoured a more conciliatory line.

Following the decimation of the Palestinian national movement in the 1936–39 rebellion against the British, and the 1948 war with Israel, the Emir gathered his Palestinian allies in Jericho in 1948. At this meeting, they agreed to the absorption of areas still held by the Jordanian Army (namely the West Bank) into Jordan.

In the 1950s and early 1960s, a new Palestinian leadership emerged that would eventually come to form the PLO in 1964. Palestinians saw the organisation as a means of asserting their authority and taking charge of their own destiny. The Jordanian government, however, feared the effects of a "dual authority" on its efforts to forge a state out of the Palestinians and Jordanian population who made up society.

The disastrous Arab defeat in the 1967 war against Israel brought these differences to a head. In the post-war vacuum, Palestinian guerrillas began to develop their strength in Jordan and soon constituted "a state within a state", effectively challenging the sovereignty and authority of the king.

In September 1970, all-out conflict broke out between the Palestinians and the Jordanian Army. By July 1971, however, King Husayn's forces had driven the guerrillas out of his country.

Palestinian embroidery, Museum of Popular Traditions.

⊘ JORDAN AND THE PLO

The 1974 Rabat Arab Summit may have upheld the PLO's sole right to represent all Palestinians, but it seriously undermined King Husayn's efforts to secure national unity in Jordan, as well as his claim to the West Bank. Successive talks between the PLO and Jordanian government failed to find a compromise until 1988, eight months after the outbreak of the *Intifada* in the West Bank and Gaza against Israeli occupation. Persuaded by popular support for the PLO in his own country, the king renounced his claims to the West Bank, but in return, the PLO promised to stay out of Jordanian politics on the East Bank. An uneasy truce has remained in force ever since.

JORDANIAN PALESTINIANS TODAY

The mark of Palestine is everywhere in Jordan, especially in the towns. Look out for the names of shops or restaurants (such as the common "Al Quds", the Arabic name for Jerusalem), the refugee camps (such as Wahdat and Jabal al-Husayn) and even the posh areas of Amman (such as 'Abdun, where you can see vast mansions funded by money made in the Gulf). Eager to improve their lot and recuperate what they have lost, many Palestinians have worked hard. They also boast the highest university graduate rate in the Arab world.

Unfortunately, they also face discrimination in terms of citizenship. All Arab states except Jordan exclude Palestinians from government bodies, and in Lebanon and the Gulf, they cannot own property or businesses without local Arab partners.

In Jordan, Palestinians dominate the private sector in banking, retail and international trade, but in the army, and until recently, the government, their influence is marginal.

Meanwhile, many Jordanians resent the Palestinian dominance of the private sector, and their growing influence in the judiciary and government. There is also resentment at the dominance and disruption of their lives caused by the ongoing Palestinian-Israeli conflict. Some Jor-

The thorny question of who is Palestinian and who is Jordanian remains one of the country's most sensitive issues.

danian nationalists have also called on Palestinians to choose between their Palestinian and Jordanian identities. They claim the Palestinians want to have it both ways: to retain full rights and privileges in Jordan whilst claiming national rights in Palestine. Recently, some Jordanians have expressed disquiet at the notion of Jordan becoming Palestine.

Controversy even reigns in the debate about the exact number of Palestinians in Jordan. Some analysts put the total figure (those who arrived in 1948 and after) at 70 percent of Jordan's population; others at just 35 percent. The reality is that it is now impossible to draw sharp lines between Jordanians and Palestinians.

The fact remains that Jordan has received more Palestinian refugees than any other country. Though most have integrated well – and make a significant contribution to Jordan's economic, political, judicial and cultural life – a large proportion languishes in refugee camps in a seemingly wretched state of limbo. There have also been disturbing accounts of Jordanian hostility towards Palestinian refugees fleeing the Syrian Civil War.

Some reports suggest figures may be as high as half a million sheltered in nearly a dozen UN Relief & Works Agency (UNRWA)-run camps around the country, including outside Amman, Marqa, Irbid, Al-zarqa' and Baqa'a. You may well pass the camp at Jarash

during a visit there. Unofficial camps are also found across the country. For more information on the refugees, contact UNRWA (www.unrwa.org).

THE FUTURE

Should a Palestinian state ever evolve out of the Palestinian Authority, King Abdullah II has declared that Jordanian Palestinians will be free to choose between a home in Palestine and one in Jordan. While a kind of confederation has been suggested between the two states, Pales-

Young Palestinian woman in Azraq.

tinian and Jordanian officials have both continually dismissed the idea – Palestinians fearing they would end up subservient to Jordan, and Jordan fearful that Israel would expel thousands of Palestinians from Israeli territory, forcing them into Jordan's and consequently upsetting the already delicate balance between the Palestinian and Jordanian populations.

Even without a Jordanian-Palestinian confederation, some Jordanians fear the expulsion of Palestinians from the West Bank by Israelis, in effect making the country more Palestine than Jordan (which some believe it already is). Whatever the future brings, Jordan's stability and welfare remain inextricably linked to its troubled neighbour, whether it wants it or not.

An Aladdin's cave of a bead shop in Al'aqabah.

Kilims from Maʾdaba on sale at the Alaydi Jordan Craft Centre, Amman.

THE CRAFT TRADITION

Read a woman's life story in her embroidery or weaving, delight in Hebron glass and jewellery and carry it all back home in functional, well-made basketry.

While Jordanian men traditionally worked outside the home, Jordanian women employed themselves inside, producing beautiful and accomplished handicrafts. They also plied their crafts, especially embroidery, while visiting one another at home, in courtyards and along footpaths, passing on to the younger generation not just millennia-old skills but their ancient oral history in the form of proverbs, folklore and family history. Though the tradition is not as widespread as it once was, Jordan's arts and crafts are experiencing something of a revival.

JORDANIAN CRAFT REVIVAL

In Europe, the US and the Middle East, increasing numbers of upmarket home-furnishing stores now stock crafts from Jordan in recognition of its quality. Stunning collections of traditional crafts such as that of Widad Kawar have also done the rounds of major museums.

Meanwhile, in Jordan itself, the revival and reputation of Jordanian crafts are being advanced by the patronage of Jordan's royal family through some excellent charitable organisations such as the Noor Al-Hussein Foundation (www.nooralhusseinfoundation.org) and Queen Rania's Jordan River Foundation (www.queenrania.jo). National development initiatives include Save the Children's Bani Hamida Women's Weaving Project, the Beit al Bawadi project (www.beitalbawadi.com) in Amman, the Made in Jordan shop (www.madeinjordan.com) in Wadi musa and the various outlets of the RSCN-run Wild Jordan Centre (www.rscn.org.jo) in Amman and many of the national parks.

Other co-operatives are springing up around the country as their advantages are recognised: they bring in work and revenue for local

Hebron glassware.

communities (often disadvantaged women), tourism to rural areas, the nurturing of new artists, the teaching of professions to those who have none and the preservation of ancient skills for later generations.

Since the 1970s, traditional crafts have also been mixed with high fashion. Pioneers include enterprising women such as Mariam Abu Laban and Leila Jurius, who began to match traditional Jordanian and Palestinian needlework with rich Middle Eastern fabrics, such as striped and watered silk. By so doing, they created elegant and classical gowns and jackets with a modern flair. Other designers have followed suit, resulting in collections modelled seasonally on catwalks at Jordan's luxury hotels. Queen Rania and Queen

Noor support this modern-traditional fashion industry, often wearing such gowns and suits for public appearances at home and abroad.

WHERE TO BUY CRAFTS

Many crafts and antiques are available in handicraft shops around the country as well as in the markets of Amman, including the excellent Suq Jara (Fawzi Malouf St, off Rainbow St; May–Sept Fri 10am–10pm). Providing a great introduction and overview and a kind of quality control for future browsing, are some excellent museums

Palestinian embroidery.

around the country. The Jordan Museum, the Jordanian Museum of Popular Tradition and the Jordanian Folklore Museum, found on either side of the Roman Theatre in Amman (see page 149) are good places to start.

EMBROIDERY

As a young girl learned the stitches, she was also initiated into her culture. Patterns, colours and fabrics revealed her village, tribe, social status, material wealth and the period in which she lived. Individuality was expressed in the way each woman assembled the pieces of her dress.

A young girl's skill in embroidery was noted by the older women and was equated with her capabilities as a homemaker. The finer her

> When browsing craft shops and markets, look out for old, wood-carved games such as the mangala, which uses a board carved in the shape of a cupcake pan. Originating in Roman times, it is still played in some Jordanian villages.

stitches, they said, the better her groom. Until quite recently, nearly every Jordanian or Palestinian girl, whatever her social class, embroidered her own trousseau. The six to 12 loosely cut robes she made were worn over a lifetime, and her bridal dress served for many special occasions – and in some cases as her shroud.

Trousseaus on both sides of the Jordan River traditionally included embroidered cushions that were as beautiful and varied as the dresses. Today, it is the cushions that have carried this art into modern-day life in Jordan: in many a home, the decor is not complete without one or more matching sets. Their colours can range from red, maroon, purple and pink, spiked with orange, green and gold, to a more sober combination that instead emphasises the artistry of the needlework. The simple cross-stitch forms the basis for the myriad designs, and the recurring motifs tend to be drawn from nature.

Contemporary pieces include large wall-hangings stitched with the "tree of life" motif and elegant quilts based on the popular "horse's hoof" design.

Palestinian cross-stick embroidery in particular is highly regarded throughout the region. Ma'daba (see page 208) and Amman are both good places to browse and buy embroidery.

WEAVING

Like embroidery, Bedouin weavings are expressions of a whole way of life. They serve many purposes in the nomadic environment: as outer walls and room dividers in the tents; as cushions and bedding-bags that make up the furniture; as rugs, coffee bags, saddle-bags and food containers, among any number of other practical uses. All are woven by hand out of sheep's wool or goat and camel hair.

It takes at least two months to transform raw wool into rugs. The work is usually shared by a husband and wife team: the husband shears the wool and washes it, and both card and spin the fleece into yarn. In the past, women dyed the wool using bark, earth, indigo, plants and insects as colourants, though nowadays the husband is more likely to deliver it to the dye master in the nearby town.

When the wool is ready, they both assemble the ground loom and the woman gets to work weaving the rug. Sometimes, two women sit side by side, passing the shuttle and beating the weft threads into place with the use of the horn of a gazelle.

For each rug, a ground loom is constructed anew, with whatever material happens to be avail-

regarded mosaic school in Byzantine times, and is also home to the famous Ma'daba Map (see page 209), the oldest surviving map of Palestine in the world, and as impressive for its scale and size as its artistry. Mosaic schools and workshops can be visited in Ma'daba.

POTTERY AND CERAMICS

Jordan's natural clay deposits have been utilised for millennia. Archaeological digs are littered with shards dating from prehistoric times, and the early Islamic period saw an exceptional blos-

Weaving cotton in Amman.

able. The stones, sticks and stakes normally used in a loom are sometimes replaced by a shovel and a couple of orange crates or ammunition boxes.

For many, it is sometimes difficult to believe that such rudimentary tools and such a simple weaving technique can produce pieces that are so exquisitely crafted. The town of Ma'daba (see page 208) is known for its variety and quality of rugs; here you can also see carpet weavers at work at their looms.

MOSAIC MAKING

This ancient art is thought to have been introduced by the Romans. Mosaics litter Jordan, some dating as far back as the 1st century BC; many are very fine. Ma'daba boasted a highly

soming of ceramic arts, as pottery in all of Jordan's main museums demonstrates. Until very recently, simple sun-cured pottery, baked in a dung and straw-fired pit, was used for food storage as well as for serving vessels and oil lamps. The most common pots were the large coil-and-slab *jarra*, often around 75cm (2.5ft) tall. Once used to store water and olive oil, and to pickle and preserve olives, these can now be seen gracing the gardens of elegant villas in Amman.

Today, talented young artists are reviving and reinterpreting this ancient art form, blending old techniques with modern ideas and technology. One of the best modern ceramicists is Mahmoud Taha, well known for his tile murals. Hazim Zu'bi and sisters Rula and Reem Atalla have introduced designs based on contemporary Islamic calligraphy and petroglyphs. Probably the best selection of pottery is found in Amman and Wadi musa.

> To maintain the right tension in the fabric, the weaver traditionally wraps the yarn around her toe in such a way that the rug, the loom and the woman become as one.

Making mosaics in a workshop near Ma'daba.

JEWELLERY

Like ceramic-making, the crafting of jewellery has a long history in Jordan. Caches of gold jewellery from the 9th to the 5th centuries BC have been found near Petra. Cameos and jewellery made of copper, bronze, silver, iron and glass from the later Bronze Age to Roman times have been unearthed near Amman. Today, gold jewellery – formerly the preserve of the royals and the upper classes – is coveted and collected by rich and poor alike. Most women of all social strata possess at least a few gold pieces. In Amman's gold *suq* you can see a huge range of people buying and selling the 21-carat jewellery. A popular souvenir for travellers is a tiny gold *dalleh* (coffee pot), a symbol of Jordan, worn on a chain.

Until recently, a Bedouin bride wore her personal wealth in her silver jewellery, retaining the right to dispose of it as she chose. The pieces were bought or sold according to the woman's whims, or the rise or fall in the family's fortunes. The silver jewellery of the Bedouin comes in a dazzling variety of designs. Several shops in Amman stock a good range and quality of Bedouin jewellery.

COPPERWARE

Evidence for some of the world's oldest known copper mines and forges have been found in Jordan (some can be seen at Al-'aqabah's Archaeological Museum; see page 264). For millennia, copper has been used to make weapons, tools and cooking utensils. Today, the ubiquitous copper coffee pot is the most common sight and can be bought in varying sizes and quality in many of Jordan's town suqs, including in Amman.

BLOWN GLASS

Hebron glass", named after the West Bank city, comes in shades ranging from cobalt blue, bottle green and turquoise, to amber, pale pink and rose. When displayed against light, for example on a sunlit window sill, the glass glows like jewels. Workshops where the glass-blowing is practised are found at Na'ur, on the old road to the Dead Sea, in Ma'daba on the way to Jabal nibu (Mount Nebo) and in the King Abdullah Gardens in Amman, where larger items are produced. Originally made from sand, the glass is now made by recycling old bottles.

BASKETRY

One of the most ubiquitous crafts in Jordan is basket-making. Baskets and trays are woven for every imaginable purpose and come in every size. Those with handles are used to store grain or carry fruits and vegetables from market, while the deep baskets with lids, large enough for a child to hide in, are used as laundry baskets. Even beehives were once plaited of cane.

Today, a basketry project begun by the Bisharat family in the northern village of Mukheibeh, on the Yarmouk River, produces baskets of split bamboo and palm leaves that are sold in flower shops all over Jordan. Large round mats are also woven from bamboo fronds by Druze women in Azraq.

📷 BUILDING ON THE PAST

The buildings of Jordan mix and match architectural styles spanning 2,000 years of history – from the Romans to the Ottomans.

Although lacking a grand urban tradition of design, such as that found in Cairo or Damascus, Jordan is nonetheless home to an eclectic range of architectural styles. As a succession of empires or civilisations swept through, each new power was influenced both by the architectural styles and devices of its predecessors and by its own native traditions.

Evidence remains from dozens of periods. The castle of Qasr al-Abd (see page 157), west of Amman, dates from the Hellenistic period (around 200 BC). Impressive Roman sites abound, from Jarash (see page 173) to the classically influenced Arabian designs of the Nabataeans at Petra (see page 227). Qasr al-mushta (see page 282), one of the "desert castles", displays a fusion of classical styles and the repetitive geometric patterns particular to Islam.

And the tradition continues. Jordan has produced some of the Arab world's most highly acclaimed contemporary architects. Although modern Jordanian architecture isn't as showy as the grand projects of the Gulf countries, home-grown architects such as Jafar Tukan and Rasem Badran are renowned for producing functional, beautiful buildings. Amman's Royal Automobile Museum is one of Tukan's finest works, a long, low building clad in untreated stone, while Badran's Dar al-Omran company designed the stunning Petra Mövenpick hotel.

The King Abdullah mosque, built in the 1980s, is one of Amman's more recent landmarks. Traditional motifs are given a modern twist.

The Urn Tomb, one of the royal tombs at Petra. The Nabataeans mined every architectural style known to them. Petra is mainly a mix of Greek, Roman and Egyptian influences.

Amman's Abu Darwish mosque.

Ammar Khammash is at once an architect, designer, academic, artist and photographer.

Ammar Khammash

Born in 1960, Ammar Khammash is one of Jordan's leading designers and architects. After his widely acclaimed PhD thesis, *Notes on Village Architecture in Jordan*, Khammash has become involved in many high-profile building projects around the country focusing on the preservation of Jordan's architectural heritage by restoring traditional buildings for use in tourism. One of Khammash's early commissions was at Umm qays (see page 183), where he employed a team of local crafts-workers and masons to help restore an Ottoman schoolhouse to serve as a tourist resthouse; the team used local materials in traditional ways. Another important project was the Dana Guest House (see page 219). Khammash is also one of Jordan's most prominent artists and photographers.

...sr al-haranah desert castle. The Omayyads built these ...stles east of Amman, but the origins of many of the ...tresses stretch back to Roman times.

...ll detail at al-Husseni mosque, downtown Amman.

Hadrian's Arch at Jarash, built in AD 129.

Hummous, falafel, tabouleh and pitta bread.

JORDANIAN FOOD

"The guest is the hostage of the host" says an old Arabic proverb, so when you're heading to Jordan be sure to pack a healthy appetite.

Food can – and should – form an important part of any trip to Jordan. In the Arab world, a good homemade spread is a way of honouring guests, and Jordanian hosts spare no effort. Jordanian people are famously hospitable and proud to play host no matter how modest their means. Four people are usually plied with enough food for eight at least. In return, hosts expect their guests to eat amply, and even when their appetites are sated – pleas for mercy will only earn them another serving.

Although a meal can feel fairly heavy, the local diet is healthy, based mainly on fresh vegetables, garlic, a mixture of spices and herbs and olive oil. These are commonly joined by a few other staples, including yoghurt, *lebaneh* (a semi-dried yoghurt, roughly the consistency of cream cheese with a flavour similar to sour cream) and *tahini* (a paste made from sesame seeds). Although the basic ingredients are limited, they are combined skilfully to create a huge and imaginative array of dishes.

FOREIGN INFLUENCE

Jordanians freely acknowledge that their cuisine is an amalgam of different Middle Eastern dishes, in particular from Lebanon, Syria, Palestine and Egypt. Common among them are *hummous, ful mutabal, falafel* and *tabouleh*. Arabs quip that these are Arab versions of fast food – albeit rather more healthy ones than burgers and fries – and hundreds of roadside restaurants are dedicated to selling them. These dishes, accompanied by a pitta-like bread that serves as a scoop, can also be served as appetisers or as part of a *meze*, a buffet of light dishes.

Harvesting olives in the north, near Umm qays.

Dishes and meals also have a degree of flexibility about them: *hummous*, for example, is equally appropriate at breakfast, or with an evening meal, while *meze*, or *muqabalat*, may be served alongside a main lunch or dinner dish but can equally well be a meal in itself. The most important aspect of dining is that it is congregational, especially in the case of lunch, the largest meal of the day, when traditionally life grinds to a halt for at least two hours for an extended family get-together.

TYPICAL JORDANIAN DISHES

Lunch usually includes a stewed dish, such as lamb or chicken, served on rice. Favourites are *muloukhieh*, a leafy green vegetable cooked with chicken pieces; *bamieh*, okra stewed in tomato sauce with garlic and lamb or beef; and *masakhen*, a dish of chicken on a bed of *shraq* (a very thin bread), smothered in onions and all baked in oil and sprinkled with a citrus-flavoured spice called *sumac*. Another recommendation is *maqloubeh*, which is prepared with lightly fried chicken (or other meat) with any fried vegetable – Jordanians have a preference for aubergine or cauliflower – stewed in a crock with uncooked rice piled between layers of chicken and vegetable. Once the

rice is cooked through, the crock is upended onto a platter before it is served – hence the name *maqloubeh*, which literally means "upside-down".

Jordanians of Palestinian origin have a penchant for a baked dish known as *fatteh*. The base for *fatteh* is Arabic bread, broken into bits, over which is layered a mixture of vegetables and meat – *fatteh hummous*; *fatteh maqdous* (with aubergine and minced meat); *fatteh djaj* (chicken) – followed by a cold topping of yoghurt or *tahini*.

Mint leaves, used as a tea to aid digestion.

Making falafel, deep-fried balls of ground chickpeas or slightly spiced broad beans.

⊘ THE RAMADAN FAST

During Ramadan, the ninth month of the Muslim calendar, Muslims traditionally observe a fast from dawn to dusk, and only eat a meal – *iftar* – after sunset. At the end of the month, Eid al-Fitr is the feast held to mark the end of the fast, when special food is eaten and alms are given to the poor.

For non-Muslim visitors, hours of business for restaurants and shops can be erratic during Ramadan, and it can prove difficult to get a meal anywhere (except in the larger tourist hotels) before sunset. It's considered respectful for non-fasters to avoid eating or drinking in public in daylight hours during Ramadan.

Stuffed vegetables are considered a mark of culinary skill. Their preparation is labour intensive, and if you are offered either *wara dawali* (minced lamb, ghee, nutmeg, cinnamon and rice stuffed in vine leaves) or *cusa mashi* (courgettes stuffed with the same), you'll know you are being highly honoured.

THE NATIONAL DISH

Jordanians proudly claim only one dish as their own: *mansaf*, a Bedouin invention that has become the Jordanian national dish. Jordanians make a clear distinction between being invited to a mere lunch or dinner and being invited to a *mansaf*. It is a true feast:

usually a whole stewed lamb, served on a steaming heap of rice and *shraq*, doused in hot *jameed* (dried yoghurt), sprinkled with *snobar* (toasted pine nuts) and served on an enormous platter. Often, the (cooked) sheep's head is placed on top. The eyeballs and tongue are considered a delicacy and are offered by the host to the honoured guest. To decline is considered a slight to the host.

This gastronomic event is reserved for special occasions, such as when hosting an honoured figure in society, or celebrating births,

the right hand, which expertly rolls the meat, rice and bread into neat bite-sized balls. (The left hand, according to the instructions of Islam, is the hand used for bodily hygiene, and should never touch food, but instead is kept firmly to the side or behind the back.) As a further test of dexterity, only the thumb, fore- and middle fingers should be used to pop the ball into the mouth, without lips and fingers touching.

It reflects poorly on a host's generosity if a guest ever reaches the bottom of the dish, but it

Grilling chicken at The Basin restaurant, Petra.

weddings or graduations, or welcoming home family members who have been abroad for a long time. *Mansaf* is prepared, eaten and discussed with a reverence usually reserved for religious ritual.

Rules govern both a *mansaf's* preparation and consumption. In Bedouin tradition, for example, the size of a *mansaf* is relative to the esteem in which the guest is held – the bigger the *mansaf*, the more honoured the guest. Generally, however, Bedouins refer to chunks "the size of a cat's head" as the standard measure by which to carve the meat (a task which should only be carried out by the host).

The dish is sometimes eaten standing and, challenging though it may seem, using only

is equally considered poor etiquette for guests to eat anything except what is immediately in front of them.

MEZE OR *MUQABALAT*

Hummous: a dip of mashed chick peas blended with tahini (pulped sesame seeds), lemon and garlic topped with olive oil. This is the most common of the *muqabalat* and for many people constitutes a meal in itself.

Baba ghanoush: a dip made of the pulp of cooked aubergine which is at its best when it has been cooked over charcoal and has a wonderful smokey flavour. When mixed with tahini and garlic, it is called *mutabal*, but the distinction is not always made.

Falafel: deep-fried balls of slightly spiced broad beans often mixed with garlic, parsley, spices and sometimes onion. Usually served as a sandwich inside hot pitta bread with tahini and salad, it's unquestionably the most popular (and ubiquitous) snack across the Arab world. Falafel is the Middle East's closest equivalent to fast food and is served throughout the day, but is particularly popular at breakfast and in the early hours of the morning with students and young people after a night out. The best are golden, crisp

Maqloubeh tends to consist of rice, lightly fried chicken and any fried vegetable.

and crunchy on the outside and bright green (showing freshness) on the inside.

Ful moudames (usually known just as "ful"): originally a pauper's meal which in time became a popular breakfast dish for Arabs of all classes. It consists of boiled fava beans, crushed garlic and lemon juice and is topped with olive oil and served with bread. Filling, nourishing and sustaining, it makes a great start to the day. Many hotels in Jordan serve it as part of their Arabic breakfast, and you'll also see many tiny street stalls selling it from large metal urns in the early hours of the morning.

Koubba (or *kibbe*) *maqliya*: a deep-fried oval-shaped ball with a meat and bulgar-wheat paste as its crust and an aromatic filling of minced meat and pine nuts in the middle. It must be eaten hot to be enjoyed. Making *koubba* requires skill; the smaller their size and the thinner their crust, the more skilful supposedly the cook that made them. The best *koubba* is found in the Jordanian home rather than the restaurants. It is sometimes served in a warm, yoghurt-based sauce.

Vine leaves: stuffed with rice and/or meat, herbs and spices.

Ma'ajanat: meaning pastries made with dough (*ajin*), such as *fattayer* and *sambusak* (small baked pastries filled with minced meat, or a white salty cheese from Nablus and herbs, or spinach and sumac, a slightly sour dark-red powdered seed).

Manaeesh: flat bread with powdered oregano and sesame seeds.

Sfeeha: a flat dough spread with spicy minced meat.

MAIN COURSES

Few things can beat the smell and taste of Middle Eastern grilled meats cooked on skewers over a charcoal fire. Some of the most common grills available in restaurants are:

Shish taouk: a delicious low-fat dish of boneless chicken pieces served with lemon juice and garlic.

Kofta kebab: spicy minced lamb.

Maqloubeh: meaning "upside-down" and made of rice mixed with large chunks of chicken, lamb or fish and vegetables moulded and turned upside down to serve.

Mansaf: see under "National Dish" above.

Mussakhan: Palestinian in origin, this dish consists of chicken quarters baked and served on pieces of flat soft bread covered with chopped onions, pine nuts and plenty of sumac.

Shawarmah: the equivalent of the doner kebab – thin slices of beef, lamb or chicken cooked on the spit and stuffed into pitta bread with tahini and pickles.

Shish kebab: cubes of boneless lamb or beef.

Excellent fresh fish and seafood can be found near the Red Sea in towns such as Al-'aqabah, though fresh fish is a relatively new phenomenon in Amman. As a rule, fish in Jordan is prepared on a charcoal fire, fried or cooked according to traditional recipes such as the famous *sayadiya*, boiled fish served on a bed of rice topped with a lemon sauce.

DESSERTS

Like many in the Middle East, Jordanians have a sweet tooth. Sweets, homemade or bought, are produced at any excuse but are particularly popular – and consumed in huge quantities – during Ramadan, Muslim and Christian feasts such as Eid and weddings. A trip to a patisserie in Jordan is well worthwhile. Many are

Mahalbiyya: a pudding made of milk thickened with rice flour and perfumed with rose- or orange-flower water.

Qatayif: cake containing a layer of soft cheese, served hot and drenched in syrup.

Look out also for the elastic-like "mastic icecream" in ice-cream parlours. It is made with the powdered sahlab root and flavoured with mastic or Arabic gum, a resin that gives it its unusual texture. It's often coated with chopped nuts. Cleverly, the sahlab root also causes it to melt slower than regular ice-cream.

Try sayadiya, the famous fish dish, in Al-'aqabah.

Tray of baklava, the most common dessert.

TEA AND COFFEE

Aladdin caves for the sweet toothed, packed with beautifully arranged pastries, cakes and sweets. The most common type of sweet all over the Middle East, albeit with many variations, is *baklava*: layers of pastry filled chopped nuts, such as almonds, walnuts or pistachios, and soaked in thick syrup.

Konafa: shredded, deep-fried dough which resembles vermicelli, filled with nuts or slightly salted white cheese.

Ataif: a medieval recipe for small, deep-fried pancakes stuffed with nuts or white cheese and coated with syrup (eaten during Ramadan only).

Ma'amoul: baked pastries with nuts or dates perfumed with rose water.

Tea and coffee are served immediately following a meal, and many Jordanians are committed believers in herbal drinks – a few of which you may need after consuming a *mansaf*. Aniseed is drunk to calm the nerves, fennel seeds to alleviate wind, camomile to clear the sinuses, thyme to ease a cough, and sage and mint may be taken to calm an upset stomach and aid digestion. *Sahlab*, a hot milk drink made with the powdered *sahlab* root and served with chopped pistachios, cinnamon and rose water, is popular in winter.

"*Sahtain!*", Jordanians will wish you after a meal – "two healths". It's unlikely to be much consolation for an overtaxed stomach.

WILDLIFE

The mountains, plains and deserts of Jordan once teemed with living creatures. The plant and animal life that has survived the modern age is beginning, with help, to flourish again.

For such a small country, Jordan encompasses dramatic variation. Snow frequently caps hills in winter, whilst summer temperatures in the desert may exceed 45°C (113°F). Different areas also experience very different climates simultaneously. While the mountains of 'Ajlun in the north and Shawbak in the south are subject to a Mediterranean climate, the main part of the country basks in a desert climate. Between these extremes are at least four other climatic zones, creating a wide spectrum of wildlife habitats.

Jordan's unfortunate sobriquet, "the Desert Kingdom", implies that the whole country is dry, flat and devoid of life. In fact, all four of the Middle East's bio-geographical regions are found within Jordan's borders: Mediterranean (the highlands of Umm qays and Irbid), Irano-Turanian (the area surrounding the highlands including Al-salt and Jarash), Saharo-Arabian (the region known as the Badia, or eastern desert, the Central Desert, Wadi Sirhan, Al-jafr Basin and Al-mudawwarah Desert) and Sudanian (the Rift Valley to Wadi Rum and Al-'aqabah). These regions are home not just to unique landscapes, but also unique flora and fauna.

ALTERED LANDSCAPES

Jordan's landscapes have changed dramatically over the years through both natural and man-made causes. A drive through Jordan's deserts, in particular, is packed with geological clues to the dramatic changes that have taken place.

The great Omayyad "castles" at Amrah or Haranah, both standing in arid desert today, are testament to changes partly wrought by man. The Omayyad caliphs were great hunters and built these castles in the heart of

Camels are ideally suited to desert conditions.

"big-game country", where natural forests provided shade, refuge and food for gazelles and other large mammals.

Destruction of tree cover, primarily for human fuel, was one of the biggest causes of change in the natural forests. Protection of surviving woodlands is now an urgent priority of the Royal Society for the Conservation of Nature (www.rscn. org.jo), an organisation that has been active in protecting Jordan's wildlife habitats and setting up wildlife reserves since 1966.

PROTECTED PLACES

Jordan currently has seven nature reserves and one protected area, with many more planned (including at Rajel, Burku and Fifa).

DANA BIOSPHERE RESERVE

The most accessible – and, some would say, the most memorable – of Jordan's RSCN reserves is the Dana Biosphere Reserve (see page 219), lying in the south of the country between Al-tafulah and Petra. Encompassing an area of 320 sq km (124 sq miles) of rugged mountains and valleys, it extends from the top of the Rift Valley to the desert lowlands of Wadi 'arabah, an elevation drop of over 1,600 metres (5,250ft), incorporating a wide variety of ecosystems from Mediterranean forest to arid, sandy desert.

Such a condensed landform results in wide biodiversity. Unfortunately, many of the animals recorded at Dana are under threat of extinction, including the sand cat, Syrian wolf, lesser kes-trel and spiny-tailed lizard.

The possibilities for exploring the area are virtually limitless: from the atmospheric guest-house at Dana village trails lead out to the Rummana campsite (see page 219) in the hills, to Nabataean archaeological sites atop local mountains and across the valley to Finan (see page 217), the location of ancient copper mines and now the site of an exceptional, eco-friendly wilderness lodge.

AZRAQ WETLAND RESERVE

Lying amid Jordan's eastern deserts is the oasis of Azraq. Extending alongside the village is an unexpected sight in the bleak, arid landscape: an area of 12 sq km (4.5 sq miles) of marshes, protected since 1977 and known as the Azraq Wetland Reserve (see page 274).

Although local pumping of water has severely depleted the oasis, Azraq remains a magnet for millions of birds passing between Eurasia, Ara-bia and Africa. Special boardwalks have been constructed over the marshes and pools, and bird hides have been set up. One of Azraq's most remarkable native species is the killifish (*Apha-nius sirhani*) – a small fish that is endemic to this desert habitat. Some 420 bird species have been identified in Azraq, which remains one of the best places to see them.

SHAUMARI WILDLIFE RESERVE

Just south of Azraq is the 22 sq km (8.5 sq miles) Shaumari Wildlife Reserve (see page 274), established in 1975. The reserve reopened in summer 2017 following a five-year maintenance

and renovation programme, complete with a new visitor centre including a meeting hall and café run by local residents. Make sure to take the guided Oryx Safari Tour to view the wild ass, oryx and other mammals.

WADI AL-MUJIB NATURE RESERVE

The rugged Wadi al-mujib Nature Reserve (see page 212), which encompasses a large area of 212 sq km (82 sq miles) of arid sandstone mountains bordering the Dead Sea, is centred on a series of free-flowing rivers in deep, dramatic gorges.

Water buffalo in the Azraq Wetland Reserve.

⊙ SAVING THE ORYX

The Shaumari Wildlife Reserve was established in 1975 to provide a safe home for the beautiful but endangered Arabian oryx. Oryx have been extinct in the wild in Jordan since 1921; the world's last wild oryx was shot by hunters in Oman in 1973.

The captive breeding programme at Shaumari, which included the introduction of new stock from other Arab countries, has helped save the spe-cies. A small herd of oryx has also been intro-duced to the desert environs of Wadi Rum, where the bedouin have vowed to protect them. In the future, it is hoped that oryx will be released back into the wild.

Established in 1988, one of the most important local residents today is the Nubian ibex, a large mountain goat which had become severely threatened through over-hunting. Nowadays, populations here and in Dana Nature Reserve are slowly increasing. The RSCN established a captive breeding centre in the Mujib Mountains, and has already successfully returned a number of ibex to the wild.

Of the long list of plants recorded in the reserve are several rare species of orchid; Jordan is home to at least 22 species of wild orchid, many of them threatened by habitat depletion. Note

Africa: hyenas, jackals and lynx. Spending a night in the forest in one of the atmospheric, well-designed wooden lodges makes a great break from the hot desert plains or culture vulturing.

DIBEEN FOREST RESERVE

In 2004, an 8 sq km (3 sq miles) area of woodland near 'Ajlun was designated the Dibeen Forest Reserve (see page 180). The first step for protecting the area was to launch a scientific survey of the land and its flora and fauna. Wildlife here is not always conspicuous, though bird life is good.

Azraq wetlands attract millions of migratory birds.

that picking wild flowers within the reserves is strictly forbidden.

'AJLUN FOREST RESERVE

Northern Jordan is home to the beautiful 'Ajlun Forest Reserve (see page 181), set over 13 sq km (5 sq miles) of hilltop forests of evergreen oak, pistachio, carob and wild strawberry trees. Set up in 1988, the focus of RSCN's efforts here is the reintroduction of the formerly extinct roe deer. A breeding herd is now under close monitoring with the aim of releasing it into the wild in the future. Other fauna at 'Ajlun include some species also found in Europe: foxes, badgers, hedgehogs and boar, birds such as jays and finches, as well as species more associated with

Jordan's national flower is the black iris, a perennial that flowers between March and April. Keep an eye out around Wadi al-Sir and along the King's Highway (Tariq al-malik). Though under threat from habitat degradation, colonies are found in protected reserves, including Wadi al-mujib.

YARMOUK NATURE RESERVE

Jordan's newest reserve was established in 2011. Stretching over 30 sq km (11.5 sq miles), it lies to the far north of the country close to the Syrian border. As well as hiking and biking trails, there's an eco-café and a shop selling local crafts. Yarmouk is home to resident and migratory water birds, as well as gazelles and other mammals.

WADI RUM PROTECTED AREA

In addition to the official reserves, an area of 540 sq km (208.5 sq miles) of sandy desert in Wadi Rum (see page 249) is also formally protected as a nature reserve, though not under the direct control of the RSCN. The local government at Al-ʿaqabah controls the area, which since 2011 has also been designated a Unesco World Heritage

Site. Visitors can overnight at one of the many Bedouin camps in or outside the protected area, when their chances of sighting desert animals greatly increase, particularly at dusk, at night and at dawn, when foxes, jackals and striped hyenas occasionally put in an appearance. Wild and semi-wild camels are also found at Wadi Rum.

JORDAN'S WILDLIFE

In addition to the mammals listed above, other wildlife visitors might encounter during their trip includes the following.

INSECTS AND REPTILES

Insect life is prolific in Jordan. In spring, colourful butterflies, such as the small copper and small tortoiseshell, migrate in large numbers. Look out also for the emerald green grasshopper and its dramatic relative, the praying mantis.

Lizards are frequently seen throughout the country. While walking through the sandstone pathways of Petra, you may well encounter the Petra wall lizard (*Lacerta danfordi*), which suns itself on the rocks in the morning light.

A sharp eye is needed to distinguish the Mediterranean chameleon, which stands motionless among the branches of bushes, following its prey with its revolving eyes and capturing it on a tongue that is as long as its body.

Although there are several poisonous snakes in Jordan, including the horned viper and the Palestine viper, visitors are unlikely to encounter them (though avoid putting hands or feet in crannies when climbing or scrambling over rock), and there are few instances of snake bites in the country. In desert areas, scorpions are not uncommon; be wary when camping.

BIRDS IN JORDAN

Relative to its size, Jordan contains a huge diversity of birdlife that duly attracts birdwatchers from all over. The diversity is partly due to the varied ecosystems, but also because Jordan lies on one of the world's major migration flyways. Twice yearly, millions of birds pass through Jordan on their way to wintering in Africa and breeding in eastern Europe and western Asia.

Spring offers the best combination of migrant birds, breeding birds and good weather, and any time from late March through to early May can be recommended.

The following guide is a selection of some of Jordan's best birdwatching sites, though there are many more.

PETRA

Petra is justifiably famous for its archaeological wonders, but the tourist tracks also allow easy access into the mountains of the Southern Rift Margin. The main avian attraction here is the resident and reasonably common Sinai rosefinch, which can be seen most easily along the *Siq*, and en route to Al-dayr.

For a chance of hearing or glimpsing the other Petra speciality – Hume's tawny owl – the best area is around the Urn Tomb (Qabr al-jarrah) or along the *Siq* at nightfall. Though you now have to leave

Petra at this time, you may be in luck later if you join the "Petra by Night" tour (see page 228).

Other typical breeding birds of the Petra area include the sooty falcon, pallid swift, rock martin, blackstart, white-crowned black wheatears, scrub warbler, orange-tufted sunbird and Tristram's grackle.

Many of the raptors that pass over Eilat in spring make use of the thermals which form over the mountains on the Jordanian side of the rift; they pass over Petra in large numbers as they head north.

The list of migrants recorded at Petra, particularly during spring, is impressive. They can drop in anywhere, especially in the vegetated *wadis* and near any trace of water.

WADI DANA AND THE RIFT MARGIN

Further north along the Rift Margin, the bird community of the cliffs and rocky areas around Wadi Dana is similar to that of Petra, but here you also have access to the birds of the higher hilltops. Specialities here include Tristram's or Syrian serin, Cretzschmar's bunting and spectacled warbler.

Blue lizard in southern Jordan.

⊘ THE CAMEL

Originating in North America about 40 million years ago and related to the llama and alpaca of South America, the single-humped Arabian dromedary of today (Camelus dromedarius) was probably first domesticated in Arabia in 2500–1500 BC, initially for milk production and later to carry heavy loads along the emerging overland trade routes.

The camel is ideally suited to the harsh conditions of the desert. It can maintain a steady speed of 5kph (3mph) for up to 15 hours. It can last about 20 days without water and during a prolonged absence of food or water, it uses up fat stored in its hump, losing as much as a quarter of its body weight.

A camel's body temperature is similar to that of a human, but it has a much wider range and does not start to lose water by sweating until it has risen to around 41°C (106°F). It also urinates only about half a litre (about a pint) per day – roughly the same as a human despite being four or five times larger. A healthy camel drinks about 20 litres (4.5 gallons) of water daily, but after long periods without water can drink almost five times this amount in just 10 minutes.

To protect against sandstorms, a camel has a good sense of smell, a double row of heavy eyelashes to protect its eyes, hairy ear openings that filter out the sand and muscular nostrils that can close fully or partially.

Near the Rummana campsite, a bird-hide and drinking pool has been established, which draws good numbers of local birds, particularly in dry periods. The bulbuls are especially frequent visitors.

The cliffs of the *wadi* provide an ideal breeding habitat for birds of prey that include the griffon vulture, Bonelli's eagle, lesser kestrel, Barbary falcon, eagle owl and other raptors.

WADI RUM

The Wadi Rum Desert is an extensive area of dramatic sandstone mesas that rise up to 800 metres (2,620ft) from the surrounding sea of sand. The majority of local specialities here can be seen close to the road between the Wadi Rum entrance buildings (and ticket office) and Rum village.

Here, in habitats of cliff faces, boulder slopes and sandy desert dotted with bushes, you may see the long-legged buzzard, desert lark, rock martin, white-crowned black wheatear, scrubwarbler, brown-necked raven, Sinai rosefinch and house bunting. A few hooded wheatears are also resident but they can be challenging to locate.

The settlement itself is good for sightings of Sinai rosefinch and Tristram's grackle, and migrants are often concentrated here or at the springs at the base of the cliffs behind the Bayt rahah.

Migrating raptors pass over the mountains, but of the local breeding species, Verreaux's eagle and sooty falcon are of particular note. Verreaux's eagle, although common in Africa, is one of the most sought-after of Jordan's specialities with birdwatchers. The best place to look for it is high over the white mountain tops of Jabal ram.

AL-'AQABAH

Al-'aqabah lies at the head of the Gulf of Al-'aqabah, an area renowned for the volume and variety of migrant birds that pass through annually. Although migrants have been spotted everywhere, including inside the city of Al-'aqabah, two areas have proved particularly good in spring and autumn: the old palms and irrigated allotments lining the beach front opposite the main mosque along to Al-'aqabah Fort, and the less salubrious sewage works. Corncrakes, wrynecks or nightingales have even been spotted on traffic islands.

The sewage treatment plant, north of the town and adjacent to the Israeli border, has extensive areas of irrigated palms and bushes, areas of reeds and open water. It is a magnet for birds, but at present can only be visited with permission from the military and the proprietors, so is probably best visited with an organised tour.

Keep an eye out for seabirds in the Gulf. The best time is in the first few hours after daybreak. Of the scarcer seabirds, Cory's shearwater, brown booby, white-eyed gull, bridled tern, white-cheeked tern and skuas can sometimes be seen.

To the south, towards the Saudi border, there are several bays where gulls, terns and waders roost.

Sinai rosefinch.

AZRAQ AND EAST TO THE BADIA

Low deserts cover much of eastern Jordan, including the region known as the Badia, but are most easily explored in the area between Amman and Azraq. Here, it's usually easy to spot the most common lark of this habitat –Temminck's horned lark. In the Azraq area, red-rumped wheatear and thick-billed lark are local specialities, as are significant numbers of wintering imperial eagles, a rare bird outside Jordan.

Sadly, due to huge quantities of water being pumped out of Azraq to supply Amman, and for agricultural projects (see page 274), much of Azraq's once famous reed beds have dried up and it is no longer the lush oasis and magnet for migrant birds in a sea of desert that it once was.

Many visitors are disappointed, but it remains one of the best birdwatching spots in Jordan. Look out, in particular, for little and Baillon's crakes, purple and Squacco herons and yellow wagtail. A single pelican has also been sighted here.

East of Azraq is the desert Badia region. Though little populated and little visited, the birdlife here is surprisingly good. One spot quite well known among birders is the pool of water that lies in the middle of the desert directly in front of Qasr burqu' (see page 285) in the far east of the country. It is here that the proposed new RSCN reserve, Burqu,

in Mediterranean areas, although this represents the southeastern limit of their range. The spectacled warbler, Upcher's warbler and black-headed bunting all breed here. In winter, Finsch's wheatears replace the summer-visiting black-eared wheatear.

THE DEAD SEA AND WADI 'ARABAH

The apparently barren shore of the Dead Sea is a good spot for sighting the little green bee-eater, Bonelli's eagle, Tristram's grackle, the fan-tailed raven and rock martins.

Camel in Wadi 'arabah.

will be established. Bird species quite commonly seen here include ringed plover, marsh harrier, sandpiper and various types of lark, including crested larks, black larks, Temminck's horned larks and the European roller.

BASALT DESERT & THE NORTHERN HIGHLANDS

The main attractions of the Basalt Desert, north of Azraq, are the dark-plumaged desert larks and basalt wheatears. These birds can be found by the roadside along the first stretch of the Al-safawi to Iraq road.

The habitats of the Northern Highlands are home to a good variety of birds not seen elsewhere. Many (such as the blue tit) are common

Further south, Wadi 'arabah provides a different habitat. However, as this is a sensitive area due to its proximity to the Israeli border, it is best explored from the side road to Fidan and Qurayqrah. Look out for the bar-tailed desert and hoopoe larks. Here, acacias also provide refuge for the Arabian warbler and Arabian babbler.

ENVIRONMENTAL PROBLEMS

THE WATER CRISIS

Alongside most other countries in the Middle East, Jordan faces a litany of environmental problems. First and foremost is a severe shortage of water and ever-diminishing supplies. It is among the most water-poor countries in the world, with ground water and subterranean aquifer diminished and its rivers reduced to around 10 percent of their original flow.

Meanwhile, recurring drought, a fast-growing population (over 2.2 percent annually by current estimates) bolstered further by the arrival of tens of thousands of refugees in recent months, and demand from neighbours, including Israel and the Palestinian Territories (thought to divert over 30 percent of the River Jordan for their own water needs), is exacerbating the problem. Only managing to replace around 40 percent of the

desertification and a dramatic drop in both the numbers and variety of wildlife. Though Jordan today is home to 81 mammal species, over the last 300 years 20 have become extinct, including Jordan's lions, cheetahs, Arabian leopards and bears. Some have been successfully reintroduced, such as the Syrian wild ass (*Equus hermionus*), oryx (*Oryx leucoryx*), roe deer (*Capreolus capreolus*) and Persian fallow deer (*Dama mesopotamica*). Other man-made problems include the ever-increasing sprawl of the cities and river and air pollution.

Verreaux's eagle owl.

Irrigation in the Jordan Valley.

amount required, Jordan is slowly running out of water. Drastic action is finally being taken in the form of the controversial Red Sea–Dead Sea Canal (see page 201), which is due to begin construction in 2018 (completion date is currently set for 2020).

DESTRUCTION OF HABITAT

Linked to population increase is another catalogue of problems: encroachment on, and degradation of, wildlife habitats through the pumping of water, overgrazing from goats and sheep (thought to number around four million), soil erosion, inefficient and sometimes wasteful agriculture (in the use of water for example) and illegal hunting have all led to

SOLUTIONS

Though Jordan's problems appear almost insurmountable, and the future bleak, the government has been attempting to address the problems over the last 20 years, for example by establishing the Royal Society for the Conservation of Nature (www.rscn.org.jo), and introducing the Protection of the Environment Law in 1995. In 2012, national campaigns were launched to try and combat the country's chronic litter problem – and habit; in 2014, an anti-littering project was backed by the British Embassy. Other plans include the Red Sea–Dead Sea Canal (construction expected 2018–2020) and the funding of solar-powered desalination stations and hydroelectric plants.

Rock climbing in Barrah canyon, Wadi Rum.

OUTDOOR ACTIVITIES

From bobbing like a cork on the Dead Sea to viewing coral gardens in the Red Sea, canyoning in the *wadis* to microlighting above the desert dunes, Jordan's visitors are spoilt for choice.

In spite of such promise, most terrain – with the exceptions of Wadi Rum and Petra – remains unexplored by outdoor enthusiasts.

TREKKING AND CANYONING

NORTH JORDAN

The green and rolling hills of north Jordan are relatively undisturbed areas, and offer great opportunities for short hikes – ruins such as 'Ajlun Castle (see page 180), Pella (see page 193) or Umm qays (see page 183) make perfect start or end points.

Within the beautiful RSCN 'Ajlun Forest Reserve (see page 181) are a total of seven trails. One, the Roe Deer Trail (less than 2km/1 mile; gentle) is self-guided – and clearly signposted around the camp; the others are all guided (reserve guides are compulsory) and range in duration (depending on the distance and your pace) from 2–3 hours to 6 hours or more. The scenic Rock Rose Trail (8km/5 miles; 3–4 hours) crosses wooded valleys and ridges on a circular path through the reserve and the nearby village communities.

Heading beyond the reserve – for instance on the 'Ajlun Castle Trail (full day; 18km/11 miles; reasonably testing) up to 'Ajlun Castle, or across country on a two-day route to Pella via the beautiful Wadi Yabis – brings you into contact with local people, who may well invite you to share a meal. You can also visit local craft co-operatives, which assist women of the community. You get a great walk, meet locals and come away with high-quality souvenirs whose proceeds go directly to a good cause. The Soap House Trail (2–3 hours; 7km/4 miles; easy) is one example.

Camel riding in Wadi Rum.

THE DEAD SEA MOUNTAINS

The rugged sandstone mountains rising above the eastern shore of the Dead Sea offer some of Jordan's most exciting, and challenging, adventure activities.

From the hot springs of Hammamat Ma'in (see page 207), it is possible to follow the steamy waters as they tumble their way through an 8km (5-mile)-long gorge down to the Dead Sea. Note, however, that this is a very challenging route: the potential for dehydration in the overheated microclimate on the canyon floor is high, and the route itself involves negotiating your way along the rocky river bed, and on several occasions abseiling past waterfalls. Routes also lead south from

Hammamat Ma'in into the protected area of the Wadi al-mujib Reserve (see page 212): the hilltop site of Herod's castle at Mukawir (see page 211) is accessible from here.

The Wadi al-mujib Reserve itself has a variety of hikes and canyoning routes, accessible both from the Dead Sea mouth of the Mujib Canyon and from the hilltops just off the King's Highway to the east, more than 1,500 metres (4,920ft) above. Note that the reserve is open from 1 April to 1 November only, unless low rainfall keeps the place open longer.

The reserve has five established trails (lasting between 2–3 hours and 6–8 hours in duration), including the self-guided Siq Trail (2 hours; easy–moderate), which leads you through the gorge from the Dead Sea road to the base of three waterfalls, including one of 20 metres (66ft) that you can climb with the aid of fixed-ropes if you wish.

Longer trails are also possible, including the Wadi Hasa Trail, a two-day trip along the full 36km (22-mile) length of the river, but most visitors opt for something less daunting.

Horse-drawn carriage in the Siq, Petra.

Hiking near the Dead Sea.

⊙ WADI RUM

Wadi Rum offers almost endless opportunities for hiking and climbing. Bear in mind you will need sturdy footwear, plenty of water and warm clothing for when the sun goes down.

There are various camping facilities at Rum offering everything from very comfortable tent-cabins (for example at Beit Ali) to a plot of sand to pitch a tent. Alternatively, if you're feeling sufficiently resourceful, you can pick your own pitch in the desert, or overnight in a genuine Bayt Sha'ar (Bedouin tent) if you're lucky enough to be invited.

The Bedouins' invitations are warm and genuine, but to avoid being thought of as taking advantage of their hospitality, a gift offered in advance of your stay is appreciated, whether in the form of cash "to help pay for dinner" or something else, though be prepared for the gift to be refused; many Bedouin are too proud to accept gifts from guests.

As the Bedouin are still a relatively traditional and conservative society, guests (male and female) should keep shoulders and legs covered when in their company.

Although hikers and climbers are relatively free to roam through Wadi Rum, its designation as a protected area means that some activities are restricted. The Wadi Rum Visitor Centre, at the entrance to the area, has full information.

Other trails include the Canyon Trail (4 hours; moderate), in which the first hour is spent in the mountains before descending into the gorge and requires some abseiling; the Malaqi Trail (6–8 hours; challenging), which requires climbing, abseiling and a certain level of fitness but takes you to a deep pool at the junction of the Mujib and Hedan rivers; the Ibex Trail (3–4 hours; easy; winter only), which is entirely in the mountains (and therefore closed in summer) but gives you the best chance of spotting Jordan's ibex (mountain goat); and the Mujib Trail (6–8 hours; not difficult but steep), which is entirely mountain-bound and takes you from 900 metres (2,950ft) above sea level to 410 metres (1,345ft) below. You will either need a car to drive the 10km (6 miles) to the start point in the mountains, or organise transport in advance through the reserve. There are stunning views from the mountains across the whole of the Dead Sea to Israel and the Palestinian Territories.

Nearby, but lying outside the reserve, are several more areas of equally stunning canyon landscapes. Here, Wadi ibn Hammad is the top choice: a full-day gorge walk heads down from a point off the King's Highway north of Karak for 12km (7.5 miles) to the Dead Sea. It passes through some beautiful terrain: the sandstone cliffs are eroded into weird shapes and striking colours, bedecked with ferns and palms and, in springtime, carpets of wild flowers.

DANA

The Dana Biosphere Reserve (see page 219) in southern Jordan offers a remarkable variety of landscapes and a similarly wide variety of hikes – easy and difficult – by which to experience them.

Standing at the guesthouse looking out over the deep and dramatic Wadi Dana valley, the most obvious route is the Wadi Dana Trail (14 km/9 miles; 5 or 6 hours), which follows the gently sloping floor of the valley from the lushness of Dana village down through increasingly desolate shrubby steppe vegetation to the arid desert of Feynan at the bottom. From the wilderness lodge at Feynan Camp (tel: 0797 487800; www.ecolodge.me/feynan), it is possible to follow a challenging four-day trail through wild, largely uninhabited hilly countryside to Petra. Local guides or the RSCN can usually help with this major undertaking. There are now 10 hiking

trails from Feynan, and also guided mountain bike trails. Bikes can also be rented at the camp.

From Dana village, another excellent walk is the spectacular Steppe Trail (8 km/5 miles; 3 hours), which winds around the head of the valley to the remote campsite of Rummana. Around 300 metres (330yds) from the camp (a wonderfully peaceful place to overnight), is a bird-hide overlooking a drinking pool, ideal for early-morning observation of birds and wildlife.

There are also four trails around the camp (three of one hour's duration; one of 2 hours); the longest

Bathing in the hot springs at Hammamat Ma'in.

is the Rummana Mountain Trail (2.5 km/1.5 miles; 2 hours), which leads up through the juniper woodlands to the summit of Jabal Rummana.

PETRA

Although most visitors to Petra limit their exploration to the ancient Nabataean sites on or immediately off the main path through the ancient city centre, there are many opportunities for getting off the beaten track.

Two of the best and most accessible short hiking routes are, firstly, to the High Place of Sacrifice, a signed route starting near the amphitheatre that leads up a steep, narrow processional way to a plateau atop Jabal Madhbah; and secondly, to the Monastery (ad Dayr), one of

Petra's grandest facades, approached on a long climbing path from behind the Petra Archaeological Museum within Petra.

More challenging routes include one to Jabal Harun, the highest peak in Petra at 1,350 metres (4,430ft) above sea level, where a small white shrine stands to Aaron (Harun), brother of Moses, who is a prophet in Islam. Climbers familiar with the area cite Jabal Harun as one of the most exhilarating of Petra's climbs and one of the most spectacular sites to pitch camp for the night, though be aware that it is a place

Snorkelling in the Red Sea at Al-'aqabah.

of great sanctity for the local people. By day, the peak is a good point for surveying the entire Petra area. Look west across Wadi 'arabah to the Negev Desert.

WADI RUM

The red sandy deserts of Wadi Rum, in the far south of Jordan, are among the most exciting locations for hiking and sports in the country.

The vast majority of visitors to Rum come in the back of a jeep. There is, however, nothing to stop you striking off across the sands on your own two feet. Simple trails include the short climb behind the Rum Resthouse to the beautiful concealed spring of Ain Shallaleh (written about in glowing terms by T.E. Lawrence in

Seven Pillars of Wisdom). Nestled up against the cliffs of Jabal Rum is a small Nabataean temple (see page 251) dating from the 1st or 2nd century AD, open and free for exploration.

Longer routes include a circumnavigation of the Jabal Umm Ishrin Massif, opposite Rum village. This could take as much as 9 or 10 hours, and involves cutting through Wadi Siq Makhras opposite the visitor centre, and then making your way along the eastern side of the massif – often through soft sand. Negotiating a route through the maze-like Rakabat Canyon, which cuts directly through the Umm Ishrin massif, is very challenging, involving plenty of scrambling up and down across ridges to bypass blind gorges.

ROCK CLIMBING

Rum's reputation as one of the world's finest environments for desert rock climbing is well earned. A handful of local guides are climbing specialists, generally with rigorous training and qualifications earned in France or the UK, and the opportunities for experienced climbers to explore the rocky cliff-faces of Jabal Rum are not to be missed. For a list of recommended guides with knowledge and experience of climbing, see page 246.

CAMEL AND HORSE TREKKING

The sandy desert of Rum also lends itself superbly to trekking by camel – and the dozens of camel guides at Rum and the neighbouring areas of Disi and Shakriyya are all well-acquainted with routes lasting from 30 minutes to a week or longer.

A highly recommended route is the one that leads through the beautiful, isolated Barrah Canyon. This can usually done with a two-day trip by camel, with the night spent camping within the canyon.

Stables in and around Shakriyya are also the base for trekking on horseback – an increasingly popular way to roam this magnificent natural landscape.

4WD AND JEEP TREKS

Treks by 4WD are a great way of touring Wadi Rum, particularly if time is short, though ideally you should leave at least half a day to get an idea of the place; much better is a full day and a night. For many travellers, a night spent "sleeping under the stars" forms one of their best memories of Jordan, however toe-curling and overused the cliché.

Trips can be organised on the spot through the visitors' centre at Wadi Rum or, better, arranged in advance with a Bedouin guide or camp (see page 246). Treks can last from one hour to several weeks with camps set up in the desert, or at established campsites.

WATER SPORTS

The Red Sea resort city of Al-'aqabah offers the opportunity to practise a wide variety of water sports, including water-skiing, windsurfing, kitesurfing, parasailing, wakeboarding and kneeboarding. Full (and decent) equipment as well as instruction is available at the hotels and beach clubs that offer these sports.

DIVING AND SNORKELLING

Again, belying the country's moniker of "The Desert Kingdom", Al-'aqabah offers some excellent diving and snorkelling, easily matching or surpassing that on offer at its better-known neighbour of Eilat in Israel.

Al-'aqabah boasts several important advantages in diving terms: calm, temperate waters the whole year round; clean, unspoilt and uncrowded reefs that are accessible from the beach as well as from boats; diving to suit all levels including absolute beginners (who can also learn and get certified here); a good variety of dive sites (from old military wrecks to colourful coral gardens); and all the myriad favourite Red Sea species plus a few "extras" such as the delightful and tiny (and not easily seen) seahorse.

For information on diving and snorkelling in Al-'aqabah, as well as recommended and reputable dive outfits, see page 268.

SWIMMING AND SPA TREATMENTS

Jordan actually boasts two shorelines: the 27km (16-5-mile) coastline of the Red Sea, and the often salt-encrusted shoreline of the extraordinary Dead Sea.

Beach facilities are well-developed at resorts along both shorelines, including five-star luxury hotels that also offer world-class and unforgettable spa experiences. See Al-'aqabah and the Dead Sea for more detailed information on resorts.

AERIAL SPORTS

Aqabah is also home to the dynamic Royal Aero Sports Club of Jordan (tel: 0797 300299; www.rascj.com), based at Al-'aqabah airport, where you can book a flight in a microlight, ultralight or small two- or four-seater plane for a short sightseeing tour over the beaches and coastline of Al-'aqabah, or for a longer trip over the spectacular desert landscapes of Rum.

Short microlighting trips as well as tandem skydiving are also available for a few weeks

Camel trekking is a great way to explore Wadi Rum.

annually in Wadi Rum itself (near Beit Ali Camp), but should be booked in advance first through the RASCJ.

Also providing spectacular views across Wadi Rum, but with more time to take them in, are hot-air balloon rides. From a launch pad next to Beit Ali camp, just outside the Rum protected area, huge, silent balloons lift into the dawn sky for a breathtaking 90-minute flight over the cliffs and sands – perhaps Jordan's greatest scenic adventure. Again, these should be booked through the RASJC in advance.

Gliding and ultralighting is also possible at the Royal Jordanian Gliding Club (tel: 0796052696; www.tipntag.com) at Marka Airport outside the city.

Grey horses are never born grey:
they are born bay, black or chestnut and change colour later on.

Along with camels, horses are highly prized amongst the Bedouin.

THE ARABIAN HORSE

This most aristocratic of breeds is spirited, intelligent and strong. The Arabian horse not only wins races but also inspires passionate poetry.

Hidden among pine trees off the road to Al-fuhis in the suburbs of Amman known as the Al Humar area (around 12km from Downtown), is the Royal Jordanian Stable (by appointment; tel: 0777 469159 or 0797 792983; email: stablesroyal@ yahoo.com; free). It is here, in a low-lying complex surrounded by fragrant clematis and roses, that the royal family's 250 pure-bred Arabian horses are stabled, attended to by a host of grooms.

The stud has come a long way since 1912, when Emir Abdullah first brought a small team of seven mares and five stallions with him from Mecca and the Hejaz in Saudi Arabia. The collection, said to be descended from those belonging to the Prophet Muhammad, and augmented by horses given to him by local tribes, formed the foundations of today's stock. At the time, Emir Abdullah's interest was recreational rather than ideological, but in the 1960s, when interbreeding with thor-

The distinctive concave-shaped face of the Arabian horse.

> *The copious amounts of manure produced by the stable's residents are said to nourish Amman's finest rose beds.*

oughbreds in the interests of horse-racing threatened the purity of the Arab breed in the region, his grandson King Husayn set up an official state stud. Initially this was based at the king's palace in Amman, but was later established at the Royal Stable in 1967.

Since the 1950s, the stable's director and patron has been Princess Alia Al Husayn (President also of the Royal Jordanian Equestrian Federation, RJEF), Abdullah's great-granddaughter (who traces her interest in Arabians to a childhood love of "a pony and a rocking-horse"), together with her son, Prince Abdul Hameed (who is responsible in particular for the endurance horses). The stud has blossomed into a thriving enterprise committed to preserving the local lines and supplying stock for Arab studs all over the world. The stable has met impressive success on the international stage, including at the annual National Horse Championship and Middle East Championship, rivalling and sometimes surpassing the famous and far better-funded UAE stables. The saddle room contains some of the countless trophies and rosettes won by both stallions and mares from the stables.

THE ARAB HORSE AND THE BEDOUIN

The Arab horse (*Equus arabicus*) is more finely boned than the thoroughbred, yet it is famed for its power as well as its beauty. Its most valuable asset historically was its power of endurance, a quality much prized by the Bedouin for the horse's ability to weather the hardship and demands of the desert. As one early 20th-century traveller noted, "The Bedouin seem to belong to the Arabian horse as naturally as the date palm belongs to the sand-dune."

Years of working, fighting and surviving together (horses were often stabled in the safety of the family tent) has forged an unbreakable bond of affection between the Bedouin and their horses which transcends other human-animal relationships in the Middle East (with the possible exception of the Bedouin relationship with the precious camel) and has inspired myriad legends, poetry and romantic literature.

The origin of the Arab remains cloaked in myth. The breed is believed to have evolved over

Roman Army and Chariot Experience at Jarash.

> *The Bedu would eulogise their horses, lauding them as "drinkers of the wind" and "the envy of all", even comparing them with magic carpets.*

4,000 years ago either in central Arabia, or the area around the Euphrates River in Mesopotamia. Tradition has it that the original strains are known as *Al Khamsa* (The Five), tracing their descent to five horses said to have been owned by the Prophet Muhammad himself.

An old Bedouin legend, meanwhile, attributes their source to the south wind: "Then God took a handful of wind and fashioned from it a chestnut horse. He said, 'I have created you, Arabian horse; I have moulded you from the wind; I have tied Good Fortune to your mane; you will fly without wings; you will be the noblest among animals...' God then blessed the horse with the sign of glory and happiness and marked his forehead with a star, and the horse leaped into space."

A Bedouin's horse was his chief pride, his partner in raiding, hunting and war. Horses were also associated with important rites of passage. Once a young male Bedu had singlehandedly captured a mare from within the midst of an enemy's camp, for example, he was admitted into the *majlis*, the distinguished council of men who gathered around the chief's camp-fire.

As a rule, mares were valued above stallions, not only for their reproductive value, but for being more manageable in warfare, and more likely to be quieter when stealth was required and the whinny of an over-excitable stallion could blow a Bedu's cover. It is believed that it is for this reason that the bloodline of Arab horses is traced through the mares.

VALUABLE TRAITS

Breeders have long waxed lyrical about the symmetry, harmony and balance of the Arab, and the famous "float", the horse's unique manner of moving that makes the animal appear to float above the ground. Physically, the principal distinguishing characteristics of the breed are: pointed ears, a concave face with a broad forehead, a large jaw, small muzzle, a short back (they have 23 vertebrae, instead of the 24 of the non-Arab), long hindquarters which should be level with the back, a high tail, and fine legs (though appearing almost spindly, they are in fact very powerful). Arabs can be grey (white), chestnut or black. Their colour at birth changes as they become adults.

The Arab's superior intelligence apparently makes it unsuitable for polo, and its independent spirit as well as its small build make it an unreliable showjumper (though they can jump well, they have a tendency to refuse). Some strains, however, make good race horses, as well as exceptional endurance horses, used as they are to extreme heat and long distances.

The Arab is most valued for its ability, when crossed with other breeds, to improve them. As a result of cross-breeding over the centuries, most other breeds contain an element of Arab in their blood, including the English thoroughbred and the pedigree hackney. Arab traits are also usually genetically dominant; even if a horse appears to lack Arab traits, these may still be passed on to offspring.

As a rule, Arabs are not bred from until they have reached the age of four, after which time mares can produce a foal every 11 months into their late teens or early 20s, with occasional rest periods in between. The Royal Stables' longest-lived stallion was 33 years old when he died; he had sired a foal only the year before.

PRESERVING DIFFERENT STRAINS

There are various strains of the Arab breed, and the Royal Jordanian Stables boasts several rare lines, such as Umm Argub and Kehilah Krush. Maintaining these lines can prove a delicate and difficult business. The Hamdani line, for instance, was almost lost in Jordan when female foals of the stud's only Hamdani mare were sold to Britain and Morocco, and the mare then went on to produce only males. In the end, the stud was forced to buy back a mare.

The stud is also committed to preserving the unique local lines, even if they are not especially beautiful or prized. The greatest threat to such lines came immediately after King Abdullah I's death. As his horses' value and heritage was not properly appreciated at the time, his stable – expensive to maintain – was disbanded. When the late King Husayn began reassembling the original stock, he found the horses

had dispersed to all corners of the kingdom. Though most were found serving with the Royal Mounted Guards and the army, one prize stallion, Ghazalleh, was found ploughing a field in the Jordan Valley.

Some of the horses hired out at Petra are thought to be pure Arabs, but the traditional means of tracking ancestry in such horses – verbally from father to son – has now broken down. To help improve the general stock at Petra, the Royal Stables lend Petra two stallions a year for mating.

Galloping through Petra.

David Roberts' El Deir, Petra.

ARTISTS' IMPRESSIONS

Jordan, and particularly Petra, have attracted a catalogue of
artists over the centuries but few have been able to do it justice.
A Scot named David Roberts proved one of the exceptions.

In the 18th and 19th centuries, Europe was
gripped by a fever: a new interest in the Classical world and the rediscovery of its antiquities. This interest, with time, extended to
the Orient, and though initially confined to
professional explorers, it soon spread to dil-
ettantes wealthy enough to undertake the
often lengthy and costly journeys involved.
These early tourists were drawn by the sights
lyrically described in travel literature (a new
and booming industry), as well as by the very
evocative images of the Orient depicted by the
artists of the day, who flocked to the region
hot on the heels of the explorers.

The development of the steamship in the
early 19th century made such travel much
easier (the Red Sea, for example, became navigable in all seasons), and by the mid-century,
touring the Middle East had become a fashionable pastime for adventurous members of
the wealthy middle and upper classes, many
who fancied themselves as amateur explorers,
archaeologists or artists.

In the absence of press photographers, it
was up to the artists of the day to capture the
image of these newly "discovered" places and,
via the time-consuming media of painting and
lithograph-making, transmit to the world the
wonders they had witnessed.

In many cases, the journeys involved were
long and arduous; there was plague and disease
to contend with, and a serious risk of losing all
baggage, not to mention one's life.

All these dangers were especially preva-
lent in the rock-carved city of Petra, which
had been rediscovered by the Swiss explorer,
Burckhardt, in 1812 (see page 241). The
inhabitants of Petra, the Howeitat and Omrah

*Local people were often used to enliven 19th-century
compositions, such as in this picture of Petra
by David Roberts.*

Bedouins, who claimed descent from the original Nabataeans, were given to such hostility
that paintings often had to be executed very
swiftly. Some tribesmen additionally believed
that the artists possessed magic powers which
enabled them to steal the ancient treasure. It
was nearly a century before the journey to the
city was considered safe.

Any artist or archaeologist worth his or her
salt would have possessed the ability to give a
rough impression of a place (and working later
from studies away from the scene was the traditional artistic practice then), but it required an
exceptional draughtsman to convey both the full

majesty and the detail of a site as glorious as Petra. As the most accomplished draughtsman of his age, David Roberts was clearly the man for the task.

DAVID ROBERTS

"Painter Davie", as David Roberts was affectionately known by friends, of whom the famous British painter, J.M.W. Turner, was one, was of humble Scottish stock.

In 1838, he set out on a tour of the Levant, starting in Egypt and travelling on to Jerusalem.

to Britain with "one of the richest folios that ever left the East".

Accompanying Roberts for this great adventure were John Pell, and John Kinnear, an Edinburgh businessman and a keen admirer of Roberts' work. Roberts himself travelled in Eastern-style clothes, which he had bought not only for protection from the heat, but also to try to make himself less conspicuous while sketching in Cairo.

One month after departing from Cairo, the party arrived at the port of Al-'aqabah,

Lithograph of Petra by Roberts.

His first stop was Cairo, where an English traveller, John Pell, took him to meet the French artist Louis-Maurice-Adolphe Linant. Linant, who had first visited Petra ten years earlier, was the first serious artist to the ancient site. His work, which was rather heavy and laboured in the traditional French style of the day, had not been widely seen. When Roberts saw Linant's paintings, the scenes nonetheless bowled him over.

The Scot had been in two minds about taking on the additional hazard and expense of visiting Petra, but one look at Linant's drawings convinced him that the rewards would be well worth the effort. Such a journey, he was instantly convinced, would enable him to return

where the men were obliged to employ as their escort, Sheikh Husayn of the Alowein, who held sway in the lands leading to Petra and had been Linant's guide a decade earlier. However, even he seemed unsure if he could provide the "Franks" full protection against the local Bedouin, and at one point he refused to continue on the journey, declaring his charges to be "all mad" for even attempting to enter the Wadi musa.

Roberts' courage and determination won through in the end, but the continuing and tangible tension created by the Arab tribes indelibly coloured his first impression of the city. Still, he wasted no time in making numerous sketches. It took all of his talent to capture the rose-red city's likeness and spirit; like others who visited it before and after him, there were moments, later admitted by Roberts, when he felt completely overawed and unable to do due justice to the ancient city.

Roberts spent a total of five and a half days at the site. It was hardly enough. He did not reach the Tomb of Aaron, nor did he get a view of the Royal Tombs from the High Place of Sacrifice. His output was nevertheless prodigious. Petra was perfect for the drama and romance that later became trademarks

> "I often throw away my pencil in despair of being able to convey any idea of it," David Roberts once wrote at his attempts to portray the magnificence of Al-dayr (The Treasury) in Petra.

There's little doubt that Roberts did indeed manage to fulfil his wish to produce one of the richest folios of the region. On his return,

Corinthian tomb and Palace tomb, part of the Royal Tombs at Petra.

of Roberts best paintings, and with Petra, he held nothing back. Though romanticised in the Orientalist tradition of the time, his drawings were on the whole remarkably accurate and well observed.

Roberts and his party apparently left Petra in good spirits and headed for Hebron. There he painted two watercolours of the town he found "almost English" in its cleanliness, and inhabited by children, "the most beautiful I have ever seen." But an outbreak of the plague forced them on to Jaffa and Jerusalem, where they joined the Easter faithful, visiting the monastery of Saint Saba, Bethlehem, Nablus and Ba'albek, among other sites on the classic pilgrims' route.

Roberts excitedly wrote: "My sketches of the East have taken the world of art by storm." Later, he expertly worked up the sketches into watercolours followed by lithographs, and published them in 1842 in the now iconic volume The Holy Land, accompanied rather incongruously by a slightly turgid text by a Scottish cleric, the Reverend George Croly.

Roberts' own reputation has gone up and down according to fashion, though his talents as a draughtsman have never been in question. The Holy Land has seldom been out of print since first published in the late 19th century, and the original lithographs (plates torn from the early editions of the book) are today extremely valuable.

WILLIAM HENRY BARTLETT AND EDWARD LEAR

English artist, William Henry Bartlett, was one of the leading topographical illustrators of his day and, like Roberts, whose style his work resembled, travelled widely in search of the "exotic". He contributed illustrations (steel engravings, drawings and watercolours) to travel books, including one he himself wrote, called *Forty Days in the Desert*. He arrived in Petra in 1845 and gushed about the "marvellous and romantic singularity" of the place. After no fewer than

faced with such magnificence. "My art is helpless to recall it to others," he complained. Writing to his sister, he conveys a strange description of Petra, food clearly not far from the front of his mind: "All the cliffs are a wonderful colour – like ham in stripes and parts are salmon colour."

Lear was there barely more than half a day when Sheikh Husayn's earlier warnings proved well-founded: he was seized by local Bedouin tribesmen who robbed him of everything from money to clothes and sent him packing.

William Henry Bartlett.

Masada or Sebbeh on the Dead Sea by Edward Lear.

seven expeditions to the Middle East, William Henry Bartlett succumbed to fever on board a ship off the coast of Malta while voyaging home in 1854 at the age of 45.

After Bartlett, came the well-known English artist, illustrator and author, Edward Lear, best known for his verse and nonsense rhymes, who embarked on his trip to Petra in 1858. Unfortunately, his journey didn't go entirely to plan. His first bit of bad luck came when, after leaving Hebron, he emerged from the Sufa Pass to find a scene of "astonishing beauty". Desperate to get out his brush, he discovered that his painting equipment was strapped to a camel that had gone a different route.

But Petra surpassed anything else he saw. And, like Roberts, he felt frustrated when

◎ LEAR'S LUCK

Ill-fated apparently from the start, Edward Lear's final setback came after his return to Britain. His major work of the trip, 'Petra', a depiction of the eastern cliff, was hung in the Royal Academy in London in 1872 directly above Whistler's portrait of his mother – a position that meant the delicate workmanship and subtle colouring was all but lost on the viewer.

"As if in mockery," wrote the critic of the London Times, "Petra is placed immediately above Mr Whistler's 'Arrangement in Gray and Black' which, thanks to its broad simplicity, would have lost nothing had the two pictures changed places, while, as they hang, Mr Lear's delicate work is entirely sacrificed."

Shepherd and his flock between
Ma'daba and Mount Nebo.

Full-body mud pack at
the Dead Sea.

INTRODUCTION

A detailed guide to the entire country, with principal
sights clearly cross-referenced by number to the maps.

*Panorama over Amman
from the Citadel.*

At just over 92,000 sq km (35,500 sq miles), Jordan is
roughly the size of Ireland, Portugal or the US state of Vir-
ginia. With natural features that range from the Dead Sea at
400 metres (1,300ft) below sea level, to mountains fragrant
with pine forests, and gorges splashed by waterfalls, plus
coral reefs, desert dunes and wheat fields, Jordan packs a
lot into its perimeters.

Jordan can be divided into three main geographical areas:
the Jordan Valley, the plateau of the East Bank, and the desert hinterland.

Jordan forms part of the Great Rift Valley – the great fissure that runs from
Syria all the way to East Africa – marked by the Wadi 'arabah, the Red Sea,
Dead Sea and the Jordan Valley itself. Running through the northern part of
the Jordan Valley is the River Jordan, which irrigates the valley and facilitates
intensive farming. This area has been cultivated for millen-
nia, and today includes the stone-age sites of Pella, and the
biblical sites of Bithani-beyond-the-Jordan and the Dead Sea.

Rising above the valley is the East Bank Plateau, marked
by a series of wadis including the Wadi al-mujib. The landscape is gentle and hilly and forested in places. 'Ajlun Forest
Reserve is found here, as is Dana Biosphere Reserve. It is
also home to some of the country's main towns: the capital,
Amman, Irbid, Ma'daba and Al-karak.

Stretching eastwards and forming the vast majority of
the landscape is the desert hinterland including the stony
wasteland known as the Badia. The Azraq Wetland Reserve
is found here, as well as the Desert Castles and, in the far
south, Wadi Rum.

*Farmers and goat herd near
Umm qays.*

Distances in Jordan are short, so a little of everything can be sampled in
a week. However, there is much to fill a longer stay (Petra alone is worth
at least two to three days) and many incidental pleasures to be sampled
along the way, including wildlife viewing in Dana or Azraq, the hot springs
at Hammamat Ma'in, a tingling full-body mudpack at the Dead Sea, or
following in biblical footsteps at Bithani-beyond-the-Jordan. Even non-
believers may find they are uplifted by more than mountain breezes on
Jabal nibu (Mount Nebo). Small it may be, but Jordan packs a powerful
punch in tourism terms.

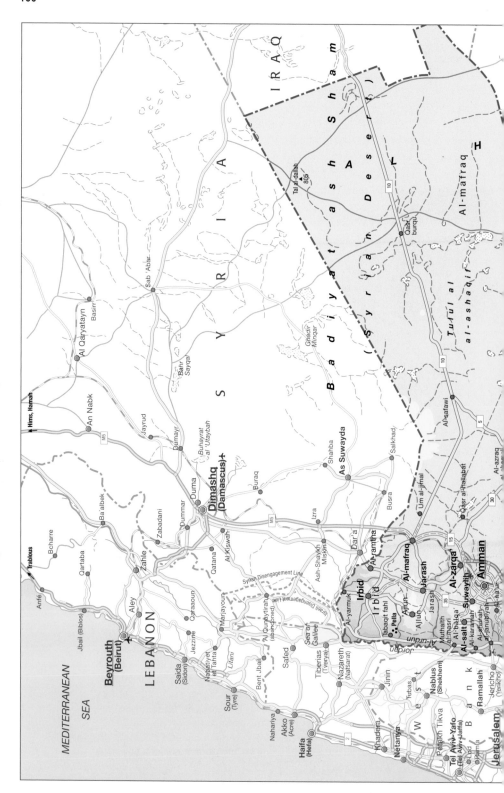

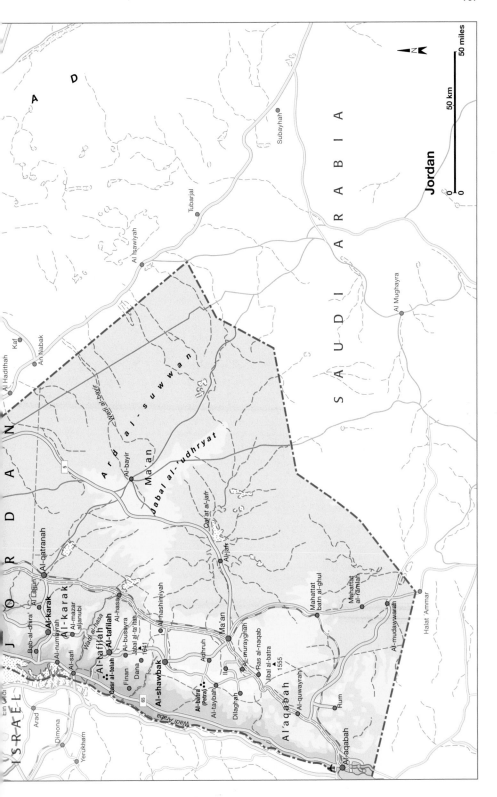

Byzantine church in the Citadel.

AMMAN

Many visitors use Jordan's capital merely as a base from which to reach more famous attractions such as Petra. But Amman holds its own in tourism terms: the city claims impressive ancient sites, important museums and a healthy cultural and social life with a lively arts scene.

Amman is both similar and dissimilar to other Middle Eastern capitals. Like many cities in the region, ancient monuments stand cheek-by-jowl with shiny modern megaliths; poverty and deprivation jostle uneasily with wealth and ostentation, and a governing minority leaning westwards co-exists with a conservative majority that roots itself firmly in the traditions of the East.

Though its origins are almost as ancient as other capitals such as Damascus, Amman's heritage is less linear and less conspicuous. With the waning and waxing of the city's fortunes, many of the monuments of its great past have vanished. Between the remnants of the ancient cities of Ammoun and Philadelphia, and the gleaming towers of the present day, is a long architectural hiatus, with most buildings dating only to the latter half of the 20th century. A handful of houses date from the 1920s and '30s during the days of the Emirate, but most are suffering visible absorption by the ever-growing metropolis.

Amman's urban landscape is famously confusing: in the older parts of town, there is little street planning and most buildings are constructed of similar size and design, in a uniform white stone that turns to mellow gold with age or the evening sun. Some streets have two names: those signposted, and those named locally, often after landmarks or locals who once lived there.

CULTURAL DIVERSITY

Amman was always a cultural crossroads that saw conquerors and occupiers come and go. Today, those influences are reflected in the range of the city's art, music, dance, cuisine and dress. Amman is the best place to discover Jordan's historic, cultural and ethnic diversity, and to witness

Main Attractions
The Citadel
Downtown
Rainbow Street
Jabal al-luwaybda
Jordan Museum
West Amman
Al Husayn National Park
Kan zaman

Map on page 146

View over Amman from the Citadel.

signs of modern cultural transition: European and American fashions are often compromised by the *hijab* (head scarf), robed imams stride to the mosque clutching mobile phones, and burkha-clad women poke at iPads in the city cafés.

Scores of unfinished buildings are reminders both of the city's continued expansion, swollen both by rural migration and thousands of immigrants from troubled regional neighbours, and of its recent economic woes. The ever greater demand on space and resources along with the current economic malaise and political restlessness have, however, failed to transform Ammanis into the jaded and cynical city dwellers found in many capitals. Locals are the city's charm, and their warmth and friendliness often surprise Western visitors. They are never reluctant to offer help (particularly when trying to navigate the city) or shy to show hospitality and generosity. After all, a local saying has it that a "guest is a gift of God".

Palestinian women in downtown Amman.

EARLY HISTORY

There is archaeological evidence that settlement in the Amman area has existed for almost 9,000 years. Ain Ghazzal, off the Zerqa road on the outskirts of the city, is one of the largest Neolithic settlements (c.6500 BC) ever discovered in the Middle East. Remarkable artefacts dating to the period can be seen in the Jordanian Archaeological Museum (Mathaf al-aathar) in the Citadel.

The Citadel (Al-qal'ah) hill contains early Bronze-Age tombs (3300–1200 BC), and the site of a late Bronze-Age temple (1300–1200 BC) near the old airport at Marka suggests that these early inhabitants were quite affluent.

By the beginning of the Iron Age (1200–539 BC), Amman had developed into the capital of the Ammonites referred to in the Bible. It was here, during a siege in the 10th century, that King David of Israel arranged the death of Uriah the Hittite, whose wife he coveted. Fortress towers ringed the outskirts of Amman (today one of the best preserved stands next to the Department of Antiquities' offices,

⊙ PHILADELPHIA

As the Roman Empire extended southward to Petra and beyond, Philadelphia found itself at the centre of the new Roman province of Arabia, and of the lucrative trade routes running between the Mediterranean as far east as India and China, as well as routes north and south. With the commerce, the city boomed and great monuments were constructed, including the magnificent Temple of Hercules (Ma'bad hiraql), the massive walls of the Citadel (Al-qal'ah) and the great amphitheatre and odeon in downtown Amman.

Philadelphia eventually grew to become the southernmost city of the Decapolis (see page 171). Along with other cities in the group, Philadelphia retained some degree of autonomy and became an important centre of Graeco-Roman commerce and culture amid a Nabataean hinterland.

near the 3rd Circle), but they were little protection against King David's determined attack. His forces toppled the Ammonites and, apart from a brief revival in the 9th and 8th centuries BC, the area was ruled successively by foreign invaders: the Assyrians, Babylonians and Persians for the next several hundred years.

Amman's history during much of this time is unclear. However, it emerged from this historical darkness during the Hellenistic period, from the 4th century BC. The city was rebuilt, expanded and renamed Philadelphia by Ptolemy II (285–247 BC), under whom it flourished.

The area was later taken by the Seleucids in 218 BC and for two centuries it continued to grow. In 63 BC, it was absorbed by the Roman Empire as Philadelphia.

Though Christians were persecuted (and martyred) in Amman during the Roman occupation, Amman later became a bishopric after the new religion was adopted, and the remains of two Byzantine churches can be found on the Citadel and in the garden of Dar al-funun on Jabal al-luwaybda. At Swayfiyah, near 6th Circle, archaeologists have discovered the mosaic floor of another Byzantine church dating from the 6th century. It is one of the few Byzantine mosaic floors found in the capital.

AMMON

Philadelphia reverted to its Semitic name, Ammon, under the Islamic caliphate in Damascus and continued to flourish as a trade centre. It soon became the headquarters of the local Omayyad governor and capital of the surrounding Belqa'a district, and its pre-eminence can be seen in the scale and majesty of the Omayyad Palace (Al-qasr al-umawi) on the Citadel.

With the shift in political power from Damascus to Baghdad under the Abbasid Caliphate (750–969), and to Cairo under the Fatimids (969–1171),

Amman's fortunes began to decline. During the Crusades and under the Mamlukes in Egypt, Amman was eclipsed by the rise of Al-karak in the south. It was not until the end of the 19th century that Amman began to regain its former status.

OTTOMAN TIMES

Under the Ottoman Empire, Amman remained a backwater, with Al-salt the principal town in the vicinity. In 1806, Amman was reported to be uninhabited, although the ancient buildings were used as temporary dwellings and store rooms by local farmers. There was plenty of water from the stream running through the valley, and Bedouin often camped nearby.

Increasingly beleaguered in Europe in the 19th century, the Ottomans sought to reassert their authority in other parts of their empire. This process coincided with the exodus of large numbers of Circassian and other Muslims from the Caucasus in the wake of wars with the Christian tsar based in Moscow. The Circassians found refuge

Byzantine Church in the Citadel.

Spice shop owner in downtown Amman.

Fruit and veg market in downtown Amman.

in the Ottoman Empire and, with the encouragement of Istanbul, some made their way to the area around Amman. The first to arrive were members of the Shabsugh tribe, and these early immigrants are commemorated in the names of streets and buildings in downtown Amman.

From the beginning of the 20th century, merchants from Al-salt, Syria and Palestine began to arrive, attracted by the opportunities for trade. However, it was the construction of the Hejaz railway which brought Amman to the centre of the regional stage once more. Linking Damascus with Medina, it passed through Amman in 1902 and was completed in 1908. The railway changed the exclusively Circassian, agricultural character of the town (see page 146).

Once again, Amman became a centre on the route from Damascus to the Holy Cities. The population began to swell, and by 1905, there were some 3,000 people in what had effectively become a market town with an increasingly cosmopolitan population.

⊘ THE CIRCASSIANS

The Circassians are an ancient ethnic group originating from the North Caucasus. From the late 18th century onwards, the Circassians lost land and autonomy to Russian expansion, culminating in their defeat in the 1864 Russian-Circassian War. Thereafter, tens of thousands of Circassians were forcibly displaced, making their way to lands in the Ottoman Empire, including the Levant. Considered accomplished and brave fighters, the Ottomans welcomed them to the empire's troubled borderlands. Today, between 1 and 2 percent of Jordanians claim Circassian descent.

The group have made a disproportionate contribution to Jordanian history. Within a few years of arrival in Amman, the Circassians had established mills along the river and a network of rough roads. Some claim they were also the first to introduce tea to the region. Mostly farmers, they tilled the land and planted fruit trees and vineyards. They were also goldsmiths, silversmiths, leather and dagger craftsmen and carriage-makers. Considering themselves men of the soil, craftsmen and soldiers, the Circassians traditionally looked down upon commerce and trading. Many have served with high distinction in public life, including as prime minister (Sa'id al Mufti, who served three times in the 1950s), as military officers and high-up public officials. In recognition of their role in Jordanian history, the Circassians make up the Guard of Honour for the royal family.

THE EMIRATE

When Emir Abdullah arrived in Transjordan from the Hejaz (modern-day Saudi Arabia) in 1920, it seemed for a while that Al-salt, the administrative centre of the area under the Ottomans, would become his capital. However, he eventually decided on Amman, marking a crucial stage in the modern history of the city. There were good reasons for choosing Amman: it was at the political and geographical centre of the region, and the Hejaz railway linked the Emir with the Hashemite heartland to the south as well as with Damascus to the north.

Amman in the early 1920s was described by a British officer as "quite big for this part of the country and built along the bottom of a narrow valley with houses up the side of the hill". But there were still no paved roads and few services.

A modest start was made at creating an administration. On 11 April 1921, the first Council of Ministers was formed. The Chief Minister set up shop in a small building by the stream. In 1923, the Emir began to build the Husseni Mosque (Al-masjid al-husayni) on a much older Omayyad one, a move which famously enraged St-John Philby (the father of British spy master, Kim Philby), one of Abdullah's advisers at the time. Two years later, Abdullah completed the construction of the Qasr raghadan (Raghadan Palace) on a hill across from the Citadel.

Amman's main streets were realigned and widened in 1925, and new shops and houses spread along them. Between 1925 and 1927, offices for the Emir Abdullah and the British Residency were built. The telegraph system was reorganised and a bi-weekly motor service was created to connect Amman with Baghdad. Amman's first telephone directory appeared in 1926, and by the following year, two newspapers were being published in the city.

The 1927 earthquake encouraged the construction of solid, stone buildings rather than the mud and wood homes introduced by the Circassians. As the *wadi* became more crowded, development began to spread up the nearby hills. Most of the ruling elite chose to settle on Jabal Amman, near the 1st Circle (Al-duwwar al-awwal).

THE MODERN KINGDOM

Despite the slow but steady change, until 1948, Amman remained a sleepy capital on the edge of the desert with no more than 25,000 inhabitants. In residential areas, many streets were still known by the name of their most important inhabitant. But after the 1948 war with Israel, the population of Jordan jumped from about 400,000 to 1.3 million in one year. There was a similar surge in the population of Amman. Better-off refugees in Amman settled in the centre and west of the city, but the vast majority settled in camps located in the east.

Following Jordan's annexation of the West Bank in 1951, merchants in Amman with an eye for opportunity prospered by serving as middlemen for West Bank importers, as well as between Palestinian producers and Arab markets. Attracted by the opportunities presented by the city, rural to urban migrants enlarged the population further still. By 1967, Amman boasted about 433,000 inhabitants and this was then boosted by the influx of more than 150,000 Palestinian refugees in the wake of the war in that year.

The economic boom in the oil-rich Arab states of the Gulf in the early 1970s had enormous consequences for urban expansion in Amman. Between 1972 and 1982, the city grew from 21 sq km (8 sq miles) to 54 sq km (21 sq miles), almost doubling in size. Building expanded yet again with the return of the 300,000 or more Palestinians and Jordanians expelled from the Gulf and Kuwait after the 1991 Gulf War. In the 1990s and early 21st century, the population of the city has been further filled with immigrants and temporary residents from Iraq (from 1990 and

⊘ Quote

Writing in 985, the Arab geographer Muqaddasi called Amman "the sword of the desert": "Lying on the border of the desert, (it) has round it many villages and wheat fields... it also has many streams, the waters of which work the mills."

Luxurious carriage used by King Abdullah in the Hejaz Railway Museum.

⊘ THE HEJAZ RAILWAY

Stretching from Damascus to Medina, the Hejaz railway was begun in 1900 under the direction of the Ottoman Sultan. It was designed to transport Muslim pilgrims to Medina in the Hejaz, reducing the month-long journey by camel, donkey or foot to four days, and offering respite from the beating sun, toll-charging Bedouin and other notorious hazards of the journey. In addition to its ostensible function, the railway also served to unite Turkey's crumbling empire.

The line was built solely with Muslim funds, and soldiers were drafted in to undertake much of its construction – it became a source of pride for the empire and a labour of devotion for the Muslim workers. Rising to a height of about 1,200 metres (4,000ft) in some points, and plummeting to 90 metres (3,000ft) below sea level at others, the track crosses 1,600km (1,000 miles) of some of the world's most testing terrain.

During World War I, the railway became a vital line of communication for the Turks. By repeatedly blowing up trains, whilst never actually severing the line, Lawrence and his Arab irregulars drew Turkish attention away from the main battle fronts. Having declined during the latter part of the 20th century, the railway was revived in 2012 and sections of it transported tourists, complete with staged Bedouin attacks. At the time of writing, however, the service had been stopped due to the civil war in Syria.

Downtown Amman.

Omayyad Palace.

2003), Egypt (2011) and Libya (2011), the latter filling many of Amman's hospitals as they sought medical treatment following the war in 2012. Since the start of the Syrian war in 2011, waves of refugees continue to arrive in Amman from the north.

In the process, the city has spilled over and merged with nearby towns like Suwaylih, Wadi al-sir and Rusayfeh. Today, the population of the Amman conurbation is estimated at over 4 million (and is expected to continue to rise to over 6.5 million by the year 2025). Unpaved roads have at last given way to paved streets and highways, and villas and high-rise apartments have replaced earlier wooden dwellings. Today, parts of the city – particularly West Amman – are indistinguishable from upmarket districts of European or American cities, with glass-and-steel office buildings lining multi-lane expressways, along with drive-through Starbucks and Burger Kings. The city sprawls, but it has retained a good deal of its original character and, in large part, its human scale.

ORIENTATION

Though born on seven hills like Ancient Rome, modern Amman now sprawls over two dozen. The Husseni Mosque (Al-masjid al-husayni) is at the heart of the city, with the downtown area extending from it to the northeast. Towering unmistakably above Downtown is the Citadel (Al-qal'ah) on Jabal al-qal'ah.

West Amman is defined by a series of junctions known as Circles (numbering one to eight), and largely represents the prosperous area of Amman, the heart of which is marked by Jabal Amman. Rainbow Street is found at the 1st Circle (Al-duwwar al-awwal).

To the north of Jabal Amman lies Jabal al-luwaybda, where some galleries can be found, including the Dar al-funun, as well as the Jordan National Gallery of Fine Arts.

Northwest of here lies Abdali, currently undergoing a massive transformation into the city's new business district. Northwest again lies Shumaysani, a busy commercial district, and beyond, the University of Jordan.

outh of Shumaysani lies Swayfiyah, an pmarket shopping area on the door-tep of 'Abdun, famously the "Million-ires' Row" of Amman.

CITADEL WALK

A great way to start a tour of Amman s by hiking the 15-minute (steep) limb from Downtown (or you can ake a taxi) to the **Citadel** (Al-qal'ah; at–Thur 8am–4pm, Fri and holidays 0am–4pm, summer 8am–6.30pm; harge; tel: 06-463 8795), which not nly gives a terrific overview of the ity's early history, but also of its eography. The Citadel also makes a reat escape from the noise and pol-ution of Downtown. It's a lovely place o wander in the early morning or late fternoon (avoid the intense heat of nidday) amid the wild fig trees and irdsong. Archaeological digs con-nue to uncover new evidence of set-ement from earliest times. However, ne best excavated sites currently are ne Roman, Byzantine and Islamic nes. One of the pleasures of the Cita-el is stumbling at any moment upon

a treasure, such as a fallen Roman capital or lion gargoyle.

After passing through the main gate and ticket office (Maktab al-tadhakir), begin with the small and unassuming **Jordanian Archaeologi-cal Museum Ⓐ** (Mathaf al-athar al-urduni). Though it's a bit dusty, musty and fusty and could do with a paint, the value and interest of the exhib-its more than compensate. Arranged chronologically, it begins with the Paleolithic period and contains a substantial collection of artefacts ranging from Paleolithic rhino teeth to child burial pots, fine Nabataean pottery and statuettes, to medieval jewellery, arms and coins. Three exhibits claim special attention: the Neolithic Ain Ghazzal figures, the ancient anthropoid and the "Amman Daedalus".

The Neolithic figures were discov-ered at Ain Ghazzal in 1983; dating to the early Neolithic period (8000–6000 BC), they lay claim to being the earliest surviving statues sculpted by man. Though unsophisticated in

Enjoying the Amman vista from the Citadel.

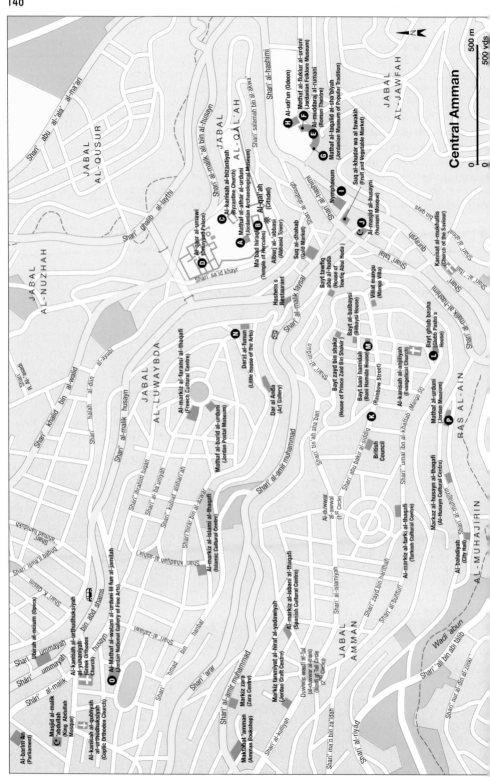

Central Amman

JABAL AL-QUSUR

JABAL AL-NUZHAH

JABAL AL-QAL'AH

JABAL AL-HASHIMI

JABAL AL-JAWFAH

JABAL AL-LUWAYBDA

JABAL AMMAN

AL-MUHAJIRIN

RAS AL-'AIN

Shari' abu 'ala' al-ma'ari

Shari' abu al-'ala' al-ma'ari

Shari' ghalib al-laythi

Shari' sa'id khayr

Shari' 'ali bin al-husayn

Shari' al-malik 'ali bin al-husayn

Shari' salamah bin al-akwa'

Shari' al-hashimi

Shari' al-hashimi

Shari' al-hashmi

Shari' khalid bin al-walid

Shari' halah al-din

Shari' al-ayubi

Shari' al-malik husayn

Shari' ibrahim tuqan

Shari' al-ba'uniyah

Shari' hiraf bin al-awal

Shari' kuliat alishari'ah

Shari' khadijah al-ashra'

Shari' al-amir muhammad

Shari' 'its 'ali sha'ban

Shari' abu bakr al-siddiq

Shari' 'umar ibn al-khatibi (Mango St)

Shari' zayd bin haritha

Shari' al-islamiyah

Shari' zayd bin humuri

Shari' al-malik al-hashimi

Shari' al-malik al-hashimi

Shari' al-muhajirin

Shari' ali bin abi talib

Shari' nur al-din al-zinki

Shari' 'ali bin abi talib

Wadi 'abun

Shari' ma'n bin za'idah

Shari' al-riyad

Shari' al-kuliyah

Shari' al-zahawi

Shari' inmad bin hanbal

Shari' 'arar

Shari' 'ammad bin muhammad

Duwwar al-awwal (1st Circle)

Duwwar wasif al-tal (al-duwwar al-thani) (West) al Tal Circle (2nd Circle)

Rainbow Street

Shari' al-amir muhammad

Shari' Umar

R. Al-'asada

Shari' ahmad hamduh

Shari' bin abdukh

Shari' ismai'l babuni

Shari' K. Qasim

Shari' Ubiah ummayah

Shari' ummayah

Shari' 'abdullah

Shari' al-malik

Shari' al-malik 'abdullah

Shari' al-tal

Shari' al-mukhallis

Shari' bin qays

Shari' Talal

qurayshi

500 m

500 yds

N

Al-barlm An (Parliament)

Masjid al-malik 'abdullah (King Abdullah Mosque)

Al-Kanisah al-urthudhuksiyah al-yunaniyah (Greek Orthodox Church)

Al-kanisah al-qubtiyah al-urthudhuksiyah (Coptic Orthodox Church)

Al-Mathaf al-watani al-urduni lil fun al-jamilah (Jordan National Gallery of Fine Arts)

Maktabat 'amman (Amman Bookshop)

Markiz zara (Zara Centre)

Markiz tanmiyat al-hiraf al-yadawiyh (Jordan Craft Centre)

Al-markiz al-isbani al-thaqafi (Spanish Cultural Centre)

Dar al-Anda (Art Gallery)

Al-markiz al-faransi al-thaqafi (French Cultural Centre)

Derat al-funun (Little House of the Arts)

Mathaf al-barid al-urduni (Jordan Postal Museum)

Al-markiz al-islami al-thaqafi (Islamic Cultural Centre)

Hashem's Restaurant

Ma'bad hiraqi (Temple of Hercules)

Mathaf al-athar al-urduni (Jordanian Archaeological Museum)

Al-kanisah al-bizantiyah (Byzantine Church)

Al-qasr al-umawi (Umayyad Palace)

Al-qal'ah (Citadel)

Alburj al-'abbasi (Abbasid Tower)

Suq al-dhahab (Gold Market)

Nymphaeum

Bayt tawfiq abu al-huda (House of Tewfiq Abul Huda)

Al-masjid al-husayni (Hussein Mosque)

Suq al-khudar wa al fawakih (Fruit and Vegetable Market)

Mathaf al-taqalid al-sha'biyah (Jordanian Museum of Popular Tradition)

Al-muddaraj al-rumani (Roman Theatre)

Mathaf al-fuklur al-urduni (Jordanian Folklore Museum)

Al-udi'un (Odeon)

Bayt zayd bin shakir (House of Prince Zaid Bin Shakir)

Bayt bani hamidah (Bani Hamida House)

Bayt al-balbaysi (Bilbaysi House)

Villat mangu (Mango Villa)

British Council

Al-kanisah al-anjiliyah (Evangelical Church)

Mathaf al-husayn al-urduni (Jordan Museum)

Markaz al-husayn al-thaqafi (Al-Husayn Cultural Centre)

Al-markiz al-turki al-thaqafi (Turkish Cultural Centre)

Al-baladiyah (City Hall)

Bayt ghub basha (Glubb Pasha's House)

xecution, the statues are remarkably xpressive and engaging.

Another alcove on the other side f the room contains two of the most triking and curious exhibits. The first f these comprises three anthropoid arcophagi. Discovered in the grounds f the Qasr raghadan in 1966, they are ery rare examples of burial practices ating from between the 13th and 7th enturies BC. Look out for the human eatures on the coffins such as the rm and hand. Just across from the arcophagi is the "Amman Daeda-us", a fine Roman copy of a Hellen-stic original. The mythical Daedalus uilt the Minoan Labyrinth in Crete, ut he is more famous for the wings e made to enable him and his son carus to escape the island. (Icarus's vings subsequently melted when e flew too close to the sun.) The ncomplete statue imparts the liveli-ess, expressiveness and sense of novement characteristic of the finest Greek work.

After visiting the museum, start a our of the Citadel at the **Temple of Hercules ❸** (Ma'bad hiraql), directly in ront of the museum as you cross the treet. The temple lies on a raised plat-orm, dedicated to the Emperor Marcus Aurelius (AD 161–180). Three gigantic olumns have been restored here.

Just beyond the Temple of Hercules s a platform with a grand view over lowntown Amman, including the Roman Theatre (Al-muddaraj al-rum-ni) and Odeon (Al-udi'un), and partly bscured, the Nymphaeum. Between t and the two minarets of the Hus-eni Mosque is the black and white Abu Darwish Mosque (Masjid abū Jarwīsh) on the hilltop behind Jabal l-Ashrafiyah. This mosque was built n the highest point in Amman by a Circassian in 1961. A panorama panel n the right of the platform points out he landmarks. From the Temple of Hercules, return to the road in front f the museum. To the right of the

museum and slightly off the road is the site of a small **Byzantine Church ❸** (Al-kanisah al-bizantiyah), marked by a number of Corinthian columns and the remains of a wall. A Byzan-tine city is thought to have existed here for hundreds of years until its destruction at the hands of the Sas-sanids (Persians).

A path leads beyond the church to the remains of an entire Omayyad city. Most Omayyad remains in the Middle East are isolated structures, so this complex has helped shed much light on Islamic urban planning, architec-ture and art. The road leads into the city's **main square**, or *suq*, where you can see the remains of several com-mercial stalls on either side. To the left are the steps that would once have led to a magnificent mosque, constructed by the Omayyads on the highest point of the Citadel.

Across the square is the **Great Audience Hall**, covered by a dome. The hall is thought to have been the main link between the palace and the rest of the city, which probably

Temple of Hercules in the Citadel.

Palestinian embroidery at the Jordanian Museum of Popular Tradition.

came under Omayyad control during the early 7th century. Archaeologists describe the building as a "cocktail adaptation of Byzantine and Sassanid work". The intricate geometric carvings inside is typical of the Sassanid style, while the cross-shaped building plan is typically Byzantine. The hall was probably used during the Omayyad period as a "hall of justice", whose second, northern doorway still opens towards the palace entrance.

Other details, in the hall and elsewhere, demonstrate how the Omayyads absorbed other cultures' artistry into their own. The remains of mosaic floors inside the palace are also indicative of the Byzantine influence, while the smooth surfaces of some walls show how the Omayyads adopted the Sassanid technique of using gypsum in their buildings.

On exiting the northern door, look for the "F" building to your left. Inside, several living quarters are situated around a central courtyard – a typical Omayyad residential arrangement, with extended families usually

Inside the Omayyad Palace.

occupying the area around each courtyard. Eight other similar dwellings have been unearthed.

Proceeding to the **Omayyad Palace** (Al-qasr al-umawi), visitors will first pass through a patio and a small entrance before reaching the **Throne Room**, from where the prince or governor, or possibly even the Damascus caliph, would have addressed visitors from behind a curtain, a Sassanian practice. The Omayyads enclosed the palace quarters in the original Roman *temenos*, or sanctuary.

Returning to the Audience Hall, you will find the remains of the **bathhouse** immediately to your left. Its style is similar to that of Roman and Byzantine baths with minor differences; for example, the Omayyads provided more generous seating in their baths, as holding congress and entertaining while bathing were favourite pastimes. You can also see the remains of the ceramic water system and an enormous restored water Cistern (Al-saharij). Continue straight towards the main road, and take a left turn for the main road to downtown Amman.

DOWNTOWN

The Roman city centre is mostly under concrete and tarmac nowadays, but the restored **Roman Theatre** (Al-muddaraj al-rumani; AD 169–77) conveys a sense of the city's former size and importance. Built into the hillside, it seats about 6,000 people and is still used for performances today. There are three bands of seats: the tiers closest to the arena were for the nobles, the second for the military and the third for the ordinary citizens. Look out for a large stone inscribed with an eye, snake, dagger and bow (just discernible), lying on the old stage near the entrance gate to the left as you come in. This stone once topped the entrance to the amphitheatre and symbolised the emperor's protection.

Two small museums at either end of the Roman stage showcase more recent times in Amman's history. The small **Jordanian Folklore Museum** ❻ (Mathaf al-fulklur; Sat–Thur 8am–6pm, Fri and holidays 9am-4pm; charge; tel 06-465 1742) to the right of the stage as you enter the theatre. It presents a cross-section of traditional Jordanian life and culture. Inside, one exhibit shows how rugs are woven, and a display case has samples of different types of embroidery. There are also some old guns and a small display of traditional musical instruments. Look out for the *mihbash* (coffee-grinder), comprising a large wooden pestle and narrow-necked wooden mortar: a good grinder can beat out extraordinary rhythms. Town life is represented by a diorama of the living room of a fine house; the desert, by a Bedouin tent; and the countryside by a small collection of agricultural implements, rakes and threshing boards.

To the left of the stage is the **Jordanian Museum of Popular Tradition** ❼ (Mathaf al-taqalid al-sha'biyah; Sat–Thur 8am–5pm; Fri 10am-4pm; charge; tel: 06-465 1760), opened in 1971 by Sa'adiya at-Tell, the wife of Jordan's then prime minister, Wasfi at-Tell. Partly built into the theatre, the museum is cool and shady, and a lesson in good design and maintenance. It contains fine examples of popular tradition, from different tribal garb and headdresses to Bedouin jewellery and handicrafts. Look out for the ornate burkhas from South Palestine decorated with British Mandate coins. A cool barrel vault to the side contains a collection of delightful mosaics originating from 4th- to 6th-century churches in Jordan. Look out for the partridge inspecting another in a cage.

Directly in front of you as you exit the theatre is the old **Roman Forum**. Not much remains of Philadelphia's old marketplace and meeting area, but if you bear right, you can walk through the old colonnade marked by a row of tall Corinthian columns. At the end of this on the left is the Roman

The Roman Theatre.

Odeon **Ⓗ** (Al-udi'un), begun in the early part of the 2nd century AD. After more than 20 years of restoration work by the Jordanian Department of Antiquities, the Odeon reopened in 1997. The intimate little theatre occasionally hosts concerts, such as those of the National Music Conservatory. Check the "What's On" section in the Jordan Times for listings, or the flyers in cafés in Rainbow Street.

Turn left along the main street past the Amman Municipality Public Library and keep left at the junction. This is called **Saqf as Sayl Street** ("the roof of the stream"), so-called because it is built over the stream which was so crucial in Amman's history. The Roman **Nymphaeum Ⓘ** (completed in AD 191), dedicated to the water nymphs, is about 100 metres/yards further up on the right. The stone wall on the street is all that remains of the original fountain complex. Though closed off by wire and neglected, the impressive ruins of the Nymphaeum are an indication of Philadelphia's status and still well worth a visit.

The Nymphaeum.

Turn right after the Nymphaeum, past the colourful and noisy fruit and vegetable market, and left at the next intersection for the **Husseni Mosque Ⓙ** (Al-masjid al-husayni). It is decorated in pink and beige stone, and a plaque on the wall reveals that the original mosque was built by Omar Ibn al Khattab, the Second Caliph of Islam (634–644). Emir Abdullah built a new mosque on the site, and restoration work was carried out by King Husayn in 1987. Though there are no must-see sights inside, appropriately dressed visitors are welcome to walk around. Women (even with headscarves) may be less welcome.

RAINBOW STREET WALK

For a stroll through the early modern history of Amman and the Emirate down to modern times, take a taxi to Jabal Amman, to where **Rainbow Street Ⓚ** (Shari' abu bakir al-siddiq) off **1st Circle** (Al-duwwar al-awwal) comes to an end in a T-junction. It was to this area that the Emirate's rich and powerful (including the current king's grandfather and family) moved following the earthquake of 1927. They replaced the old Circassian houses of dried mud and wood with more secure stone houses, and the beautiful houses and mansions in characteristic white and sometimes pink stone that are dotted along the route tell the history of Jordan prior to 1948. Rainbow Street is also increasingly the home to new cafés, restaurants and art galleries, which are well worth a visit. One of these is the café-cum-gallery, Duinde Gallery (daily noon–2am; free), which is a cool, atmospheric and relaxed place for a mint tea or coffee. The artist owner displays his work on the walls.

The first house on the left (as you walk back up Rainbow Street) once belonged to a leading Palestinian historian, Aref al Aref, who came from Jerusalem in the early 1920s to work

with Emir Abdullah. Next on the left is the **Mango Villa** (Villat mangu) with its curving balconies. The present structure dates from the 1950s, but an earlier part of the building is around the corner in Shari' 'umar bin al-khattab. It was owned by two Palestinian brothers, Hamdi and Ibrahim Mango, who made their fortune from cloth and thereby founded one of Amman's foremost business families. Back on Rainbow Street, the compound on the right belonged to Sa'id al Mufti, a prominent Circassian who served as prime minister during the Emirate (see box, page 142). The current structure dates from the post-1927 period. Look out for the traces of the old Circassian buildings in one of the houses in the compound, with a low roof and long porch.

Turn left along Omar Bin Al Khattab Street (Shari' 'umar bin al-khattab) (formerly Glubb Pasha Street), which curves for about 100 metres/yards before coming to No. 40, where high walls on the right surround **Glubb Pasha's house** (Bayt ghlub

basha). Go back along the street for 10 metres/yards, walk up the stairs on the same side as Glubb's house, and pass the Evangelical Church (Al-kanisah al-anjiliyah), built in 1949, and the Ahliyah school, founded in 1926 by the Christian Mission Society of England. Just across the road, near the junction with Rainbow Street, is the house where the late King Husayn and Prince Hassan were born and lived with their father, King Talal. Compared to some of the mansions hereabouts, it is a modest building. The family was relatively poor in those days, and Emir Abdullah could accommodate only his immediate family at the Raghadan Palace (Qasr raghadan). Straight on across Rainbow Street and just past a stone house on the corner, which once belonged to the Mara'i family of Syrian merchants, is what has become known as the **Bani Hamida House** (Bayt bani hamidah). This is the salesroom and administrative centre of a successful crafts project involving local Bedouin women. Beautiful

Tip

Amman's taxi drivers aren't always familiar with tourist sights, the smaller hotels or restaurants. Ask a local to write your destination's name in Arabic, with the area, nearest circle or landmark. If it still draws a blank, ask the driver to telephone the place for directions.

Downtown Amman's fruit and vegetable market.

King Abdullah Mosque.

flat woven rugs and other items are on sale. The house used to be home to Major Alec Kirkbride, who was the British Resident (first ambassador) in Jordan for many years.

The **Bayt al-balbaysi,** of white stone, and the **Bilbaysi palace**, of alternating pink and white, are straight ahead. The story goes that Ismail Bilbaysi came to the East Bank in the early 1900s to work on the Hejaz railway as an unskilled labourer. He went on to become a delivery man for Shell – at the time, motor fuel was sold in containers holding 20 litres (4 gallons), which required a strong man such as Bilbaysi to shift – and then moved on to selling. In time, he became Shell's sole agent in Jordan, and made his fortune in World War II.

Bilbaysi built the palace in 1954 and allowed King Abdullah to house his guests here (there was still no room at Raghadan). The king rewarded Bilbaysi by making him a Pasha. Locals say that Rita Hayworth stayed here when shooting *Salomé*.

Rainbow Street.

Take the steps down past the high walls to the left, which enclose the **house of Prince Zaid Bin Shakir** (Bayt zayd bin shakir), a relative of the king and ex-prime minister and Commander of the Armed Forces. Prince Zaid's father was one of Emir Abdullah's closest allies during the Arab Revolt.

Turn left for about 30 metres/yards and take the stairs down to the next street. The Rashdans' house is situated on the right. The Rashdans were from Irbid in the north and worked in government, reflecting once more Emir Abdullah's efforts to unite all parts of the country.

Go straight down the road for 100 metres/yards, keeping right at the fork, to the **house of Tewfiq Abul Huda** (Bayt tawfiq abu al-huda). Tewfiq Abul Huda was one of Emir Abdullah's earliest allies and prime minister of Jordan on several occasions. His home was built in 1927, and designed in the style of a Lebanese mountain house. The mason who planned and constructed the upper storey was a Lebanese Druze, Shekeeb Abu Hamdan. Go back towards the fork in the road. A small stone structure in a car park in front is all that remains of the **house of Ibrahim Hashem** (Bayt ibrahim hashim). He was also with Emir Abdullah from very early on, and locals joke about how he and Tewfiq Abul Huda used to take turns as prime minister.

Fifty metres/yards down the road to the right, a set of stairs lead down to Shari' al-amir muhammad. Cross the road and turn right past Shari' 'umar al-kaiyam. A small alley to the left leads to an Ammani institution: **Hashem** restaurant (off Shari' al-malik faysal; open 24 hrs; tel: 06-463 6440), one of the oldest in the downtown area. It was first opened by a Turkish immigrant in 1956 and has just opened its third branch. It sells Arab fast foods, like *hummous* (a closely guarded house

recipe) and *ful* (beans). All classes of Jordanians (from King Abdullah and his wife to early morning workers and TV celebrities) meet and eat here; nearby is the famous Ammani patisserie Habiba (daily 7am–midnight; tel: 06-5538 044), whose speciality is *konafa*, deep-fried sticks of dough filled with cream cheese and syrup.

Shari' al-amir muhammad and Shari' al-malik al-husayn (or Al-salt) streets intersect a few metres further along the main street. The Cairo Hotel still bears bullet holes in its walls which are a relic of the 1970 conflict between the Jordanian Army and the Palestinian Resistance Movement.

JABAL AL-LUWAYBDA

Return to Shari' 'umar al-kaiyam and climb the street past the row of white "service" taxis. Keep heading right all the way uphill, then turn to the left when you reach the top. It is a steep climb to this area of town, known as Jabal al-luwaybda, but worth the effort.

In front is the restored Hamud house, now known as the **Darat al-funun**

(Little House of the Arts; Thur–Sat 10am–7pm; free; www.daratalfunun.org), which was once home to Peake Pasha (see page 63). The house has been beautifully renovated by the architect and artist, Ammar Khammash, and is now arguably the city's leading art centre, containing exhibition space in two buildings, a peaceful and shady outdoor café, a large rambling, sloping garden with the ruins of a 6th-century Byzantine church (Al-kanisah al-bizantiyah) at the bottom, and a collection of art books in the centre's "library". Founded by Khalid Shoman, the centre exhibits works of both well-established artists from the whole of the Middle East, and promising local artists, whom it aims to "nurture". Regular activities include exhibitions, workshops, talks, and in summer, musical recitals and concerts in the evocative ruins of the Byzantine church. The small sculpture displayed near the entrance of the gallery is by Mona Saudi, a leading Jordanian sculptor, whose monumental *Architecture of the Soul* sits outside the Institut du Monde Arabe in Paris.

Darat al-funun art gallery.

Around the Darat al-funun lie a handful of galleries, including the excellent **Dar al-Anda**, (Sat-Wed 10am–6pm, Thu 10am–4pm; free) around 100 metres/yards west of the Darat al-funun on the same street. The galleries have changing exhibitions as well as workshops, talks and so on. Returning to the top gate of Darat al-funun, then climbing north past the Luzmila Hospital, takes you to the Luwaybda roundabout. A 10-minute walk northwest of here along Shari' al-kulliyah (College Street) takes you to the **Jordan National Gallery of Fine Arts** Ⓞ (Almathaf al-watani al-urduni lil funun al-jamilah; winter Wed–Thur, Sat–Mon 9am–7pm, summer 9am–5pm, during Ramadan 9am–2pm; charge), which houses the country's best collection of contemporary Middle Eastern artists as well as up-and-coming Jordanian ones. The exhibits are well-presented, lit and captioned on three floors, and there's an excellent upmarket gift shop belonging to the Zara chain.

JORDAN MUSEUM

Due south of Rainbow St (Shari' abu bakir al-siddin) and Mango St (Shari' 'umar ibn al-khattab) in an area known as Ras al-Ain is Amman's newest museum, the **Jordan Museum** Ⓟ (Mathaf al-urduni; Sat–Mon and Wed 10am–2pm; tel: 06-4629317; www.jordanmuseum.jo), constructed in late 2009 in an impressive, custom-designed modern building. Funding shortfalls long delayed its opening. It is now undoubtedly Jordan's top museum, containing world-class exhibits on Jordan's history and culture, as well the country's key archaeological collections (including the Dead Sea Scrolls). Laid out over around 2,000 sq metres (21,500sq ft) over two floors, the exhibits are well-displayed with life-size dioramas, interactive displays and good information panels. The museum also contains a restaurant and café, bookshop, seminar room and gift shop. Audio and museum guides are available. Check out the website for updates. Entrance for foreign visitors is 5JD.

King Abdullah Mosque.

Just west of the museum lie two other sleek new buildings: Amman's City Hall (Al-baladiyah) and the Al-Husayn Cultural Centre (Markaz al-Husayn al-thaqafi), both designed by the modernist Palestinian-Jordanian architect, Jafar Touqan. Both serve as cultural venues for art exhibitions, talks, concerts and other events. Check the Jordan Times' "What's On" section for current listings.

WEST AMMAN

Amman covers a large area, spiralling out in all directions over the city's more than 20 hills from the central hub of Downtown. You're unlikely to have much reason to explore the populous, low-income neighbourhoods of north, east and south Amman, but the relatively wealthy areas of **West Amman** hold virtually all the city's hotels and upmarket restaurants, and you may well find yourself staying here. Although there are few major sights here, just strolling the streets, or sipping a cappuccino at a terrace café and indulging in some West Amman people-watching, can give an interesting insight into a part of the city in stark contrast to the chaos and hubbub of the Downtown.

The **Abdali** district is home to one of the capital's most distinctive landmarks, the King Adbullah Mosque (Masjid al-malik 'abdullah), with its giant blue dome; it dates from the 1980s.

Up the hill is **Shmisani**, a lively, traffic-bound neighbourhood of offices, restaurants and grand hotels, including the Marriott and Le Meridien. Clustered along Shari' al-Nahdah, and in the streets adjacent, are shops, fashion boutiques and fast-food outlets. Local residents love to spend an hour or two over lunchtime or after work at one of the many terrace cafés, drinking coffee, smoking an *argileh* (water pipe) and watching the world go by – and the cafés stay busy into the small hours.

Other interesting areas lie on the south side of the great ridge of **Jabal Amman**, which runs from 1st Circle (Al-duwwar al-awwal) westwards for several kilometres to 8th Circle at the city limits. Just south of 4th Circle is **'Abdun**, the wealthiest area of the capital. Its central roundabout, 'Abdun Circle, is surrounded by upmarket restaurants, noodle and sushi bars, patisseries and chocolate shops and music outlets, while the millionaire's row of Shari' al-qahirah, leading west, is lined with some of the most grandiose and ostentatious domestic architecture in the country. Nearby, just below 6th Circle, is Al-**Swayfiyah**, a dense network of narrow streets packed with shops of all kinds – from groceries to designer homeware, *haute couture* to ice-cream parlours.

Shari' al-makah, a busy boulevard leading from near 5th Circle into the northwest area of the city, hosts, at its western end, **Mecca Mall** (Makah mall), one of the biggest covered shopping malls in the country – and a sight worth seeing. Spread over five floors, it encompasses hundreds of shops,

Trendy Noodasia restaurant in 'Abdun Circle.

cafés, eateries, a cinema, a bowling alley, a kids' adventure complex and more. An afternoon in the mall with the urban middle-class is just as authentic – and sometimes as fascinating – a Jordanian experience as an afternoon in the desert with a Bedouin guide.

AL HUSAYN NATIONAL PARK

Lastly, on a hill overlooking the western fringes of the city, is the **Al Husayn National Park** (Hadiqat al-husayn al-wataniya), the city's largest green space, established by King Abdullah II in honour of his father, and a favourite spot for extended family picnics and outings, especially on Friday afternoons.

On the highest point of the hill, in landscaped gardens, is the peaceful, airy and well-designed **King Husayn Memorial** (Nusb al-malik husayn al-tidhkari). Nearby is another tribute: the **Royal Automobile Museum** (Mathaf al-saiyarat al-malaki; Wed–Thur, Sat–Mon 10am–7pm; Fri 11am–7pm; charge; tel: 06-541 1329), celebrating Husayn's passion for motor cars and motor racing. The collection undoubtedly ranks

Café in Jabal Amman.

as one of – if not the – greatest private collection of motor vehicles in the world. Among the splendid models on display are a 1916 Cadillac, a 1940 Buick, a 1947 Lincoln and a 1952 Aston Martin. The vehicles are superbly displayed around a path that leads through a purpose-built hanger lit with powerful spotlights. The exhibits are accompanied by informative panels that introduce the vehicle as well as the make. Even for non-car buffs, the museum is a fascinating visit. Nearby is the **Children's Museum** (Mathaf al-atfal; Wed–Thur, Sat–Mon 9am–6pm; Fri 10am–6pm; charge, children under one free; tel: 06-541 1479), opened in 2007, which contains toys, gadgets, educational and interactive displays designed to please all children from toddlers to teens. Exhibits range from the cockpit of an airliner and a walk-through inner ear to a mini planetarium and a child's ATM. Though noisy, it's imaginative and well-designed.

AROUND AMMAN

Wadi al-sir, one of the loveliest valleys in Jordan, also contains one of the most interesting, least known and underrated ancient monuments in the Middle East. The *wadi* lies about 12km (8 miles) west of Amman, beyond 8th Circle and past the village of Wadi al-sir itself. The scenery is spectacular at any time of the year, but the best time to visit the valley is in spring, when the landscape is verdant and lush, and the slopes are dotted with poppies and wild irises. A trip here amid sweet-smelling meadows and the sound of water and birdsong makes a very welcome break from the commotion, car fumes and dust of Amman. Around the end of March, the famous black iris starts to bloom in this area.

The road winds down the valley to the river and passes through several small villages before reaching **Iraq al-Amir**, Caves of the Prince; two of the caves bear ancient Hebrew inscriptions. The road continues only a little

urther, ending at **Qasr al-'abid**, the Palace of the Slave, perhaps the most mportant palace to have survived in he Middle East, dating from the Hellenistic era. The ruins are impressive for their sheer size and sturdiness and their state of preservation. The ground around the building is strewn with beautiful objects, including fallen columns and capitals, giant millstones and broken gargoyles. Look out for the ion carvings on the ruins.

Nearby and signposted lies the excellent **Iraq al-Amir Women's Project** (Sat–Thur 9am–5pm; Fri and other imes by appointment; free; tel: 0775 931563; no landline). Opened in 1993 by Queen Noor, the project is managed and run by a co-operative of 34 spinsters, who produce well-made artisanal products including rugs, pressed flowers, pottery, olive oil, shawls and drawings. Visitors can wander around and visit the kilns, workshops and loom and see the women at work.

Just south of Amman, on a hilltop 12km (7 miles) from 7th Circle, off the airport road, is **Kan zaman**, a renovated 19th-century complex of stables, storehouses and residential quarters and now a major tourist attraction. The complex belongs to the prominent Jordanian family, the Abu Jabers. The family's forefathers moved from Nazareth to Al-salt in the early 1800s. By the middle of the 19th century, they were growing cereals and raising livestock from their hilltop base.

Kan zaman (which translates as "once upon a time") opened in 1989. It combines an early 20th-century atmosphere with some of the best crafts that Jordan has to offer. The stone-paved courtyard is lined with attractive shops selling handicrafts, jewellery and spices. Visitors can smoke a hubble-bubble at the coffee shop, or eat excellent Arabic food at the restaurant in the renovated stables. Be prepared, too, for the skirl of bagpipes, a popular Jordanian sound, and to see the waiters dance an Arab *dabkeh* here. There is also a piano restaurant at the other end of the courtyard called Al-baydahr, which translates as "the threshing floor". The restaurant serves local food that is cooked in the traditional *tanoor* clay oven.

Playing inside the Children's Museum.

⊘ THE SEVEN SLEEPERS

Lying around 8km (5 miles) from Downtown in the southeastern suburbs of Amman in the village of Rajib (look out for the huge mosque complex), on the road to Sabah, is a site that claims to be the location of the Cave of the Seven Sleepers. According to legend (including references in the Quran), seven Christian boys fleeing persecution at the hands of the Roman emperor Trajan sought sanctuary in a cave. There, God made them sleep 309 years, awaking to Byzantine Christian rule. Attempting to buy food with Roman coins, they were brought before the Christian king, where a miracle was declared. Besides the caves themselves (which contain a row of small tombs), are the remains of two mosques, and 500 metres/yards west of the cave, the remains of a Byzantine cemetery.

📷 CAFÉ SOCIETY IN AMMAN

From smoke-filled dens to slick cyber cafés and organic eco-cafés, the coffee-drinking industry in Amman has transformed itself into a diverse and lucrative business.

In Jordan and the Middle East, coffee is the lifeblood of society. It is the foremost symbol of hospitality in every home and at every social occasion, from engagements to funerals. In business, a deal sealed over coffee becomes a binding commitment.

But, as Jordanian society undergoes rapid social change, so do its coffee-drinking habits. Internet cafés today can be found in many towns and villages of Jordan, and modern European-style cafés are becoming increasingly fashionable in the cities. The university city of Irbid has long claimed to have more internet cafés packed into one kilometre of road than anywhere else in the world.

Blue Fig Café near 'Abdun Circle in Amman.

A THIRST FOR MORE THAN COFFEE

The organic Wild Jordan Café.

When Books@Café, Jordan's first internet café, opened in 1997 in Amman's famous Rainbow Street, the country's alternative youth – until then an untapped sector – were attracted in droves, drawn by high-tech communication, occasional live international music, and an escape from the strict social rules governing public interaction between the sexes. More recently, organic cafés, such as the excellent Wild Jordan Café, and gallery cafés, such as the Darat al-funun and Duinde cafés – all in Amman – have started sprouting up.

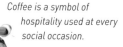

Coffee is a symbol of hospitality used at every social occasion.

Argilehs (water pipes) and internet access often accompany the coffee.

A coffee with a smoke

In the Downtown area of Amman, coffee houses and their patrons remain rooted in tradition. These cafés, often cloaked in the heavy and sweet-smelling haze of the *argileh* (water pipes) are most busy after work. During the day, they are the haunt of the old, the retired and the unemployed, who exchange news and gossip and occasionally conduct business over a *finjan* (demitasse) of Turkish coffee or a cup of tea (served sweet and strong like the coffee but often flavoured with mint). Amid the gloom, heads bow intently over games of *taoleh* (backgammon), *tarneeb* (trumps) and card games, or newspapers, interspersed with lively discussions.

For a taste of one of these basic but atmospheric places, head for Peace Café in Amman's Downtown. Do as the locals do: bag a seat on the balcony, suck at an *argileh* and watch Amman go by. More used to tourists (and women travellers – these coffee houses are traditionally the domain of men) is the ever-popular Al Rashid Court Café in the Downtown area. For a more modern, trendy take on the traditional coffee house, seek out the very popular Afrah Restaurant & Coffeeshop next to the Farah Hotel in Downtown, located in a traditional Ammani town house.

...é des Artistes in the upmarket neighbourhood of ...al Amman.

Modern coffee shops offer young Jordanian women a place to catch up and socialise.

The road from Al-salt to the Dead Sea.

Ottoman-era architecture in Al-salt.

AL-SALT AND ENVIRONS

Though practically a satellite of Amman today, for long periods in the region's history, Al-salt was the most important settlement between the Jordan River and the eastern desert.

Benefitting from a clement climate, a plentiful supply of water and fertile soil, Al-salt has attracted settlers since at least the Iron Age. Located on the "frontier of settlement", the town additionally provided security from marauding Bedouin. It was also well placed on the north–south and east–west trade routes linking the interior with Jerusalem, Nablus, Nazareth and the Mediterranean coast. Al-salt's golden age was at the end of the 19th century and the beginning of the 20th, and it is the legacy of this period that makes Al-salt unique in Jordan. The town's mixed Muslim-Christian population, and its trading tradition, have to this day helped create an atmosphere of tolerance and co-existence.

Roman tombs on the outskirts of the town are a legacy of Al-salt's Roman period. Then during the Byzantine era, Al-salt became known as Al-saltos Hieraticon. In the 13th century, a fortress was built on the site of the Citadel by the Mamluke Sultan al Malik al Mu'azzam, who was based in Cairo. Destroyed by the Mongols in 1260, the fortress was rebuilt a year later by a second Mamluke ruler from Egypt. Six centuries later, in 1840, it was demolished again by the forces of another Egyptian potentate, Ibrahim Pasha. The Citadel is now the site of a large mosque that towers over the modern town.

Al-salt inhabitant.

By the early 19th century, Al-salt was a prosperous frontier town on the edge of the Ottoman Empire and the desert. Useful to all, it was ruled by none. In 1806, the people of Al-salt were said to be "free from every kind of taxation and to acknowledge no master". Down to the present day, Al-saltis have a reputation for being stubborn, independent and proud.

The town was also the centre of lucrative trading between the region and urban industries in Palestine. Al-saltis were the middlemen for the

Main Attractions

Muasher House
Latin Monastery
Abu Jaber House
English Church, Hospital & School
Hammam Street
Al-salt Archaeological Museum

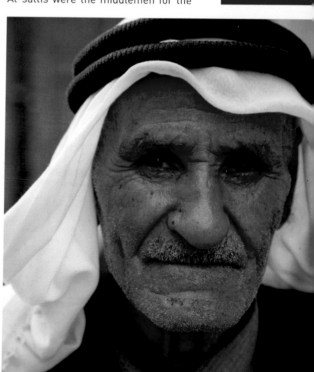

Map on page 172

supply of raw materials (3,500 camel-loads annually by the mid-19th century) collected by local Bedouin for use in the tanneries of Jerusalem and the soap factories of Nablus. Raisins and grapes were also exported to Palestine. Travellers of the time wrote of a flourishing town with shops stocking cotton from Manchester, England, as well as locally produced goods. From 1867 onwards, the town's fortunes boomed.

AL-SALT'S GOLDEN AGE

In the mid-19th century, the Ottomans sought to reassert control over their empire in the Middle East. As part of this process, the Belqa'a region was incorporated into the area governed from Nablus, and an administrator, with military forces at his disposal, was sent to Al-salt. The Ottomans also encouraged migration and settlement from other parts of the empire, and people began to flock in from Nablus, Nazareth, Jerusalem and further afield in search of opportunities in agriculture, trade, construction and government.

Al-salt began to expand and the new construction reflected its new status. An Ottoman administrative office was built on what was to become the town square. In 1866, the first modern Christian church was built and the Church Missionary Society set up the first hospital. As trade increased, shops spread along Hammam Street and houses sprang up on the lower slopes of the hills meeting at the town centre.

Al-salt's fortunes began to decline after World War I. The first blow came when Emir Abdullah chose Amman as the capital of the new Emirate of Transjordan. The irreversible shift in political and economic power concluded with the Arab-Israeli wars of 1948 and 1967, when Al-salt was cut off from the Mediterranean and its mother markets in Nablus and the rest of Palestine.

While this dealt an economic blow to the town, the resultant slowdown in growth and development has seen fewer of its old buildings bulldozed for new reinforced concrete ones – as has

Stopping for a rest.

⊙ MERCHANT HOUSES

As Al-salt was settled, made secure and organised by the Ottomans, merchants were drawn from Palestine and beyond. Al-salt had plenty of home-grown merchants too, including the Sukkars, Muashers and Sakets; all names well known in Jordanian public life and politics to this day.

These families celebrated their good fortune by constructing fine houses, many of which have survived. Made from local yellow limestone, they incorporate a variety of indigenous and European styles. Typically, they consist of one to three storeys, an inner courtyard and domed roof. The Abu Jaber mansion (built 1892–1906), with frescoed ceilings painted by Italian artists, is considered the region's finest example of a 19th-century merchant house.

happened elsewhere. The town centre and other buildings remain almost as they were 100 years ago, and provide a rare example of a late-19th century Arab town in the era of the Ottoman Empire. Following a new tourism-led, part Japanese-funded (by Japan International Corporation Agency – JICA) impetus to preserve Al-salt's Ottoman heritage, a series of street panels have been installed that indicate self-guided walking trails around town. An accompanying brochure, *Al-salt Heritage Trail,* containing a small map, is available at the Tourist Office and museums.

A WALK AROUND AL-SALT

Buildings in **Al-salt ❶** climb a tight cluster of hills. On a hill to the left, just before entering the town, is Al-salt secondary school, the first of its kind in the country. Built in 1924, it attracted teachers and pupils from all over the Arab world and a list of alumni reads like a *Who's Who* of Jordan. Straight ahead, a modern mosque dominates the town centre from the Citadel (Al-qal'ah), the site of the 13th-century Qal'at al-mamlukress. Below, look out for the older yellow stone houses gleaming amidst modern concrete ones.

Start at what locals know either as Shari' al-dayr (Monastery Street, after the monastery up the road), or Shari' al-baladiya (Municipality Street, because it leads to the old Municipality building). On the southern side of the street is what locals call the **Muasher house** (Bayt al-mu'ashshar). A Christian merchant family, the Muashers are long-time residents of Al-salt from the Dababneh tribe believed to have originated in the Hawran region in the south of modern-day Syria and Lebanon. In fact, this house originally belonged to the Abu Jaber family, who built it at the turn of the 20th century and later sold it to the Muashers. The house is unmistakable for its

intertwined, liquorice-like columns on the second floor.

Walk back along the same street and up towards the town square. Older buildings on the left-hand side belonged to the Hamud and Nabir families. Note the narrow stairs off the main street leading to the remains of other Ottoman-era houses up the hill.

The **Latin Monastery** (Dayr al-laltinis) is on the right-hand side as you approach the square, behind high walls. The complex contains the oldest public building (1871) in Jordan's modern age, a church (1890) and a fine courtyard, which was the site of important meetings between local notables and British officials from Palestine in 1921 prior to the establishment of the Emirate. There are two steel doors on the street; ring the bell to go inside or ask around for the guardian.

ABU JABER HOUSE AND AROUND

The large 19th-century house to be seen on the left when entering the

Muasher house.

Smoking argilehs (water pipes) at a traditional café.

square is the **Abu Jaber House** (Bayt Abu Jabir, on Shari' al-amir hasan bin talal; daily 8am–5pm; charge; tel: 05-355 5652). Its sheer size and eye-catching balconies make it the most impressive building of its kind in the town. Emir Abdullah (the great-grand-father of the present king) stayed at the Abu Jaber house when he first arrived from the Hejaz in March 1921; the guardian will point out the room. Restored in October 2010 in a joint JICA-Jordanian venture, the building now houses a well-designed, semi-educational museum spread over two floors that documents Al-salt's colour-ful history and culture. Displays include exhibits on Al-salt's ancient trad-ing produce, its educational system, and traditional dress (look out for the famous *khahga* traditionally wrapped three times around a woman and worn right up to the 1950s in Al-salt).

Keep heading left up the town square. A small entrance to the left beyond the Abu Jaber building and a row of shops leads up to a number of old houses behind the new government buildings on

the square. Climb up the steps to where they fork. The house in front belonged to the Muasher family; the mansion at the top of the stairs to the right was built by the Sukkars, a Christian family from the Dababneh tribe. According to locals, Emir Abdullah also stayed at this house. Note the European-style roof perched on the top storey.

To the right of the Sukkar house, along a small pathway behind the new government buildings, is a one-storey house which belonged to the Khateeb family from Jerusalem. Next door is a good example of the "peasant-style" houses that characterised Al-salt prior to 1860. The ruined building has one storey and, inside, two stone arches supporting the remains of a wood and clay roof.

Continue down the stairs past the house of the Saket family, old resi-dents of Al-salt, to the town square. Cross the road and go back towards the Abu Jaber house and the mod-ern **fountain** near the bottom of the square. This may be the site of Al-salt's first fountain.

Near the fountain, directly across the square from the steps to the Muasher and Sukkar houses, a small yellow-walled lane leads up to the **English Church, Hospital and School** (Al-mustashfa al-ingilizi). The first door on the right is to the church, built in 1926. The second one higher up with E.H. (English Hospital) engraved on it leads to the hospital (1882–1923) and the school, the very yellow build-ing on the left, which is now disused. Stand a while in the old schoolyard and enjoy the view over the town. You can also visit the church and hospital; ask around for the guardian in the square (near the fountain below). The hospital contains a few items of old furniture including an old piano, an 1890 bridal chest from Jerusalem, some old medi-cal instruments and an old bellows, as well as broken crockery from the old hospital kitchen.

Hammam Street.

HAMMAM STREET MARKET AND AROUND

Go back down the steps and take the second left into **Hammam Street** (Shari' al-hammam). This vibrant and colourful narrow street is a working market. The yellow stone buildings are only about 100 years old, but the ambience goes back hundreds more years. Fruit and spices and other goods are on sale here, and a few metres along, just after a small entrance on the left, is the curving facade of the Touqan building (Binayat Tuqan). It is said that the Touqans fled from Nablus in the mid-19th century. About 50 metres/yards further on, steps on the left lead to the Nabulsi house (Bayt al-nabulsi). Note the wooden *mashrabiya* balcony, whose delicately carved wooden screen allowed women to see out without being seen by passers-by.

Return to Hammam Street and, walking along it, pass a right-hand turn leading to the main street. Next on either side of the road are properties belonging to the Mehyar family, who may have arrived in Al-salt from Nablus in the 1860s or earlier. A little way along is the carved minaret of the "small mosque", built in 1906. This building, too, reflects the confidence and wealth of Al-salt's golden age.

On reaching the main road, turn right. On the left is the newly renovated Touqan House (Bayt Tuqan), built between 1900 and 1905, which has been converted into the **Al-salt Archaeological Museum** (Mathaf al-aathar, on Shari' al-mada'in; daily, summer 8am–6pm; winter 8am–4pm; charge; tel: 05-355 5651), which displays objects unearthed from excavations in the Al-balqa' region. Exhibits, arranged thematically, are well-displayed, lit and captioned and range from "The Dolmen Landscape" and "Death & Burial" to "Temples & Towns" and "From Forts to Villages". The museum is also worth visiting for its architecture: the entrance hall, in particular, provides a good example of the vaulted roofs which characterise

these old houses of the well-to-do – cool in summer, warm in winter – and upstairs there is a typical interior courtyard containing a café and toilets.

AROUND AL-SALT

There are various sites of interest within easy access of Al-salt. Lying around 25 minutes' drive (minibuses travel here) southeast of Al-salt is the hilltop town of **Al-fuhis**. Known for its fine fruits (particularly apricots and peaches) and 19th-century churches (the town is very largely Christian), it also boasts a few remaining old stone cottages, a grassroots crafts initiative, a carnival in August and a music festival in December. It is also the site of a famous restaurant, the Zuwwadeh Restaurant, a great place for a lunch stop on your way to or from Amman.

Around 40 minutes by minibus southeast of Al-salt lies the Arcadian-like **Wadi al-sir,** and 10km (6 miles) west of Wadi al-sir is **Iraq al-Amir,** site of some old caves. Nearby is an impressive ancient palace, the **Qasr al-'abid** (see page 157).

Pulses and beans on sale at the market on Hammam Street.

Packing manakeesh at a flat bread bakery.

The Cardo (main street) at Jarash.

JARASH AND THE NORTH

North Jordan has the country's most spectacular historical sites after Petra – including Jarash, one of the world's best-preserved Roman cities – as well as some of the country's most beautiful scenery.

Jordanians love the area for its greenery. For Ammanis especially, the sweet-smelling valleys, thick forests or peaceful, undulating landscapes make a welcome change from the congestion, dust and sprawl of Amman. The drive north from the capital is an enticing one, as the landscape changes from rugged browns to vibrant greens. Keen Classicists, meanwhile, prick up their ears at the mention of the region, known internationally for one of the largest and best-preserved Roman cities in the world, Jarash.

REGION OF THE DECAPOLIS

The area of north Jordan and south Syria – roughly from Amman to Damascus – was often referred to during the Roman era as the region of the Decapolis, meaning the "10 cities" in Greek. This was a region of great wealth, due to its rich agricultural lands, plentiful water from rainfall and perennial springs and rivers, valuable mineral resources, and its strategic location along some of the most important trade routes of antiquity. The spice, incense and silk routes all passed through or near the Decapolis.

Little surprise then, that this region should be dotted with some major archaeological sites, several of which can be visited on an easy day trip from Amman that additionally takes in the

three main topographic and climatic zones of the country – the semi-arid eastern desert, the central highlands, and the Jordan Valley to the west. The four most important sites in the northern highlands and desert plateau are Jarash, Umm qays, 'Abilah and Um al-jimal.

In their historical sweep, the antiquities of north Jordan cover a timespan of well over 5,000 years – from the establishment of cities in the Early Bronze Age to the Ayyubid/Mamluke settlements of the medieval Islamic

⊙ Main Attractions
Jarash
'Ajlun
Irbid
'Abilah
Umm qays
Um al-jimal

📍 Maps on pages 172, 175

Young goat-herder near Umm qays.

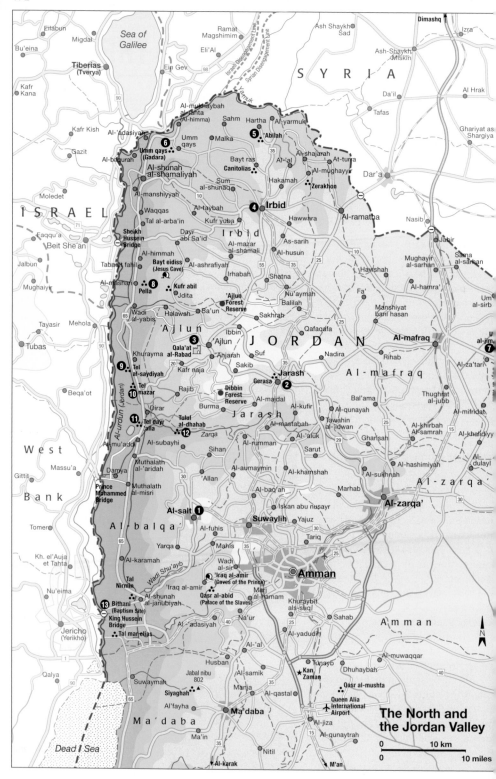

The North and
the Jordan Valley

| 0 | | 10 km |
| 0 | | 10 miles |

era – and almost all of the major sites have continued to be inhabited right through to the 21st century.

The area contains many smaller ancient sites and areas of natural beauty. The north is the most fertile part of the Jordanian plateau because of its higher altitude and greater rainfall. The best time of year to visit is the spring, when the plains are covered in wheat and barley and the verges in wild flowers, and the rolling hills leading down to the Jordan Valley are carpeted in grass. The area is predominantly agricultural, with only a few medium-scale industries and service firms making up the balance of the economy. Many parts of the semi-arid eastern desert fringe turn green in spring, thanks to the seasonal farmers who tap run-off water or underground aquifers.

JARASH

Jarash ❷ (ancient Gerasa; summer 8am–5pm; charge), lying just south of the modern city of Jarash, is only a 45- to 60-minute drive north from Amman depending on traffic.

Despite the passage of time, and trials of Jordan's sometimes troubled history, this is still one of the best-preserved Roman cities in the world, and the spectacular ruins are rivalled in Jordan only by those of Petra. Yet while Petra relies partly on the amazing beauty of its natural setting for its impact, Jarash is a man-made treasure, built over fertile rolling highlands.

As part of the Roman Decapolis, Jarash enjoyed a high degree of prosperity, wealth and civic development. Its diversity of economic activity – iron-ore mining, agriculture and trade – supported a rich culture quite at home with luxurious living. Greek inscriptions at the South Theatre (Almasrah al-janubi) give the names of wealthy donors and indicate a civic-minded society that numbered at least 20,000 during the city's golden era.

The monuments of Jarash also tell the tale of the empire's decline. The fragmented remains of splendid baths indicate the destruction wrought by successive earthquakes, while a concentration of churches – many built out

Hadrian's Arch, Jarash.

⊘ THE DECAPOLIS RIDDLE

The term Decapolis has never been found on coins, inscriptions or literary sources originating in the area; all ancient references come from literary sources elsewhere. For this reason, the Decapolis has always been something of a riddle: scholars still debate whether the term refers to a formal league or confederation of 10 cities bound by commercial, political and security bonds, or to something less systematic. Though it is mentioned in the New Testament as a "region", Roman-era references suggest it may have been an administrative district, created when the general Pompey conquered the region in 63 BC.

Modern scholarship now agrees that at its height in the Roman period, the Decapolis was probably a loose association of geographically contiguous Graeco-Roman provincial cities that shared cultural, commercial and political interests. Different lists of Decapolis cities from several historical periods provide the names of more than 10 cities, indicating that the definition of the region also changed over time. The most recent scholarship identifies the cities as: Philadelphia (Amman), Gerasa (Jarash), Pella, Gadara (Umm qays), Raphana and Capitolias (Bayt ras) all in Jordan; Scythopolis (Beisan or Bethshean) and Hippos (Hippus or Sussita) in Israel; Damascus, and Canatha (Qanawat) in Syria.

The Nymphaeum at Jarash.

Roman Army and Chariot Experience, Jarash's Hippodrome.

of stones taken from pagan temples – testify to the rise of Byzantium, by which time Jarash, the Roman entity, was almost over.

ANCIENT GERASA

Graeco-Roman Jarash as we know it today (Gerasa then) was first built by the Greek armies of Alexander the Great in the 2nd century BC. It flourished as a provincial trading city after the Roman general Pompey conquered the region in 63 BC. Along with its compatriot Decapolis cities of Philadelphia, Gadara and Pella, the city reached its peak in the 2nd century AD, when the Pax Romana (uniting and stabilising the empire) allowed regional and international trade to flourish and encouraged local investment by wealthy merchants and landowners.

Jarash is a fine example of the grand provincial urbanism found in all Roman cities in the Middle East, comprising paved and colonnaded streets, soaring hilltop temples, handsome theatres, spacious public squares and plazas, baths, fountains and city walls pierced by monumental towers and gates.

In the 1990s, the Jordanian Department of Antiquities' Jarash International Project brought together archaeologists and architects from eight countries (the US, France, Poland, Spain, Italy, Australia, the UK and Jordan) to excavate new areas while conserving and restoring monuments. Their ongoing work has clarified nagging ambiguities about the earliest (Hellenistic) and latest (early Islamic) phases of the city's life. It has confirmed that Jarash survived virtually without interruption for over 1,000 years – spanning the Hellenistic, Roman, Byzantine and early Islamic (Omayyad and Abbasid) periods, from the 2nd century BC to the 9th century AD.

Beneath its external Graeco-Roman veneer, Jarash is at heart a unique entity: a subtle and fascinating blend of the Orient and the Occident. Its architecture, religion, languages, and even the names of its citizens in antiquity

reflected a process by which two powerful cultures initially clashed but ultimately meshed and coexisted – the Graeco-Roman world of the Mediterranean basin, and the ancient traditions of the Arab Orient.

ANTIOCH ON CHRYSORHOAS

The first Classical settlement was a Hellenistic one founded in the 2nd century BC, which was called Antioch on Chrysorhoas (or Antioch on the "Golden River", the Hellenistic name of the perennial stream which still runs through the city). Little of the Hellenistic city has been excavated, as most of it was removed when the Romans rebuilt it in the 1st and 2nd centuries AD.

The Romans who arrived in 63 BC quickly adapted the former Nabataean name Garshu into Gerasa. At the end of the 19th century, the Arab and Circassian inhabitants of the then small rural settlement, in turn transformed Roman Gerasa into Arabic Jarash.

In ancient times, the roads linking Jarash with Philadelphia to the south,

Bosra and Damascus to the north, and Pella to the west, would have been well travelled by local traders, international caravans and Roman legionary troops. When the Emperor Trajan occupied the Nabataean kingdom in south Jordan, north Arabia and Sinai in AD 106, the area underwent another major reorganisation. Half the Decapolis cities found themselves within the Roman province of Syria, while others, including Jarash, fell under the jurisdiction of the new province of Arabia.

But this reorganisation had little impact on the fortunes of these towns, which continued to develop. On the heels of peace came local investments in agriculture, industry and services, which in turn boosted both regional and international trade.

As Jarash flourished for the next 200 years thanks to the income from exports and taxes from trade, it expanded towards its meandering city walls, and filled many of its urban spaces with public structures that still stand.

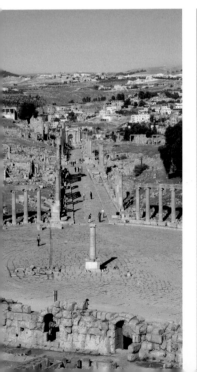

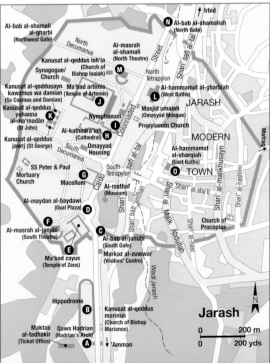

Oval Plaza, Jarash.

WALKING TOUR OF JARASH

Today, you can sense Gerasa's prosperity even before you arrive at the South Gate (Al-bab al-janubi): the first monument you reach on the road from Amman is the impressive triple-gated **Hadrian's Arch**  (Qaws Hadrian) standing alone some 450 metres/yds south of the city walls. It was built to commemorate the Emperor Hadrian's visit to Gerasa in AD 129, when the city fathers planned to extend the city walls to link up with the arch, which would then form the town's main entrance from the south. However, the project was never completed, and the arch remains standing alone.

After buying tickets at the Ticket Office (Maktab al-tadhakir; daily 8am–6pm, last entry 5pm; charge; tel: 02-635 4653) beneath Hadrian's Arch, visitors pass through the monumental archway to the **Hippodrome** just beyond. The focus of much recent excavation and restoration, it is now home to chariot racing again in the form of RACE's new spectacles (see box). Shows take place five days a week

(with sufficient numbers of visitors) all year round. Beyond the hippodrome you can still see the remains of a small Byzantine funerary church.

Visitors then enter the city proper just as the Roman-period inhabitants did – through the monumental, delicately carved **South Gate** (Al-bab al-janubi), now adjacent to the modern Visitors' Centre (Markaz al-zuwwar) and restaurant. The gate has been reconstructed by a French-Jordanian team. Immediately inside it is a marketplace with a 3rd-century AD olive press visible in a room now below ground level.

From the South Gate, walk up into the spacious **Oval Plaza** (Al-maydan al-baydawi), a skewed oval-shaped space measuring 90 by 80 metres (295 by 262ft) in size, with a fine colonnade. These columns were largely remodelled in the 2nd century, with Corinthian capitals and columns replacing the Ionic ones.

The Oval Plaza's non-symmetrical shape is unusual for classical cities, but is explained by its distinct role

Chariot racing at the Hippodrome.

served to reconcile the two different axes of the Cardo (Shari' kardu, or main street) and the Zeus Temple, which were aligned neither on a straight line nor at 90-degree angles. The plaza allowed the east–west axis of the Zeus Temple to fit into the north–south axis of the Cardo and the rest of the city. Visitors who walk into the plaza from the south find themselves naturally turning towards the north, to the start of the Cardo.

High to the west, overlooking the plaza, is the 1st-century AD **Temple of Zeus** Ⓔ (Ma'bad zayus). The temple combines a Classical appearance with the Oriental tradition of siting cultic installations on hilltops (like the biblical-era "high places") and surrounding them with a *temenos* (an enclosed holy precinct). Recent excavations on the terrace in front of the temple have uncovered some pre-Roman, Hellenistic cultic structures, including an open-air altar.

Immediately west of the temple is the **South Theatre** Ⓕ (Al-masrah al-janbi), ancient Gerasa's main gathering place for stage entertainment; completed in the early 2nd century AD, it could accommodate 3,000 spectators. Inscriptions in Greek give the names of some of the wealthy Gerasenes who donated money to help pay for its construction. The Greek numbers still visible would have reserved the seats for their wealthy patrons. Today, with much of its stage area restored, and its acoustics as sharp as ever, the South Theatre is back in business and hosts the main events at the annual Jarash Festival of Culture and Arts (see page 178). There is a fine view from the rim of the theatre overlooking the Oval Plaza and much of the city.

ALONG THE CARDO

The Oval Plaza leads visitors into the 12-metre (40ft)-wide and 800-metre (2,600ft)-long **Cardo** (Shari' kardu, or main street), the architectural spine and focal point of ancient Gerasa. In the 2nd century, the original Cardo was widened into its present Corinthian configuration (except at its northern end). The city's most important

South Theatre, Jarash.

structures were arranged around the Cardo, including markets, temples, fountains and other public buildings.

As you walk up the street, you pass a series of important monuments, most of which are announced by large, thicker columns that stand out against the street colonnade. Four such taller columns mark the **Macellum** G on the left, the old food market. A short way beyond, where the Cardo connects with the first of the city's two main cross-streets, the **South Decumanus** (Shari' janub dikmanis), is a junction known as the **South Tetrapylon**. A richly carved entrance midway along the Cardo heralds a Roman temple that was transformed into a church in the Byzantine period; it is now known as the **Cathedral** H (Al-kathedra'iah). Next to it is the **Nymphaeum** I (public fountain), on which you can see tiny fragments of the original coloured paint from the Roman/Byzantine period still clinging to one upper-level niche.

A little further north is the stately **propylaeum** (entrance) and processional way leading up to the **Temple of**

Flamenco performance at the Jarash Festival.

Artemis J (Ma'bad artimis; daughter of Zeus, sister of Apollo, and patron goddess of the city). Her hilltop temple with soaring bronze-coloured columns is nestled in a spacious, colonnaded *temenos* measuring 162 by 121 metres (531 by 396ft); it was approached via a processional way that started across the river in the area of the modern city.

When the Byzantine Empire and Christianity penetrated the region in the 4th century, some of Gerasa's pagan Roman temples were transformed into Christian churches. Many new churches were built from cut stones and columns taken from Roman-era buildings that had collapsed from the frequent earthquakes which plagued the region in antiquity. With the discovery of more churches in recent years, we know of close to 20 churches in Byzantine Gerasa, some of them still sport their mosaic floors. The **complex of three churches** K dedicated to **St George, St John** and **saints Cosmas** and **Damian**, west of the Temple of Artemis, has the best-preserved mosaics from the 6th

⊙ JARASH FESTIVAL

For two or three weeks every July, the ruins of Jarash come alive with a vibrant arts festival. Performances span countries and cultures and range from an Italian-produced *Rigoletto* or Spanish flamenco on the steps of the Artemis Temple, to Lebanese traditional songs and Chinese acrobats in the South Theatre.

Inaugurated in 1981 by Queen Noor, the event is much anticipated. As the events' organiser put it: "The festival offers an opportunity for Westerners to see Arabic folklore, hear Oriental music and experience Middle Eastern culture. It also provides Jordanians with the chance to see art and cultural events of the West." During the festival, handicrafts are sold along the Cardo (Shari' kardu), providing the perfect showcase for the Bedouin rugs, blown glass, embroidered gowns and other crafts.

century; their subject matter includes representations of various animals as well as the churches' benefactors and bishops. Some of the church mosaics are also on display in the little museum diagonally opposite the Macellum.

The massive **West Baths** (Al-hammamat al-gharbiah) were never excavated and remain in their state of collapse following a spate of successive earthquakes more than 1,000 years ago. Just to the west of the **North Tetrapylon** intersection with the North Decumanus (Shari' shamal dikmanis) is the **North Theatre** (Al-masrah al-shamali), which served as a performance stage as well as the city council chamber; you can still see the names of the local tribes that were represented in the city council engraved on the seats in Greek.

Beyond the North Tetrapylon is the **North Colonnaded Street**, a stretch of the original Cardo which was never widened or resculpted in the Corinthian order; it retains the more human-scale dimensions of Jarash during the 1st century AD, and leads to the large but ungainly **North Gate** (Al-bab al-shamaliah), whose strange shape was, like the Oval Plaza, a means of reconciling the different axes of the Cardo and the external road entering Jarash from Pella.

BEYOND THE CARDO

From the Cardo, the Roman town expanded towards the city walls, forming different quarters for housing, commerce and cultic activities. At the height of its prosperity in the 2nd and 3rd centuries, Jarash and its immediate suburbs may have accommodated some 20,000 people. They were served by a splendid array of public facilities, including temples, theatres, markets, baths, plazas, fountains and a hippodrome. The massive **East Baths** (Al-hammamat al-sharqiah), in the centre of the modern town, indicate the extent of the city's spread, as well as the monumental size of some of its public facilities.

Many of the Roman structures were rebuilt or modified in the Byzantine era, when Gerasa ceased to be important for international trade. The city fortunes gradually dwindled,

Souvenir stalls at Jarash.

and successive attacks by Persian and Muslim forces in the early 7th century AD made Jarash's historical course change once again.

After 636, the city fell to the control of Islamic forces emerging from Arabia. When the Islamic world's capital shifted from Omayyad Damascus to Abbasid Baghdad in AD 750, Gerasa lost its strategic location on the road between Damascus and Islam's heartland in Arabia. As a result, its fortunes faded slowly thereafter, and the town could support little more than small squatter occupations after the 9th century.

AROUND JARASH

Well worth a visit or picnic in the cool conifer glades is **Dibeen Forest Reserve** (daily summer 8am–5.30pm; winter 8am–3pm; charge), lying around 15km (9 miles) southwest of Jarash (see page 104). Short trails (some marked) wind through the fragrant Aleppo pine and oak forest. You really need your own transport to get around. There is currently no visitors' centre

here or any accommodation or facilities, though there's a controversial Dubai-funded plan under construction to build a large number of luxury chalets over the next 10 years.

'AJLUN

One of the best-preserved examples of medieval Islamic military architecture in the Middle East is **'Ajlun Castle ③** (Qala'at al-Rabad; Sun–Thur 8am–6pm; charge; tel: 02-642 0956). It was built between 1184 and 1188 by Izz ed-Din Ousama, one of the most capable generals and governors of the Islamic leader Salah' ad Din (Saladin), who defeated the Crusaders, evicting them from Jordan in 1189. The castle became the base from which Islamic forces defended this region against Crusader expansion (see page 43). Enlarged in 1214, two gates, seven stout towers and a 15-metre (50ft) moat formed its defences. In 1260, the Mongols managed to destroy much of the castle, but its strategic and naturally defensive position was recognised by the Mamlukes, who quickly rebuilt

Medieval 'Ajlun Castle.

. The Ottomans occupied it during the 7th century but it was damaged again, this time by earthquakes in the 19th and 20th centuries.

Built on top of Mt 'Auf at 1,250 metres (4101ft), the views from the top over the Jordan Valley are spectacular, especially from the keep. Though there's not much to see inside the castle bar piles of cannon balls and a small but interesting museum, the maze of galleries, chambers, vaults, towers and staircases are atmospheric, evocative, and in summer, cool. Buy tickets from the tourism office in the car park below the castle.

AJLUN FOREST RESERVE

Lying 9km (5.5 miles) from 'Ajlun amid the oak forests of the 'Ajlun highlands is the beautiful, RSCN-run 'Ajlun Forest Reserve (daily 8am–6pm; charge; tel: 02-647 5673). Though covering an area of just 13 sq km (5 sq miles), it contains more than its fair share of flora and fauna (see page 104), as well as seven, all-ability hiking trails that weave through the forests (see page

111). The reserve also supports local community craft ventures which you can visit as part of the trails or by car. A night in one of the tented bungalows or cabins makes a fabulous escape from the commotion and pollution of the cities or the heat of the lowlands.

IRBID

A trading centre to its farming hinterland for thousands of years, **Irbid** ❹ is now Jordan's second largest city, with a population of nearly 2 million. Historically, it relied on a combination of agriculture and trading, which are still its main economic activities, along with a newer source of revenue: students. Since 1977, Irbid has been home to the famous Yarmouk University (Jam'at al-yarmuk), considered one of the best centres of higher education in the Middle East. Apart from some fine late 19th-century houses and public buildings in the city centre and a number of museums, Irbid also has a buzzing vibe generated by its 35,000 students.

Worth a visit are the cluster of museums (Sun–Thur 10am–3pm;

Agricultural worker during the olive harvest.

View from 'Ajlun Castle.

free; tel: 0777 646911) in the grounds of the university: the newly refurbished **Museum of Jordanian Heritage Numismatic Halls** (Mathaf al-turath al-'urduni) has interesting exhibits on the history of money; the **Heritage Museum** (Mathaf Jarash lil-athar) displays a beautiful collection of Bedouin jewellery; and the very well-presented **Museum of Archaeology & Anthropology** (Mathaf al-athar wa al-anthrubulujya) has excellent dioramas and information panels tracing the history of mankind in Jordan. Exhibits range from Stone Age graves and 500-year-old giant storage jars to fine Roman jewellery and mosaics, and a reconstructed Bedouin tent. There's also a life-size model of a traditional Arab smithy and pharmacy.

In the town centre, the **Bayt As Saraya Museum** (Bayt Mathaf al-saraya, on Shari' al-baladiyah; Sun–Thur 8am–6pm, Sat 10am-4pm; free; tel: 02-724 5613) exhibits well-presented artefacts around the courtyard of a lovely Ottoman villa, ranging from Mamluke pottery to Graeco-Roman

Students on Yarmouk University campus, Irbid.

sculpture and Islamic inscriptions It is the mosaic collection that reall stands out: sophisticated, well-pre served, colourful and brimming wit life and charm, they are unmissable Nearby, the Ottoman-era **Bayt 'arra** (off Shāri'al-hashimi; Sun–Thur 8am– 3pm; free; tel: 02-724 0874) is the for mer residence of the famous Jordania nationalist, poet and political activist Mustafa Wahbi Al Tal (better known a "Arar", 1897–1949). The house contain manuscripts, personal belongings an photos of Arar.

'ABILAH

The scattered remains of **'Abilah ❺** ar not frequently visited by foreign tour ists today, but the site is well wort exploring for those who have the time The large site, undiscovered unti 1982, is located amidst verdant field of barley, olive trees and cucumber a the modern 'ayn Quwaylbah spring, 20-minute drive north of Irbid. Whil several impressive ancient structure have been excavated (and an America team of archaeologists currently visit

every summer), including churches, aqueducts, tombs, gates and public buildings, 'Abilah is especially fascinating because so much of it remains unexcavated. Surface remains hint tantalisingly at what lies below, and you get a real sense of exploration and discovery clambering among the enigmatic ruins.

The two hills that make up the site were occupied almost continuously from the Neolithic to the early Islamic period, roughly from 7000 BC–AD 800. The site flourished for such a long period because of its abundant water and agricultural resources, as well as its strategic location alongside ancient trade routes.

Rising on one hilltop to the south of the site are the limestone and basalt columns, capitals and other ruins (including remains of mosaics with blue St Andrew's crosses and an altar) of a 7th- to 8th-century basilica. The large semicircular depression in the hillside is where the theatre once stood, while the path to the bridge over the stream hints at the route of the

Roman road – look out for the beautiful basalt paving stones and white marble columns. Elsewhere, the massive column drums and Corinthian capitals scattered incongruously in agricultural fields conjure up images of long-buried temples, baths or marketplaces that still await discovery.

The site also includes an extensive cemetery with some of Jordan's finest Roman and Byzantine-era painted tombs. Unfortunately, thieves in the 1980s and 1990s removed much of the contents but they are still interesting to see. You can usually locate the guardian of the site who, for a small tip, will fetch the key, unlock the small gates protecting the most interesting tombs and shine a torch on the evocative frescoes and old niche tombs within. To be sure, call ahead: Dhefaleh Obidat (0772 280230) speaks Arabic only, so enlist help if necessary.

UMM QAYS

The most dramatically situated Roman-era town in Jordan is **Umm qays** ❻ (Roman Gadara), about two

Herding goats near Umm qays.

Harvesting olives near Umm qays.

hours by car from Amman. Sitting on a long, high promontory, the views from here are breathtaking. As the guides like to point out, it overlooks four countries: Jordan (the North Jordan Valley), Syria (the Syrian Golan Heights), Israel and the Palestinian Territories (Lake Tiberias or Sea of Galilee) to the northwest.

The city was established in the Hellenistic period and grew to form part of the famous Decapolis, when it was known as Gadara (see box, page 186). It continued to flourish as a strategic trading town for nearly 1,000 years, well into the early and medieval Islamic eras. Its name in Arabic is thought to be related to the word *maqass*, which means junction in Arabic; the city stood at an important junction on land trade routes linking the vital north–south roads with the east–west passage to the Mediterranean Sea.

Umm qays is also unique in another way: it consists of two quite distinct historical components – the ancient town and ruins, and the well-preserved late 19th-/early 20th-century Ottoman town clustered on the summit and largely built from stones reused from the classical town below.

WALKING TOUR OF UMM QAYS

From the **Ticket Office** (Maktab al-tadhakir; daily, summer 8am–6pm; winter 8am–4pm; charge), a paved Roman road leads to the ruins. Rising up on the right is the restored but impressive **West Theatre**, made of black basalt, which once seated 3,000 people. Just beyond lie the basalt columns and remains of the 6th-century **basilica** (ruined by earthquakes in the 8th century), and adjacent **courtyard**, which is strewn with beautifully carved black sarcophagi. The colonnaded main street and a side street are clearly lined with the remains of **shops**.

Turn west (left) along the east–west running Decumanus Maximus (colonnaded street). In Roman times, it ran from Gadara all the way to Pella, Avela and other important towns. Along it can be found the remains of the 4th-century **baths**, various **mausoleums**, a **city gate** and the faint outline of what

Umm qays.

was once a very large **hippodrome.** If you walk down it for about 350 metres/ yds, keeping an eye out for the city gate (a circular tower) to the left, you'll see a black basalt tomb just beyond the gate (which can be seen more clearly from the foot of the nearby flight of stairs). It is here that Jesus is said to have performed one of his miracles (see page 186).

Turning right off the Decumanus Maximus leads to the ruined **Temple of Zeus** (Ma'bad zayus), **tombs** of various dates, and the remains of the **North Theatre** (Al-masrah al-shamali), whose stone was much plundered by the Ottomans in the construction of their village. Gadara was renowned during the classical era as an inspired city of the arts, famous for producing notable playwrights, poets, satirists, orators and philosophers.

The **Ottoman village** is located on the Acropolis and is notable for its large houses arranged around central courtyards. Several houses have been restored and two, in particular, are being used again: the **museum** (same hours and entry price as Ticket Office) in Bayt al-rusan, and the German archaeological dighouse in Bayt Malkawi. The museum contains an original Ottoman well that's still in use and some finely carved Roman-era sculpture, including the large, headless, marble Tyche or "Seated Goddess of Gaddara", which once stood in the West Theatre, as well as a collection of old Roman, Byzantine and Islamic coins, Byzantine sarcophagi, 4th-century mosaics and marble statuettes.

UM AL-JIMAL

The first glimpse of the black city of **Um al-jimal ❼** forms one of the most startling and memorable impressions of Jordan. Rising coal-black against the horizon, from afar it looks like the skyline of a modern metropolis. Up close, abandoned, ruined and silent, it has the ominous and sinister air of an ill-fated ghost town. The city is particularly eerie when visited in the early morning haze of winter.

Lying around 10km (6 miles) south of the Syrian border, Um al-jimal is

Church Terrace at Umm qays.

situated at the edge of the eastern Basalt Desert plain, close to the junction of several ancient trade routes linking central Jordan with Syria and Iraq. Remains of the Roman road can still be seen today by taking a 10-minute drive to the west to the village of Ba'ij.

The city was inhabited for some 700 years, from the 1st to the 8th century, in three different stages: as a rural village in the 2nd and 3rd centuries (founded possibly by the Nabataeans), as a fortified Roman town in the 4th and 5th centuries, and as a prosperous farming and trading city from the 5th to the 8th century.

The key to Um al-jimal's success was its inhabitants' ability to store winter rainwater in a series of covered and open reservoirs, which supplied water for human and animal consumption as well as irrigating summer crops. As a stable and organised settlement with a reliable source of water and food, Um al-jimal developed into a major caravan station. After surviving a number of events, including the Persian invasion, plagues and minor earthquakes, the city was destroyed by a major earthquake in AD 747.

Um al-jimal's ancient lineage has still not been decided: Thantia and Surattha have both been proposed as possible candidates. A walk through the ruins reveals a wide range of structures typical of a modest provincial town that lacked a formal urban plan – unlike the monumental splendour and imperial propaganda of more important towns such as Jarash, Gadara and Philadelphia. Nonetheless, Um al-jimal is unique in providing insight into provincial life at this time, and largely avoided the pillaging and vandalisation that more famous sites suffered until 2014, when tomb raiders extensively damaged the excavation sites searching for jewellery, gold and ceramics.

Among the most interesting structures are the tall **barracks** with their little **chapel**, the dozen or so **churches**, several large enough in size to have been **Cathedrals**, the numerous open and roofed **water cisterns** served by conveyor channels, the dozens of **domestic houses,** including one dubbed the **Sheikh's House** for its large size, elaborate stairways and stables, and the cluster of **shops** (often around a common courtyard). Along the east side of town is the outline of a **Roman fort**, and the remains of several **town gates**.

Many of the structures at Um al-jimal still stand two storeys high, thanks to the excellent engineering used in antiquity. Look out for examples of the very common "corbelling" technique, in which long flat slabs of basalt stone were laid over intersecting stones to form the roof of a typically long and narrow room or building. Arches were used to make the buildings larger, and well-designed windows and doors (many still in place) helped to relieve structural pressure from the weight of the building material.

⦿ GADARENE SWINE – FACT OR FABLE?

Umm qays – ancient Gadara – has another claim to fame: it was the reputed site of one of Jesus' most famous miracles: the miracle of the Gadarene swine. According to the bible, it was here that Jesus cast the demons from two madmen into a herd of pigs, which then rushed down the hillside to be drowned in Lake Tiberias (Matthew 8:28–34). Versions in Luke (8:26–39) and Mark (5:1–20), talk of only one possessed man, who lived among the tombs chained and guarded.

In the 1980s, a German archaeological team excavated a 4th-century Byzantine church thought to be built over a Roman tomb where Jesus is supposed to have performed this miracle. Interestingly, excavations of the crypt in 1988 discovered a skeleton bound in chains about the legs. Even more enigmatically, the remains of the church lie squarely on top of the mausoleum, with a hole cut in the centre of the floor that gave a clear view into the tomb.

Archaeologists now postulate that the church, with its "peep hole", may have been built to honour the spot which Christian lore identified as the place where Jesus performed the miracle, and that the opening into the crypt from the church floor is testament to the church's significance as an early pilgrimage site.

Ruins of a Byzantine church, Um al-jimal.

Growing lettuce in a polytunnel in the Jordan Valley.

THE JORDAN VALLEY

The fertile land of the Jordan Valley has attracted settlers since biblical times; evidence of its remarkable past civilisations is the principal draw for today's travellers.

The Jordan Valley is the kingdom's Garden of Eden. It elicits a feeling of abundance mixed with a sense of history and spirituality, enveloped in a landscape that is striking for both its physical beauty and its many biblical associations. Archaeological evidence of early civilisation abounds in the valley, and although it is obvious that man settled here out of economic necessity – the land is some of the most fertile in the region – it is equally obvious, especially at dusk or after a soak in one of many steamy, hot springs, that life must have seemed good here too.

The valley today still thrives. It constitutes an integral part of Jordan's economy, as attested by the swathes of banana plantations, citrus orchards and vegetable farms. The Dead Sea's invigorating minerals attract large crowds of weekenders, especially in the spring and autumn. At the southern limits of the sea, travellers along the highway might notice salt "mushrooms" cropping up from the water. These odd protrusions, appearing like misplaced snow sculptures, mark the potash extraction fields, the source of a multi-million dinar industry.

Most importantly, the valley, river and sea form a natural border with Israel and the West Bank. The valley plains bear witness to Jordan's

turbulent recent history, and remnants of the Arab-Israeli conflict, although slowly disappearing, can still be found. Houses that were casualties of the successive wars can be seen not far from the river, whose ever-dwindling waters are a reminder that this vital resource must be shared equitably and responsibly between three countries – a bone of contention that continues to this day.

THE JORDAN RIFT VALLEY

The Jordan Dead Sea region forms part of the Great Rift Valley (see box).

Map on page 172

Main Attractions
Pella
Ancient Tels
Bithani-beyond-the-Jordan
Dead Sea

Farm workers on the Lisan Peninsula near the Dead Sea.

Due to its low altitude, the valley is a natural hothouse characterised by mild winters, hot summers, rich agricultural lands and important mineral resources. Since the mid-1970s, it has benefited from a governmental programme of integrated rural development based on exploiting the area's agricultural and mineral resources while providing a range of social services for its growing population.

It wasn't always so settled. In the early 20th century, the valley was an inhospitable and dangerous place, known more for its malaria and occasional banditry than its economic potential. In the early 1960s, the valley's permanent farming population of some 40,000 people was almost entirely uprooted during the politically turbulent and violent period of 1967–72 following the Arab-Israeli conflict. In 1973, the integrated development effort was launched by the Jordan Valley Authority to encourage small, family-based farming units to cultivate the land. However, a dire water shortage and world trade requirements continue to demand a radical shift in the way the valley is utilised.

HISTORY OF THE VALLEY

The valley's water, land and warm climate have encouraged people to live, hunt and farm here since the earliest days of human history. There are over 200 known archaeological sites in the Jordan Rift Valley, and hundreds of others await discovery. The oldest evidence for human activity, stone tools discovered in the Wadi Himmah region in the northern valley, date back almost 1 million years – to a time when the region probably looked very similar to today's savannah grasslands in East Africa.

Evidence of some of the world's earliest campsites and semi-permanent villages comes from excavations near Pella, dating from the Natufian and Kebaran periods (10,000–18,000 years ago). The advent of year-round farming and live-stocking settlements in the Neolithic period (8000–4500 BC) is also attested at several sites, though the most famous Neolithic village in the valley is across the river in Jericho. Large

Stunning view over the Jordan Valley.

⊙ JORDAN'S RIFT VALLEY

Jordan's Dead Sea region forms part of one of the world's greatest geological phenomenon: the Great Rift Valley. Running from Turkey all the way to East Africa, it was formed by geological upheavals millions of years ago. The Jordan valley in its present form started to take shape between 100,000 and 20,000 years ago, as a result of the contraction of a saltwater sea that originally covered the entire 360km (223-mile) stretch from the Red Sea to Lake Tiberias (the Sea of Galilee). It initially formed an inland lake – Lake Lisan – before shrinking again to leave behind Lake Tiberias and the Dead Sea. These two inland water bodies are surrounded on all sides by dry plains interspersed with side valleys (wadis) flowing from the eastern and western highlands.

ites such as Pella show an almost unin-
errupted sequence of human occupa-
ion going back at least 4,000 years, from
he Bronze Age to the present.

ELLA

Lying in the foothills of the northern valley just above the modern town of Al-
mashari, **Pella** ❽ (dawn to sunset; free)
may be Jordan's richest site in terms of
its historical sweep and architectural
remains. It boasts a beautiful natural
setting of rolling green plains (gold in
summer as the barley ripens), lush plan-
ations and forested hills, watered by the
perennial Wadi al-jirm stream. Below,
lies the plain of the Jordan Valley, and on
a clear day, you see all the way to northern Palestine and Israel and discern the
hills of Haifa on the Mediterranean coast.

Though Pella's gate should be
manned, it's not currently, so come
early in the morning to escape the
heat of the day. A team of Australian
archaeologists visiting for one or two
months every two years are excavating
the Canaanite temple and Ommayad
ruins. The Pella Museum above the

Resthouse remains sadly empty; the
refurbishment project which began in
2007 has ground to a halt.

The name Pella dates from the Hellenistic period, when soldiers of Alexander the Great named their new imperial
settlements after the Macedonian birth-
place of their leader. The site is known in
Arabic as Tabaqit fahil (the name of the
nearby village). "Fahil" retains a linguis-
tic link with the ancient names of Pella
and Pihilum. Archaeological excavations
have revealed a series of both major
walled towns and modest settlements
at Pella for most of the past 6,000 years.

The site's impressive historical significance and continuity is owed to its rich
natural resources and strategic location
at the intersection of major north–south
and east–west trade routes.

On the central main mound of the
site, where the archaeological dighouse is located, the earliest visible **mudbrick house** and **fortification
walls** (in the deep trenches on the
south side) date from Bronze and Iron
Age walled towns spanning the period
2000–600 BC.

Pella ruins.

On the south side of the main mound is the recently unearthed Canaanite temple, believed to date to around 1250 BC and dedicated to the god of the Canaanites, Baal.

The Roman and Byzantine periods are represented by the ruins of a Roman gate near the entrance at the base of the main mound, the small **theatre** by the stream, which dates to the 1st century AD and once held up to 500 people, and the 5th-century colonnaded **civic complex** and **church** above it (reached over a monumental **staircase**).

To the east of the civic complex lie the traces of a Roman **nymphaeum**. Lying to the southeast of the civic complex on an adjacent hill is the Byzantine **east church**, which dates to the 5th century. Nearby, Tel Al-husun contains **Byzantine tombs** carved into its steep hillside, and above, the remains of a **Roman temple** and **Roman-Byzantine fort**.

Near the main site, sadly closed to visitors behind a large fence, are the impressive remains of the Byzantine **west church**, thought to date to the 5th to 6th centuries and numbering among the largest Byzantine churches in Jordan and the Levant.

The remains of **domestic houses**, **shops** and **storehouses** of the early Islamic (Omayyad) period are well preserved on the central mound; later Islamic structures can be seen at the 9th- to 10th-century Abbasid domestic area excavated in **Wadi al-khandaq** (in the valley north of the main mound) and in the restored 13th- to 14th-century **Mamluke-period mosque** on the main mound.

A 90-minute drive from Amman, Pella can be comfortably combined in a day trip with the Dead Sea, 'Ajlun, Jarash or Umm qays.

AROUND PELLA

There are various sites of interest around Pella that can be easily visited in a morning or afternoon with your own transport. The manager of the Pella Countryside Hotel can provide directions or act as a guide.

Less than 2km (1.2 miles) from the Resthouse lies a picturesque **natural rock arch** that spans rock over the

Main archaeological site at Bithani-beyond-the-Jordan.

Wadi Himmah. It's a popular place locally for a picnic.

Around 5km (3 miles) southeast of Pella is the extraordinary site of **Kufr abil,** which boasts dozens of Paleolithic dolmens spread over a hillside (locals claim there are over 100). Around 15km (9 miles) east of Pella lies **Bayt 'aydis,** the site of the so-called Jesus Cave (known locally as Kahf al-Messih), where, according to local tradition, Jesus stayed on his way to meet John the Baptist before his baptism. Apart from a stunning setting amid olive groves and barley fields where cicadas and turtle doves call, there are breathtaking views to Lake Tiberius, Umm qays, the (often snow-capped) Hebron Heights and northern Syria, as well as the cave itself, some old Roman rock-cut tombs thought to date to AD 21, an old Roman olive press with run-off channels carved into the rock, and an ancient olive tree. Nearby lie the ruins of a church with the remains of mosaics (though most have been extracted).

ANCIENT TELS

The entire Rift Valley is dotted with ancient tels (artificial mounds formed by the cumulative debris from ancient settlements built of stone and mud-brick). Three of the most striking can be visited in the centre of the valley (west of the main road), and some of their excavated walls can be seen (though the sites have not been fully excavated and there is little if any information for the lay visitor) and few remains bar bare traces of ruins and shards – though the views are often spectacular.

The long double mound of **Tel al-saydiyah ⑨** was an important regional walled town for most of the Bronze and Iron Ages (3300–600 BC), and was also the site of a large caravanserai in the early Islamic period. It has been inconclusively associated with the biblical sites of Zaphon and Zarthan.

The smaller **Tel mazar ⑩** to its south (and visible from the summit of Saydiyah) was a substantial settlement in the Iron and Persian periods, from the 11th to the 4th century BC.

The most dramatic of the three mounds is the 30 metre (100ft)-high **Tel dayr 'alla** ⓫, towering over the main road at Dayr 'alla village. Excavations have revealed almost continuous human habitation from 1600–400 BC, when it served variously as township, cultic centre, metal workshop, grain store, farm and a seasonal migration site. Its summit lies 200 metres (656ft) below sea level and some archaeologists believe it is the biblical site of Succoth.

About 7km (4.25 miles) east of Tel dayr 'alla are the twin hills called **Tulul al-dhahab** ⓬ ("the little hills of gold"). Excavated architectural remains and pottery shards indicate that both hills were fortified settlements in the Early Iron Age and Late Hellenistic/Early Roman periods. Remains of slag and furnaces confirm that iron smelting took place here. Ore came from the nearby Mugharat Wardah mines, 4km (2.5 miles) to the north. Scholars in the 19th century identified these twin hills with the biblical sites of Penuel, where, according to the Genesis story, Jacob wrestled all night with an angel; and

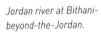

Jordan river at Bithani-beyond-the-Jordan.

Mahanaim, where David was told of the death of his son Absalom, though neither of these site identifications has yet been verified by archaeological evidence.

BITHANI: THE BAPTISM SITE

A few kilometres north of the Dead Sea lies **Bithani-beyond-the-Jordan** ⓭, otherwise known as the Baptism of Jesus (or, in Arabic, Al-maghtas, or the Place of Dipping).

For many years, this site lay in a closed military zone on the banks of the River Jordan. Following the 1994 peace treaty between Jordan and Israel, archaeologists returned to the area, and were able to uncover well over 20 ancient sites in the short, 2km (1.2-mile) stretch of the Wadi al-kharrar, a small sided valley. These included several Byzantine churches, baptismal pools from the Byzantine and Roman periods, caves that had been inhabited by hermits and monks, and ancient hostels able to house dozens of pilgrims.

A host of accounts written by medieval pilgrims and travellers – the

details of which often exactly matched the physical remains, as well as very accurate descriptions of the topographical make-up of the Wadi Kharrar area – very rapidly convinced both Jordanian and international opinion that this area, on the east bank of the river, was indeed where **John the Baptist** (revered by both Christianity and Islam) had been active, and where he may indeed have baptised Jesus Christ.

Whatever your religious convictions – and the site is sacred to Jews, Christians and Muslims alike – there's no question of its historical significance. It was here evidently that John the Baptist preached, that Jesus met him and at least four other apostles, and above all, that Jesus was baptised. As a result, a new religion was born and a new Testament begun. For Christians, this is where it all began.

The site (www.baptismsite.com), which is best visited in the early morning before the heat becomes unbearable, is signposted off the main Amman–Dead Sea highway. Enter the main gates, and after a short drive on an access road, you reach a gated compound housing the visitor centre (daily, Apr–Oct 8am–6pm; Nov–Mar 8am–4pm, last entry one hour before closing; charge; tel: 05-359 0360) with toilets and some small shops selling refreshments.

Under new regulations, all vehicles must be left in the car park. A site shuttle bus (which departs every 30 minutes) takes visitors for a tour around the sites accompanied by an English-speaking guide included with the admission ticket. "Easy Guides" (audio guides) are available in English, French, Spanish, Italian, German and Russian. Brief stops are made at designated parking stops at the major sites (although some travellers complain they are too brief).

In 2015, the site was inscribed by Unesco on its World Heritage list. Churches from around the world are falling over themselves to buy (limited) plots of land at the latest must-have holy site; 12 new churches will overlook the Jordan River. Future plans include chronological tours and lodging for pilgrims. In recent years the site has received many special visitors, including royalty, heads of state and religious leaders, such as Pope Francis in 2014.

ELIJAH'S HILL

"Parking 1" gives access to a set of remains at the head of the Wadi Kharrar. The main focus of attention is the low, rounded hill of **Tel Mar Ilias**, or Elijah's Hill. According to tradition, this was the spot from where the Old Testament prophet Elijah was taken up to heaven in a chariot driven by horses of fire.

In front of the hill is a single, freestanding arch, raised here in 1999 over the foundations of a rectangular 5th- to 6th-century Byzantine church. The arch is made from 63 stones, to commemorate the death, at the age of 63, of King Husayn. In March 2000, the church was renamed the **Church of John Paul II**, after the late pontiff stood on this spot to bless Jerusalem (to the west) and Jabal

Church of St John the Baptist interior, Bithani-beyond-the-Jordan.

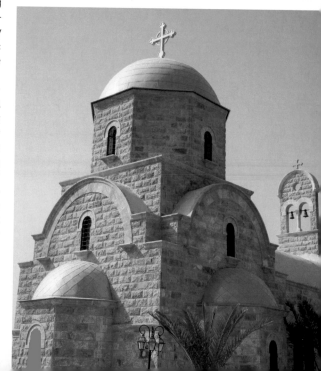

Floating in the Dead Sea.

nibu (Mount Nebo), to the east. The ruins of the rectangular prayer hall close by are believed to date from the 3rd century AD, making this one of the earliest Christian places of worship anywhere.

Nearby is a network of water channels and cisterns, while the hill of Tel Mar Elias – a few metres away – also features several Roman baptismal pools, still with their original plaster and steps intact leading down for the purpose of group baptisms in antiquity.

On the west side of the hill is a small Byzantine church, while round on the northern side is a large, **late-Byzantine church** beneath a modern shelter. Its apse features a black meteorite – perhaps a commemoration of Elijah's fiery ascent to heaven – while its floor is covered with an intricate mosaic, with a long inscription in Greek dating the church to the early 6th century.

Part way along Wadi Kharrar, accessed from "Parking 2", is the impressive **Large Baptismal Pool**, designed to hold 300 people at a time.

On an outcrop above the pool stands the **Pilgrims' Station**, a hostel for

Inside the Church of St John the Baptist.

those who came to pray and be baptised. Surrounding the hostel are a series of hermits' caves.

FLOOD PLAIN

To the west, the *ghor*, or broad floor of the Jordan Valley, dips down to the *zor*, the deep channel of the flood plain of the river itself, set in a bleak moonscape of chalky marl cliffs and hummocks. From "Parking 3", set amidst this eerie landscape, paths penetrate what the Old Testament describes as the "jungle of the Jordan" – a dense, thorny thicket of tamarisk bushes. If you're visiting outside the summer season, water may well also be flowing all around, from the dozen or so springs which rise here.

In a clearing rise the remains of the Byzantine **Church of John the Baptist**, built by the Emperor Anastasius in the 6th century, with its apse and mosaic floor still discernible.

A path through the bushes leads on to the modern **Church of St John**, unmistakable for its gleaming gold roof, built by the Greek Orthodox Church (who owns this site) and inaugurated in 2005. Inside are colourful and well-executed murals of saints. Opposite it, steps lead down to a wooden platform built on the **River Jordan** itself – these days little more than a shallow, murky stream, but nonetheless dramatic for its historical and religious associations. The river remains an international frontier: in plain view opposite stands an alternative Israeli-run baptism site, built in what is now the West Bank. Soldiers keep a wary watch on both sides.

THE DEAD SEA

Part of the famous Great Rift Valley, Jordan's **Dead Sea** remains one of the country's top attractions, and lies less than an hour's drive from Amman. The area continues to draw visitors from around the world for its unique water qualities, climate and historical and spiritual significance.

About 15km (9 miles) to the south re the ruins of Al-numayrah, a candidate for Gomorrah. Interestingly, the tories of "brimstone and fire raining own" would be consistent with factual ccounts of earthquakes and eruptions aused by the movement of the Rift alley continental plates.

Excavations near Al-safi (long associated with Zuwwar) at Dayr ain abatah, he "Cave or Sanctuary of Lot" (see age 216), have unearthed a basilica hurch and small cave, possibly used y Lot and his daughters.

About 15km (9 miles) south of the Marriott Hotel are the columns, pools nd the harbour of ancient Callirhoë, he bathing complex built by Herod the Great for his palace at Machaerus.

Sitting amidst the dramatic mountains of the biblical kingdoms of Moab, Ammon and Edom to the east, and the olling hills of Jerusalem to the west, ts buoyant saline waters are warm and he shoreline is coated in a therapeutic mud, rich in minerals.

More and more hotels offer therapeutic treatments for skin disorders and other diseases. Recognising the potential of health and spa tourism, hotels with huge spa complexes attached continue to be built along the Dead Sea shoreline despite the world economic downturn. The Crowne Plaza Dead Sea Resort attracts visitors who can enjoy treatments in their luxury, Roman-style Sohum Spa.

Many travellers feel that a trip to one of these spas is a must-do when at the Red Sea, and famous visitors who have treated themselves to spa treatments in the past include King David, Queen Cleopatra and King Herod the Great. Those offering the most luxurious and pampered experience (over 70 treatments including massages, body scrubs or body wraps – or all three in one session – plus access usually to spa pools, Jacuzzis, steam rooms, saunas, private beaches and Dead Sea water-filled pools) include the **Anantara Spa** (daily 10am–10pm; www.spa.anantara.com/deadsea) at the Kempinski Hotel; the award-winning **Zara Spa** (daily 8.30am–8.30pm; www.zaraspa.com), one of the biggest spas in the region at

The Dead Sea.

Dead Sea mud is mineral-rich and has therapeutic uses.

the Mövenpick Resort & Spa; and the 20-year-old **Dead Sea Spa** (daily 8am–6pm; www.dssh.jo), the first hotel to offer spa treatments with a firm (and widely acclaimed) medical focus, particularly for skin diseases. Qualified medical staff (including a resident dermatologist) can prescribe treatments.

It is possible to stop and swim at any place along the coast, but bring fresh water if possible to remove the glutinous residue left on the skin. Most visitors pay to use the facilities at one of the beaches or resorts, or park near one of the in-flowing streams.

Many of the beaches, both private and public, also have pots of mud that you can help yourself to beside the sea. Many of the hotels also allow non-guests to use private beaches and facilities for the day, or you can head to the new, private beach at **O Village** (daily 9am–7pm; charge; tel: 05-349 2000), south of the main hotels, or the (private) **Amman Beach Tourism Resort** (daily, summer 9am–10pm, winter 8am–5pm; charge; tel: 05-356 0800) or the cheapest option, the

Amman Public Beach (daily, summer 9am–10pm, winter 8am–5pm; charge; tel: 05-389 6531) next door.

Salt deposits, sometimes in the form of bizarre shapes and formations, are visible along much of the coast south of the resort area.

A worthwhile excursion around 10km (6 miles) from the Dead Sea resorts is to wind up the vertiginous road to the **Dead Sea Panoramic Complex,** from where there are stunning views over the surrounding mountains, the Dead Sea and Israel. The **Dead Sea Museum** (Sat–Thur 9am–5.30pm, Fri 9am–4pm; charge) has interesting, informative and well-displayed exhibits on the geology, flora and fauna of the Dead Sea and its history. Next door is the excellent **Panorama Restaurant** (daily noon–midnight; until 10pm in winter; tel: 05-349 1133), newly managed by the Six Senses group and serving imaginative and well-prepared international and Lebanese-style dishes and wine, as well as snacks such as pizza, pasta, burgers and sandwiches.

Mosaic showing Jesus being baptized at the Bithani-beyond-the-Jordan site.

⊘ HOLY TEXTS

Historically, the Dead Sea has played a central part in both biblical and koranic stories. Several sites on both sides of the lake qualify as potential candidates for the "Five Cities of the Plain" – Sodom, Gomorrah, Admah, Zeboiim and Zuwwar – which, according to Genesis, were obliterated by God in a rage possibly around 2300 BC.

One of these sites, Bab al-dhira', has been excavated, revealing a strong town wall and a huge cemetery; this could be the site of Sodom. It's signposted after the road south to Al-karak turns away from the Dead Sea. Many of the items found here are exhibited at the museum in Al-karak Castle – sadly more famous as the site of a 2016 terrorist attack, claimed by ISIL, which left 10 people dead (see page 217).

THE DEAD SEA

One of the world's geological wonders may be facing extinction unless a radical solution can solve its challenging problems.

The Dead Sea is the lowest place on the earth's surface and among the world's hottest, lying around 400 metres (1,310ft) below sea level. Though many large *wadi* systems empty their silty floodwaters from the surrounding mountains into it, there is no outlet for the sea itself. This, combined with the soaring air temperatures, produces a high rate of evaporation – almost 10 million tons of water per day. The evaporation leaves a residue of salts and minerals (magnesium chloride, sodium chloride, bromide salts and potash) close to saturation point, giving the sea its famously glutinous texture and surface and creating the buoyancy for which the sea is famous. With a salinity rate of over 30 percent, the Dead Sea is almost ten times saltier than any ocean.

Unfortunately, this unique geological phenomenon is poorly; some say the Dead Sea is dying. A series of environmental pressures have taken their toll, including population growth on both sides of the sea and the related demand for water as drinking water for rapidly growing populations and for agriculture. Much water has been diverted from the River Jordan – a major source of water for the sea – for irrigation on both banks such that its annual flow into the Dead Sea has dropped to a trickle. In the 1930s, 1,300 million cubic metres (45,000 million cubic feet) of water flowed through the Jordan each year. Today it's down to between 200–300 million (7000 million cubic feet), half of which is untreated waste water effluent from fish farms and raw sewage.

As a result of all this, the Dead Sea is slowly drying up, with a drop in the sea's water level of 15 metres (50ft) in the last 50 years alone. The current rate of decline is approximately 1 metre (3.3ft) a year. Take a look at the tell-tale salty white water marks showing way above the current level along the coast. This drop is affecting not just the Sea itself, but also ecosystems on the land and shore, including the surrounding oases and wetlands, as well as groundwater levels. The demise of the Dead Sea would also have a devastating impact on tourism in the region.

When the matter finally caught international attention, various solutions were put forward. The winning proposal – and the most economically, politically and environmentally viable – was the idea of constructing a canal to connect the Dead Sea with the Red Sea. With water piped to the southern shores from Al-'aqabah, Dead Sea water levels can in theory be restored to historical levels, hydroelectricity can be produced using the 400-metre (1,300ft) drop in water levels between the two seas and a desalination plant (using renewable hydro-static energy rather than fossil fuels) can potentially turn the Red Sea feedwater into water for both urban and agricultural use.

The canal will not come cheap. Recent costing estimates put the construction of the canal alone in the region of US$800–900 million, with financing to be found mainly by the Jordanian and Israeli governments. It is hoped that the private sector will finance the desalination plant and other ventures.

The World Bank commissioned a US$15 million feasibility study into the viability of the plan, including the environmental impact; this was given the thumbs-up in mid-2012 and public opinion appeared to turn finally in favour of the project, now known officially as "The Red Sea-Dead Sea Water Conveyance Project". The project is currently underway, with the first stage scheduled to begin in 2018 and due for completion in 2020.

Salty white water marks reveal the Dead Sea is shrinking.

Dana village.

THE KING'S HIGHWAY

Twisting its way through a mountainous landscape, the ancient King's Highway connects some of Jordan's most spectacular historic sites, including Ma'daba, Al-karak, Shawbak and Petra.

The **King's Highway** (Tariq al-malik) winding south from Amman to Arabia is an ancient route, along which traders, armies and pilgrims have passed for more than 3,000 years. As early as 1200 BC, Moses addressed the Edomites: "Let us pass, I pray thee, through thy country: we will not pass through the fields, or through the vineyards, neither will we drink of the water of the wells: we will go by the King's Highway, we will not turn to the right hand nor to the left, until we have passed thy borders" (Numbers 20:17).

The route mutates from narrow country lane to wide highway and back again. What changes little is the landscape, which is almost always scenic. The Highway plunges down into major and minor *wadis* (valleys), the most spectacular of which is the formidable Wadi al-mujib. In spring and early summer, while winter rain water flows through the valley beds, the mountain slopes explode with blankets of dazzling flora. Around every corner is either an archaeological or natural treasure, inviting travellers to stop and explore.

THE ROUTE SOUTH

Three options exist for the route south: the winding but scenic King's Highway (250km/155 miles between Amman and Petra), the duller but faster Desert Highway (265km/165 miles;

Ma'daba Map in St George's Church.

see page 221) or the Dead Sea Highway, which can be picked up outside Amman, passing the length of the Dead Sea, through Ghor al-safi and continuing south to Al-'aqabah.

Perhaps the most practical option, which combines the best of the scenery with all the major sights, is to drive along the King's Highway via Ma'daba, Jabal nibu, Umm al-rasas and Al-karak, and then cross to the Desert Highway (Al-tariq al-sahrawi) for a faster route south. This route takes about 12 hours if you stop off and see

○ Main Attractions
Jabal nibu (Mount Nebo)
Ma'daba
Wadi al-mujib
Al-karak
Sanctuary of Lot
Dana
Shawbak Castle

Map on page 206

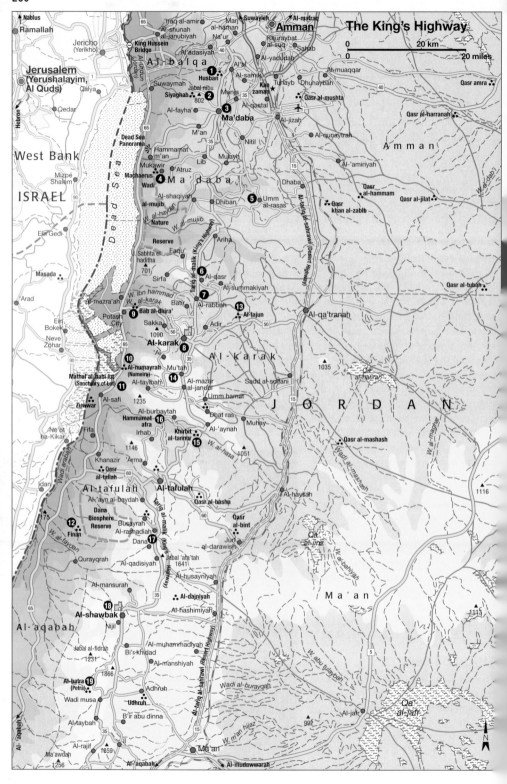

The King's Highway

he sights; two full days are recommended for a more leisurely tour.

There are good hotels in Ma'daba, s well as the beautiful RSCN guesthouse and campsite at Dana, centrepieces of the stunning Dana Nature Reserve. Leaving Amman on the airport road, travellers can approach Ma'daba, 33km (20 miles) to the south, either directly or as an interesting diversion via the ancient biblical site of **Husban** ❶.

HUSBAN

ake the Na'ur exit about 10km (6 miles) along the airport road, and the left fork when the road splits at Na'ur. The pools of Husban are mentioned in the Song of Solomon: "Thy neck is as a tower of ivory; thine eyes like the fishpools in Heshbon [Husban]..." (7:4). The only evidence of Husban today is the archaeologists' trenches visible on top of a tel crowned by several impressive 19th-century village houses on the right-hand side of the main road. Tels, formed by the accumulation of debris from successive cities resulting in a layer-cake effect when excavated, are common throughout Jordan.

JABAL NIBU (MOUNT NEBO)

"And Moses went up from the plains of Moab unto the mountain of Nebo, to the top of Pisgah, that is over against Jericho... And the Lord said unto him this is the land which I sware unto Abraham, unto Isaac, and unto Jacob saying, I will give it unto thy seed. I have caused thee to see it with thine eyes, but thou shalt not go over thither. So Moses the servant of the Lord died there in the land of Moab, according to the word of the Lord." (Deut. 34:1, 4–5).

Jabal nibu ❷ (Mount Nebo, Arabic: Jabal Siyaghah; daily, summer 8am–6pm, winter 8am–5pm; charge; tel: 05-325 2938), site of the demise of Moses, has been a place of pilgrimage since the early days of Christianity. The traditional pilgrimage route included Jerusalem, Jericho, Ain Moussa (the springs of Moses) and Jabal nibu, and ended with a restorative bathe in the **hot springs of Hammamat Ma'in**.

⊙ Fact

The basilica-church at Jabal nibu (and the mosaics inside it) reopened in 2016 following nearly 10 years of restoration. A visit is worthwhile to wander the chapels and museums, admire the views and enjoy the atmosphere of this cool and tranquil place.

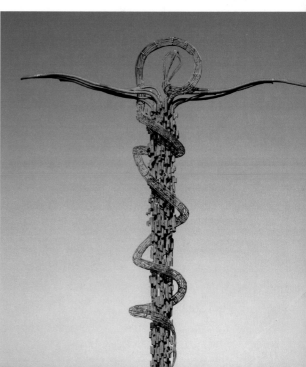

Bronze snake on the cross at Jabal nibu.

⊘ NEBO'S CHURCHES

In AD 394, the intrepid Roman pilgrim, Egeria, set out from Jerusalem on a pilgrimage to Jabal nibu. Crossing the Jordan River and trekking up the Wadi Husban and its tributaries all the way to the spring of Moses (today marked by a large eucalyptus tree), she then scrambled up to the little Church of Moses erected by very early Christians. Two centuries later, by the 6th century, this small, square chapel had expanded into one of the most extensive monastic complexes in the Middle East. Excavations started by the Franciscan Biblical Institute of Jerusalem in 1933 have exposed the early three-apse basilica-church (still in use for services) and the monastic buildings surrounding it. Today, a modern monastery to the southwest of the church has joined the more ancient churches.

The **view** from the platform in front of the main basilica church is stupendous and best seen early in the morning or at sunset. The Promised Land spreads out to the west, the dark-green mass of the Jordan Valley masking the ancient city of Jericho, the roofs of Jerusalem and Bethlehem glinting on the hills opposite, and the opaque expanse of the Dead Sea shimmering below. The **bronze snake** on a cross outside the church was designed by Fantoni of Florence and symbolises the serpent lifted up by Moses in the desert and Jesus on the Cross.

The **basilica** itself dates from the 6th and 7th centuries, although the earlier chapels, baptistry and memorial to Moses are incorporated into the fabric of the building. The most significant **mosaic**, dating to AD 531, is that in the old baptistry to the left of the main entrance. The central field, enclosed in a plait-border, depicts hunting and pastoral scenes including exotic animals – zebra, zebu (humped ox), spotted camel, lion and ostrich. Most of the central aisle mosaics have been removed for restoration and preservation, and are now displayed on the walls of the modern building. The memorial to Moses, which the pilgrim Egeria reported, probably survives as the raised structure near the pulpit at the east end of the south aisle. Pieces of the mosaic which decorated this early church can be seen near the altar, including a simple cross. Near the chancel are the tombs of early monks, visible through metal trap doors in the nave.

MA'DABA

Set amid the fertile Ma'daba plains and surrounded by rolling fields of barley, wheat and tobacco, **Ma'daba ❸** boasts an attractive natural setting. Relatively affluent, culturally mixed (more than a third of the population is Christian, and a good number of immigrants have made their home here) and well used to tourists, the town has a relaxed, laid-back air that many travellers take to. It also has a good range of hotels, restaurants and cafés, as well as well-touted attractions.

The town's skyline of church spires and minarets gives a clue to its history: in common with many of the settlements along the King's Highway, Ma'daba seems to have been abandoned in the 18th and 19th centuries, but by the end of the 19th century had been resettled by Christians from Al-karak. Today, the town thrives both as a market centre (attracting Bedouin and their animals from the surrounding area) and as a growing tourism destination.

Ma'daba traces its origins to biblical times, but it is as the seat of a Byzantine bishopric and the centre of mosaic production that this "City of Mosaics" is most famous (see box, page 210). Made from local stone, Ma'daba's mosaics were inspired by pattern books circulating at the time throughout the Byzantine world. These pattern books ensured a certain amount of uniformity to the designs, although individua

Hammamat Ma'in hot springs.

reativity on the part of the craftsman as both encouraged and appreciated.

After the **Visitor Centre** (Shari' abu akir al-siddiq; daily, May–Sept 8am–om, Oct–Apr 8am–5.30pm; tel: 05-325 563), a useful interpretive centre nowing a 10-minute film on Ma'daba's istory in a traditional 19th-century wnhouse, the impressive **Ma'daba rchaeological Park** (Mahmiyat athar la'daba; daily, May–Sept 8am–5pm, ct–Apr 8am–4pm; combined ticket) ext door makes a good first stop. here are the remains of a colonnaded oman street here, but the highlights re the mosaics, such as the 1st-cen-ary Machaerus Mosaic (immediately oposite the main entrance), the oldest osaic fragment in the country. There re more outstanding mosaics under e modern shelter over the **Hippolytus all**, a Byzantine villa dating to the 6th entury AD. Look out for a semi-naked nd cross Aphrodite spanking the ever-nischievous Eros, along with other enes, including the Three Graces and our Seasons. More charming mosa-s are found in the early 7th-century

Church of the Prophet Elias, and in particular, the **Church of the Virgin Mary,** with its elaborate curvilinear and geometric patterns. Housed in the same complex at the exit is the **Ma'daba Institute for Mosaic Art & Restoration** (Sun–Thur 8am–3pm; free), set up by the government in 1992 to teach students the arts of both mosaic making and mosaic restoration.

Nearby, to the northwest, is the **Archaeological Park II** (May–Sept Sun–Thur 8am–5.30pm, Oct–Apr Sun–Thur 8am–3pm; free), also known as the **Burnt Palace** after its destruction by an earthquake and fire around AD 749. Built at the end of the 6th century, the palace is thought to have been a lavish private villa, judging from the quantity and quality of its mosaics and rooms. In the same complex are the ruins of the 8th-century **Martyrs Church**.

A short walk northwest lies the Greek Orthodox **Church of St George** (daily, summer 8am–7pm, winter 8am–6pm except Fri 8–9.30am and Sun 8–10.30am during mass; charge), which contains the 6th-century **Ma'daba Map** (Kharitat

Ma'daba.

Ma'daba). It was discovered by builders during the construction of the church in 1898, itself on the site of a Byzantine. With delightful realism, the map portrays the physical characteristics of the Eastern Byzantine world, including its rivers, valleys, the Dead Sea and its neighbouring hills and towns. The centrepiece is Jerusalem, with its Church of the Holy Sepulchre. The area depicted stretches from Tyre and Sidon to the Egyptian delta and from the Mediterranean all the way to the Eastern Desert. Its special significance lies in the fact that it is the oldest surviving map of Palestine, and its remarkable scale. Though impressive in its scope, detail and size, its original dimensions are thought to have measured up to 25 metres (82ft) long containing over two million tesserae (pieces of stone). An **Interpretation Centre** is found to the right of the church as you enter.

Admiring the mosaics at Ma'daba Archaeological Park.

Around 600 metres/yds due south of the Ma'daba Map, under a modern shelter, lies the **Church of the Apostles**. The large and very fine mosaic floors of the body of the church were completed in

Mosaic workshop.

AD 578 by one Salomios, whose name appears around the central medallion. This medallion depicts a personification of the sea, Thalassa, emerging from the ocean against a background of leaping fish, open-jawed sharks and an octopus. Look out for the delightful little green parrots, a recurring motif. Also housed here for display and safe-keeping are mosaics from Byzantine houses.

The **Ma'daba Museum** (Shari' haya bint al-husayn; summer Sat–Thur 8am–6pm, Fri 10am–5pm; winter Sat–Thur 8am–4pm, Fri 8am–3pm; combined ticket), containing the **Folklore Museum** (Mathaf al-fulklur) are overlooked by many visitors but also merit a visit. Housed in a cluster of old Ma'daba houses, they contain an excellent collection of mosaics and artefacts recovered from various locations in the city, as well as an ethnographic section containing a collection of traditional costumes and jewellery.

A short walk northeast of the Ma'daba Museum up the hill takes you to Ma'daba's largest church, the **Latin Church, Belfry & Shrine of the Beheading of John the Baptist** (Shari' talal;

⊙ MA'DABA'S MOSAICS

Common motifs, which look back to the Hellenistic/Roman world, include scenes of hunting, fishing and pastoral pursuits; representations of well-known buildings; mythological scenes; marine or riverine scenes; and depictions of animals. Such motifs remain common to the mosaics produced along the King's Highway today – numerous workshops around Ma'daba still produce lovingly made pieces. During the 7th and 8th centuries, however, the figures of humans and animals in many mosaics were extracted and replaced by patches of blank *tesserae* (the small stones of which a mosaic is composed). This is as likely to have been the result of the iconoclastic movement among Christian communities during that period, as the result of Muslim destruction of figural representation, as is popularly claimed.

immer daily 9am–7pm, winter 9am–
2m; free). Though this impressive
uurch only dates to the early 20th cen-
ry, it's worth a visit for the remarkable
:cavations in the church's foundations
which have unearthed a Moabite-era
ell, Roman vaults and other cham-
ers), the exhibition of old photographs
 Ma'daba in the chapel, the (slightly
arish) shrine to John the Baptist, and
e church facade, which incorporates
oman architectural features including
olumns and capitals. The 90-step climb
ncluding a metal ladder for the last
art) up the narrow belfry is worthwhile
r the panoramic views over Ma'daba
id beyond.

The renovated **Dar al-Saraya** is
cated just north of the Latin Church.
 former Ottoman administrative
Jilding, the contents of the Ma'daba
useum are tipped to be relocated
ere. Competing rumours suggest it
ill become a restaurant.

IUKAWIR

venty kilometres (12 miles) southwest
 Ma'daba on the King's Highway is a

signpost on the right indicating the direction of **Mukawir** ❹, the site of the notorious palace of Machaerus, identified in
the New Testament as the place in which
Salome danced in exchange for the head
of John the Baptist (Mark 6:21–29).

Mukawir lies on a stark but spectacular promontory (700 metres/2,295ft)
overlooking the Dead Sea and protected
on three sides by deep plunging ravines.
The royal fortress on top of the steep
hill is that of Herod the Great. Dating to
30 BC, it is a replacement of an earlier
structure and is similar to Herod's other
mountaintop abodes west of the River
Jordan: Herodium, Alexandrum and
Masada. The site has been undergoing
extensive restoration by the Department
of Antiquities and the Franciscan Institute, although few walls of any height
remain standing. Nonetheless, the views
from the palace make the 15- to 20-min-
ute walk rewarding. A small café sells
refreshments beside the car park.

UMM AL-RASAS

Lying 33km (20 miles) south of
Ma'daba, **Umm al-rasas** ❺ can be

*Mukawir, site of
Herod's palace.*

*St George's Church,
Ma'daba.*

⊙ Fact

The Mujib Nature Reserve, like many of Jordan's reserves, face a litany of challenges: overgrazing and illegal hunting, but above all the siphoning off of water from the wadis to supply the demands of the Dead Sea resorts, cities such as Amman and nearby industries.

reached either from Dhiban on the King's Highway or from the Desert Highway. This ancient square-walled town probably dates from the Roman period. Two churches have emerged from the large expanse of ruins in the southeast of the town, both boasting good 6th-century mosaics depicting the standard repertoire of fruit trees, animals and geometric and floral patterns. The northern church was constructed in 586, and its mosaic depicts scenes of the church's benefactors carrying out daily tasks. The figures have been carefully blotted out during the iconoclastic movement so as to render them unrecognisable, but in the southeast corner a personification of a season was hidden by the stone base of a pulpit, and so has been preserved. The southern church was floored in two stages. According to an inscription, the mosaic of the presbytery was laid in 756 by Etaurachius of Husban; the main mosaic of the central nave and small lateral nave was remade in 785. Both churches were still in use well into the early Islamic period.

Mosaics at St Stephen's Church, Umm al-rasas.

About one hour from the ruins stands a dramatically isolated stone tower, most likely the residence of the Christian ascetic hermit of the 5th or 6th century.

WADI AL-MUJIB AND MOAB

Nothing prepares one for the plunge into the gash across the plateau which is the spectacular **Wadi al-mujib,** measuring up to 1km (0.5 miles) deep and up to 3.5km (2 miles) wide. The King's Highway twists and winds its way down 900 metres (almost 3,000ft) to a dam at the bottom of the *wadi*. On the way, look out for the Roman milestones on the southern edge marking the course of the Roman road. At the north side of the wadi, there's a good vantage point to admire the views and spot buzzards or other birds of prey soaring at eye level.

Running for nearly 75km (45 miles) from the Desert Highway almost to the Dead Sea, the Wadi al-mujib is popularly known as Jordan's Grand Canyon, encompassing in the western section the 215 sq km (83 sq miles) **Mujib Nature Reserve**. For more information on the RSCN-run reserve's flora and fauna, see page 103, and on its excellent hiking options, see page 112. A hike through the canyon and waterfalls is not to be missed. The **visitor centre** (Apr–Nov daily 8am–4pm; charge tel: 0799 074960; www.rscn.org.jo), just before the Mujib Bridge 28km (17 miles) south of Amman, can organise a trek along one of its five established trails, as well as guides and accommodation in one of its 14 basic chalets that overlook the Dead Sea.

Emerging through walls of basalt rock at the top of the *wadi*, the road once again passes through a wide open plateau of rolling wheat and barley fields. This is southern Moab, an area known for centuries for its independence of spirit. The King's Highway then passes through small but thriving villages, all with conspicuous and often ewly constructed schools to cope with ordan's rapidly expanding population. n **Al-qasr** ➏, there is an early 2nd-entury Nabatean temple that has ever been excavated. To the west of he main road through **Al-rabbah** ➐ re the well-preserved remains of a toman temple, probably converted to church and then reused in the 19th entury as a village house.

AL-KARAK

l-karak ➑ (daily, summer 8am–7pm, vinter 8am–4pm; charge; tel: 03-235 216) has always been valuable because f its strategic position at the head of he Wadi al-karak leading west to Pal-stine. The visible remains of the castle ate mainly from the Mamluke era.

Originally, access was by small tun-els hewn through the rock and these re still visible under the impressive acade, which links four square towers bove a stone *glacis* (a slope, often arti-cially strengthened).

A boardwalk takes visitors through ourist souvenir stalls and along the dge of a fosse en route to the entrance f the castle. There are superb views long the way down to the Dead Sea.

Al-karak is a castle to be explored; here are many dark passages, cavern-us holes and the occasional sheer drop many of them unfenced, so beware).

Because the castle was occupied nd altered by successive powers right own to the brief Independent Republic f Moab in 1920, it is difficult to sift one eriod historically from another. Much lso remains buried beneath modern l-karak.

The steps down to the **Mamluke ower Court** lead to a **museum** housed n one of the castle's many long galleries nd containing artefacts from excava-ons and early photographs of Al-karak aken by England's Edwardian explorer, ertrude Bell. The inner wall of this ower Court sits on Crusader founda-ons but is largely Mamluke. The outer all is also Mamluke, dating to the time of Sultan Baybars, who was responsible for constructing the towers along the city wall. Look out for his emblem, the lion, inscribed on the walls.

Turning sharp left at the entrance, walk up into an impressive two-sto-rey gallery which used to double as a football pitch for the local boys. Look through the narrow arrow slits onto one of the original Crusader entrances, now a blocked-up doorway in the rough stone wall in a projecting bastion to the east.

Once through this gallery, turn right along a narrow passage past a relief of a male torso, which many guides tell you is Salah' ad Din, better known to the English-speaking world as Sala-din, the famous nemesis of the French crusaders, Richard the Lionheart and Reynald de Chatillon. In fact, this is a fragment of a Nabataean sculpture which was found on the site when the Crusaders started building in 1142. There are side rooms leading off the passageway, including the castle bak-ery, crucial for sustaining the garrison in times of siege, as were, even more importantly, the castle Cistern.

⊘ Fact

In August 1868, a missionary in Dhiban made an extraordinary discovery: a black basalt stone inscribed in the ancient tongue of the Moabites. Unfortunately, a local dispute regarding its ownership led to its destruction, but thanks to papier-mâché casts already taken, most of the stone, known as the Mesha Stele, was slowly pieced back together and now resides in the Louvre Museum in Paris. Casts can be seen in many museums in Jordan including Amman's Jordanian Archaeological Museum (see page 145).

Al-karak town.

MOAB – ITS LAND AND PEOPLE

The modern region of Moab has a long history; in fact little has changed since biblical times for either the land or its people.

The land through which the King's Highway passes south of Amman is often referred to by its biblical name, Moab. Most of the Book of Ruth takes place against this background – an open limestone plateau of rolling rounded hills, which rises from about 900 metres (2,950ft) to the peak of **Jabal shihan** south of the Wadi al-mujib.

Dhiban, on the King's Highway, situated between Mukawir and Umm al-rasas, was the one-time capital of Moab when the modern-day region of Jordan was split into the kingdoms of Ammon, Edom and Moab. The town is also famous for the black basalt stone, known as the Mesha or Moabite Stele, erected here around AD 840 by Mesha, King of Moab. On it, the king records his liberation of the land of Moab with the help of the Moab god, Kemosh, from the hands of the Israelites, as well as the many monuments he built. The inscription at Dhiban is of huge

interest both to historians and linguists, as a rare example of the Moabite language and unusual corroboration of the Bible.

The plateau that forms the land of Moab today is at its most beautiful in spring (late March to May), when a green carpet lines the hills along with scarlet anemones, black irises, wild gladioli, and yellow heavy-scented mimosa, and fire-station-red poppies border the road and fields and fill the **Wadi al-mujib**.

By summer, hollyhocks and caper bushes take over against a background of intense activity as first the harvesting then the threshing, takes place. The tinkle of bells heralds flocks grazing the stubble – just one example of the way in which agriculture and pastoralism successfully co-exist in this region.

The same land is in fact used by several interest groups: the nomadic tribes herding sheep, goats and, less commonly, camels, who live in black goat-hair tents; the semi-nomadic tribes who live in village houses for part of the year, but then exchange these for black tents in the spring and autumn when they follow the grazing and move out to the fields for harvest; and the villagers, who live mostly in modern, concrete houses.

Occasionally, encampments of smaller sacking or canvas tents are seen on the outskirts of villages. These belong to the gypsies, who carry out "dentistry work" (putting in gold teeth) and sing and dance at weddings. Gypsies can be distinguished by the vibrantly coloured dresses of the women as well as the tents; Moabite women traditionally dress in black. The latter are also known for their long braided hair, which falls down the front of their dresses while their heads are covered by tiny black tulle scarves.

The men of the region are less distinctive and opt for either Western dress or for a long, plainly coloured *dish-dash* (floor-length "shirt"). They reserve any form of sartorial individualism for their *hatta/keffiyeh* (headcloth), which varies in design from red-and-white check to snowy white and is often worn at a rakish angle. On high days and holidays men wear an *abayeh* over the *dish-dash*, a finely woven cloak of wool or linen often trimmed with gold. The status of the man is indicated by his *agal*, the cord which holds the *hatta* on the head, and which was originally designed for the tying up of camels.

Moabite women traditionally dress in black.

Emerging from the gloom of the passage, you will find yourself in the ruined **Crusader chapel** just to the right, and ahead, the three-storey Mamluke keep: there is a great view of the castle and its surroundings from this point. The keep lies at the southern end of the Citadel and replaces an earlier Crusader construction. The Crusader defences on this southern side would have been set up against the siege engines of Saladin, which would have been placed on the high ground opposite. Saladin twice besieged the castle, then occupied by his arch-enemy Reynald de Chatillon, first in 1183 and then in 1184. Reynald had been harrying Muslim caravans and sailing vessels, and had managed to get within one day's march of Mecca. During the siege, Saladin, in an extraordinary act of chivalry, suspended his fire on the tower because it was occupied by the newly married Isabella, sister of the king, and Reynald's stepson. Both sieges were eventually relieved by Baldwin IV marching with a garrison from Jerusalem, and Al-karak did not finally capitulate until 1189.

Turning in the other direction and looking down, you can see the excavated 14th-century reception hall of al Nasir Muhammad's palace. Here, the sultan would have received guests and supplicants. Its cruciform design with four *diwans* opening on to an unroofed courtyard is typical of that period (and mirrors a similar building at Shawbak).

The town of Al-karak, like Ma'daba, is a market centre for the surrounding villages and its Bedouin communities. Like Ma'daba, it is also a mixed Muslim and Christian community. In fact, the Christian population of the Al-karak area boasts a long history that far predates the Crusades, and some of the villages to the north of the town are thought to be up to 95 percent Christian.

In Al-karak's town centre, the suq is well worth a wander, not only for the cool and tranquil interiors of the old Ottoman-built shops, but also to browse goods that range from threshing forks, sheepskins and richly roasted coffee beans to sacks of bark for medicinal purposes, goat-bells, blue-beaded Fatima's Hands

Natural rock salt formation known as Lot's wife, near the Dead Sea.

Al-karak castle.

for warding off the evil eye, and rolls of Bedouin tent-cloth. At the top of the main street, several eateries offer freshly made and delicious *falafel*, *ful*, and *hummous*. On the first sharp bend on the road out of town, look out for the old dyeing shop with its vats of colour, and an original Ottoman school built on the orders of Sultan Abdul Hamid in the late 1890s.

West of the King's Highway and running parallel with it, is a road that runs through the **Southern Ghor**, an intriguing area along the southeast coast of the Dead Sea with many important historical associations. The road is easily accessed from Al-karak.

BAB AL-DHIRA' AND AL-NUMAYRAH

Both Bab al-dhira' and Al-numayrah are considered plausible candidates for the sites of Sodom and Gomorrah. In the Genesis account, God destroyed Sodom and Gomorrah as a sign of his displeasure with the wickedness of the cities' inhabitants. Abraham's nephew, Lot, was saved by fleeing to the hills with his daughters; his wife was less fortunate. For the crime of looking back upon the scene of devastation against God's strict instructions, she was transformed forever into a pillar of salt.

Bab al-dhira' ❾ (near the junction of the Dead Sea and Al-karak roads) was inhabited for more than 1,000 years from around 3300 to 2000 BC during the Early Bronze Age. Interestingly, for much of that time it was also used as a cemetery by nomads, who brought their dead for burial here in multiple shaft tombs and large charnel houses.

Al-numayrah ❿, 14km (9 miles) to the south, is a large, walled town on a hilltop that existed for about a century during the Early Bronze Age III period (*c.*2750–2350 BC), before suffering a violent and fiery fate according to the 40cm (16in)-thick ash layers that have been revealed by excavations.

Together with Bab al-dhira' and Al-numayrah, the remains of other Early Bronze Age sites in the area can also be seen at **Fifa**, **Khanazir** and **Safi**. These five sites may be the most probable candidates for the Five Cities of the

Shop owner in Al-karak town.

Plain mentioned in the Book of Genesis, namely Sodom, Gomorrah, Admah, Zeboiim, and Bela (that is, Zuwwar).

SANCTUARY OF LOT

Lying 2km (1.2 miles) northeast of Al-safi and well signposted off the King's Highway, is a spot known as the **Sanctuary of Lot** ⓫ (Mathaf al-nabi lut). It forms part of a ruined Byzantine monastic complex that includes the remains of a church with mosaic floors, a reservoir, living quarters, and burial chambers as well as the actual cave. The site has long attracted pilgrims as the supposed site where Lot and his daughters took refuge after the destruction of Sodom.

In fact, some ceramic artefacts found in the cave date from around 3000 BC – the date attributed to the destruction of Sodom. An inscription mentions Lot by name, and the complex appears to have been used from the 5th to the 8th centuries. The site is also identified on the Ma'daba mosaic map as the Monastery of Saint Lot.

Constructed nearby is the "Museum of the Lowest Point on Earth", housed in an imposing semicircular building inaugurated in 2005 to showcase the geological and historical heritage of the area.

FINAN

A 15-minute drive to the south brings you to the turn-off for **Finan** ⓬, half an hour to the east and accessible for the last part of the journey only by 4WD vehicle (which can be organised in advance by the camp). Finan is a sprawling copper-mining complex that was one of the biggest in the ancient world. It has been associated with the biblical site of Punon. Several hundred shaft mines in the area were exploited for their rich ore during the five and a half millennia from the Chalcolithic to the Mamluke periods (c.4000 BC–AD 1500). Still visible above ground today are enormous slag heaps from several different periods, and remains of the large Roman-Byzantine town's water systems, agricultural fields, smelters, water-powered mill and at least two churches. Near the ruins is Finan Ecolodge, a solar-powered eco-friendly hotel founded and owned by the Royal

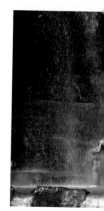

Bathing in hot springs.

Sanctuary of Lot.

⊙ 2016 AL-KARAK ATTACK

On 18 December 2016 at around 3pm local time, a group of gunmen opened fire on two police patrols in Al-karak, in a terrorist attack that was later claimed by ISIL. The assailants then headed for the castle complex, where they attacked a police station before taking refuge in the citadel. The result was initially assumed to be a hostage situation – with the castle surrounded by police and security forces – but the tourists were in fact in a different part of the castle, unable to leave. The grisly attack, which mainly targeted Jordanian police, left 10 dead (seven security force members, two civilians and a Canadian tourist) and at least 29 people were injured.

⊘ Tip

As well as mammals such as the beautiful ibex, Dana Biosphere Reserve is a great place for observing resident and migratory birds. A bird hide in front of a drinking pool has been established at Rummana Campsite.

Society for the Conservation of Nature but latterly managed successfully by a private enterprise.

AL-LAJUN, MU'TAH AND MAZAR

An interesting stop on the way to or from Al-karak and easily accessible from the town, is the excavated legionary fortress of **Al-lajun** , equidistant from the King's and Desert Highways. The name Al-lajun is probably a corruption of the Latin *legio*; the legion in question being the Legio IV Martia.

The square fortress was probably built in AD 302 during the reign of Diocletian, and contains all the standard features of a garrison town: the central *principia* (headquarters), the barracks, defensive towers and a monumental gateway within the wall.

Al-lajun numbered among the forts which guarded the eastern frontier of the Roman Empire, which ran north–south near the line of the Desert Highway. The buildings on the hill above the site belong to the late Ottoman period, when a Turkish garrison was stationed here to guard

Dana village.

the spring and the communication lines between Al-karak and Qatrana.

Continuing south along the King's Highway from Al-karak, the road passes through the neighbouring towns of **Mu'tah**  and **Al-mazar al-janubi**, site of the first battle between the Muslims and Byzantium in 632, and of Jordan's third university. The Companions of the Prophet Muhammad who fell during the battle were buried at Al-mazar al-janubi, and the town remains an important Muslim pilgrimage centre today; several Shia' sites are currently being renovated and reconstructed. There is also a small Islamic museum displaying coins and ceramics.

The road meanders on through rural landscape until reaching **Wadi al-hasa**, the ancient boundary between Moab and Edom. Edom was a Nabataean Iron Age kingdom which differed from Moab in that it was made up of small stretches of cultivatable land between steep valleys. The side valleys contain traces of the Nabataean terracing that harvested and exploited the water run-off.

KHIRBIT AL-TANNUR

On the southern side of Wadi al-hasa, on top of a high isolated hill, lies the Nabataean temple of **Khirbit al-tannur** . The path to the summit is not signposted, but lies exactly 2.7km (1.6 miles) from the turning to the Tannur dam if coming from the north, or exactly 2km (1.2 miles) after the turnoff to Hammamat afra if coming from the south. It's a fairly steep climb to the summit but is worth it for the views from the top. Though there's not much to see bar the remains of walls and the odd fallen column and capital, it's quite an atmospheric place. Bedouin have set up camp at the base; it's polite to let them know where you're heading.

The temple itself was built between the 1st century BC and the 1st century AD, and is dedicated to the gods, Hadad and Atargaris, local versions of the main Nabataean gods, Dushara and Allat. The whole structure was richly decorated with fine sculpture, which now lies in the Archaeological Museum in Amman (see page 145). Traces of the temple survive in low walls outlining the outer paved courtyard and altar in the north-east corner. A doorway leads to an inner smaller courtyard, in the centre of which stood the shrine and main altar. Animal sacrifices were made on these altars.

HOT SPRINGS OF AL-BURBAYTAH AND HAMMAMAT AFRA

Exactly 2km (1.2 miles) from Khirbit al-tannur, a signposted turn-off leads around 12km (7 miles) to local hot-spots (particularly busy at the weekend), **Al-burbaytah** and, around 5km (3 miles) beyond that, **Hammamat afra** , famous for their hot springs – including one, known as the *miqlah* – "frying pan" – that bubbles away at 52°C (125°F). Of the two, Hammamat afra (daily 7am–10pm; tel: 0796 274020; charge) has the best facilities, which includes separate bathing and changing areas for men and women, a small shop, café and restaurant, and basic (and none too clean) cabins or tents. Above the springs, hidden amid the boulders, are various caves, including one which local police claim is an old Byzantine church.

The King's Highway then climbs out of the Wadi al-hasa onto the long plain of **Al-tafulah,** where Lawrence fought his only pitched battle against the Turks in January 1918. The region is also famous for its olives, which can be seen blanketing the side of the *wadi* leading down from Al-tafulah.

DANA

After passing the ancient site of **Busay-rah**, ancient Bozrah and possible capital of the Edomites, the road passes the Al-rashadiah cement works and, just below, the village of Dana.

Dana sits at the head of a magnificent *wadi* running west into the Wadi 'arabah, once the site of early copper mines. Today, Dana is a delightful historical hamlet dating from the 15th century and made up of a collection of old stone houses at the edge of a dramatic precipice and surrounded by fertile orchards. It is one of the very few villages or towns in Jordan that remain mostly unmarred by uncontrolled concrete construction.

The surrounding area forms part of the very beautiful **Dana Biosphere Reserve** (www.rscn.org.jo; charge), part of the RSCN Wadi Dana Project, Jordan's largest reserve, and boasts four quite distinct ecosystems. A research facility to study the local flora, fauna (including the rare ibex) and archaeology is ongoing, as is an initiative to revive village life (many of its former residents have migrated to more modern towns) and restore the old village houses, turning them either into living quarters or handicraft and organic foodstuffs centres.

The Wadi Dana Guest House, as well as many of the other village hotels, offers commanding views of the spectacular Wadi 'arabah and makes a wonderful retreat for a day or two, as does the Rummana Campsite deep

Detail of Shawbak castle.

View over Dana Biosphere Reserve, Wadi 'arabah.

inside the reserve, and the exceptionally atmospheric Finan Ecolodge at the western end of the park, where there are also bike trails and bikes for hire.

For more information on Dana's excellent trekking, see page 113. The **visitor centre** (daily 8am–3pm; www.rscn.org.jo; tel: 03-227 0497) at Dana can provide the latest information on trails, as well as a basic map and guides. For more information on Dana's flora and fauna, see page 103 and visit the little **museum** inside the Dana visitor centre.

SHAWBAK CASTLE

Lying east of the main road running through **Al-shawbak ⑱** town, the first sight of the castle on its isolated hill is impressive. Shawbak, or Montreal as it was known, was the first outpost of the Kingdom of Jerusalem in Outrejordain and constructed in 1115 by Baldwin I. It was later eclipsed by Al-karak when its commander, Pagan the Butler, realised the strategic value of the latter.

Like Al-karak, most of the visible defences in fact belong to post-Crusader times and the two castles share similar

Shawbak castle.

histories. Shawbak was taken over by the Ayyubids and then the Mamlukes, whose extensive reconstruction is recorded in inscriptions on the outer face of the towers. The original entrance to the castle was through a triple gate arranged on a bent axis as found at 'Ajlun Castle.

The **Crusader church**, with its bird's-eye view of the old village, is above the entrance. Apart from this and several rooms along the arched corridor on the northeast side of the castle, there are no other positively identified Crusader buildings.

Although the water was usually brought up from springs at the base of the hill, in times of siege a deep and steep passageway within the castle walls led down to the spring. The passageway is still accessible but the steps are worn, crumbling and unlit and considered too dangerous to venture down (some visitors have and regretted it).

A **palace/reception hall**, similar to the one at Al-karak, has been excavated. It was probably built by al-Mu'azzem Isa al-Adil, the Ayyubid governor of this area, at the end of the 12th century. The Ottoman village, including the old post office, is close to the entrance.

Below Shawbak Castle is the **shrine of Abu Suleiman al-Dirany**, probably Ayyubid or Mamluke in date. Hennaed hand-prints adorn the internal walls of the shrine, imprinted by women who come to offer votive prayers.

From Shawbak, the road continues straight to Wadi musa and Petra. If you arrive towards sunset, you might consider taking a picturesque side road signposted to Hesha and the Ammareen Campsite, on the right-hand side of the road shortly after the 20km (12-mile) sign to Wadi musa. The road winds up through the scrub-oak forest and emerges on the escarpment, revealing a panoramic view of the rock-massif around Petra and Beidha, a particularly impressive sight in the setting sun. The road then snakes down to the modern village of Wadi musa.

THE DESERT HIGHWAY

Though used by most travellers as a speedy north-south conduit, the Desert Highway has its own particular history and draw.

The alternative to the sight-packed journey along the King's Highway is to take the Amman-Al-'aqabah Desert Highway (Tariq al Bint in Arabic, or Maiden's Way) towards Ma'an, before turning off west to Wadi musa. With a dual carriageway all the way to Ma'an, the journey from Amman to Wadi musa can be done in three hours.

This parallel route to the King's Highway was in fact a 16th-century Ottoman creation; Maiden's Way is thought to refer to an Ottoman princess's preference for this route. The new road was intended to replace the ancient route, although water scarcity and the caprices of, at times, unfriendly tribes, occasionally prompted recourse to the King's Highway.

Travelling down the Desert Highway during the Hajj season today, you will encounter convoys of pilgrim-packed buses sporting flags from as far away as Turkey. Part of the Desert Highway's history and raison d'être lies in its role as a conduit for Muslim pilgrims from Damascus to Medina, and on to Mecca.

AL-QA'TRANAH AND HISA

The major truck stops of Al-jizah, Al-qa'tranah and Al-haysah were also traditional stops for the Hajj caravan, and each modern town hosts an Ottoman fort which once guarded the cisterns and reservoirs so vital to this valuable caravan. The fort at Al-qa'tranah, built in 1531, has been restored with financial help from the Turkish government.

Pervasive white dust heralds the phosphate mines at **Hisa**. Phosphate and potash from the Dead Sea are today Jordan's most important exports, and the old Hejaz railway is still used to transport phosphate down to Al-'aqabah. Apart from the mine camp and truck stops, the only "villages" along the highway belong to recently settled Bedouin, who often use their concrete houses and tin shacks for storage or as animal shelters rather than for dwelling.

MA'AN

In Ma'an town centre, just across from the bus station, is Ma'an Castle, a 16th-century Ottoman fort similar to the one at Al-qa'tranah. Signposted 3km (2 miles) east of Ma'an, near the old railway station, is the King Abdullah I Palace, a modest villa where Abdullah stayed in the winter of 1920 on his advance towards Damascus. Though the building used to contain a museum, its contents have been removed to Amman.

From Ma'an, a scenic route to **Wadi musa** takes you southwest for a little way before diverting to the right, via **Al-taybha**, an old village perched on the edge of the escarpment overlooking Petra and the Wadi 'arabah. A little way south of Ma'an, the winding descent of the **Ras al-naqab** demands careful driving, but look out for the Nabataean and Roman twin towns of **Al-humaymah al-jadidah** on the way.

Section of the Desert Highway.

Bedouins overlooking the
Treasury at Petra.

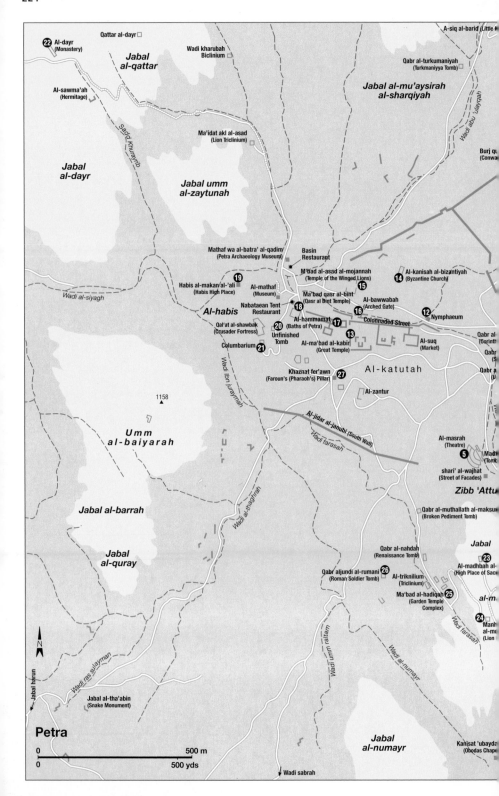

22 Al-dayr
(Monastery)

Qattar al-dayr ☐

Jabal al-qattar

Wadi kharubah
Biclinium ☐

Qabr al-turkumaniyah
(Turkmaniyya Tomb) ☐

A-siq al-barid (Little

Al-sawma'ah
(Hermitage)

*Jabal al-mu'aysirah
al-sharqiyah*

Burj qu
(Conwa

Jabal al-dayr

Ma'idat akl al-asad
(Lion Triclinium) ☐

Jabal umm al-zaytunah

Mathaf wa al-batra' al-qadim
(Petra Archaeology Museum)

Basin
Restaurant

M'bad al-asad al-mojannah
(Temple of the Winged Lions)

14 Al-kanisah al-bizantiyah
(Byzantine Church)

Wadi al-siyagh

Habis al-makan al-'ali
(Habis High Place)

19 Al-mathaf
(Museum)

15

Al-habis

Nabataean Tent
Restaurant

Ma'bad qasr al-bint
(Qasr al Bint Temple)

Al-bawwabah
(Arched Gate)

18

16

12 Nymphaeum

Qabr al
(Corinth

Qal'at al-shawbak
(Crusader Fortress)

20

Al-hammamat
(Baths of Petra)

17

Colonnaded Street

Qabr
(S

Unfinished
Tomb

13

Al-ma'bad al-kabir
(Great Temple)

Al-suq
(Market)

Qabr a

Columbarium

21

1158 ▲

Khaznat fer'awn
(Faroun's (Pharaoh's) Pillar)

27

Al-katutah

Al-zantur

Umm al-baiyarah

Al-jidar al-janubi (South Wall)

Wadi farasah

Al-masrah
(Theatre)

5

Wadi
(Tomb

shari' al-wajhat
(Street of Facades)

Zibb 'Attu

Jabal al-barrah

Jabal al-quray

Qabr al-muthallath al-maksu
(Broken Pediment Tomb)

Jabal

Qabr al-nahdah
(Renaissance Tomb)

23

Al-madhbah al
(High Place of Sac

Qabr aljundi al-rumani
(Roman Soldier Tomb)

26

Al-triknilium
(Triclinium)

Ma'bad al-hadiqah
(Garden Temple
Complex)

25

al-m

24 Man
al-m
(Lion

N

Jabal harun

Wadi ras sulayman

Jabal al-tha'abin
(Snake Monument)

Petra

0 _____ 500 m
0 _____ 500 yds

Jabal al-numayr

Wadi sabrah

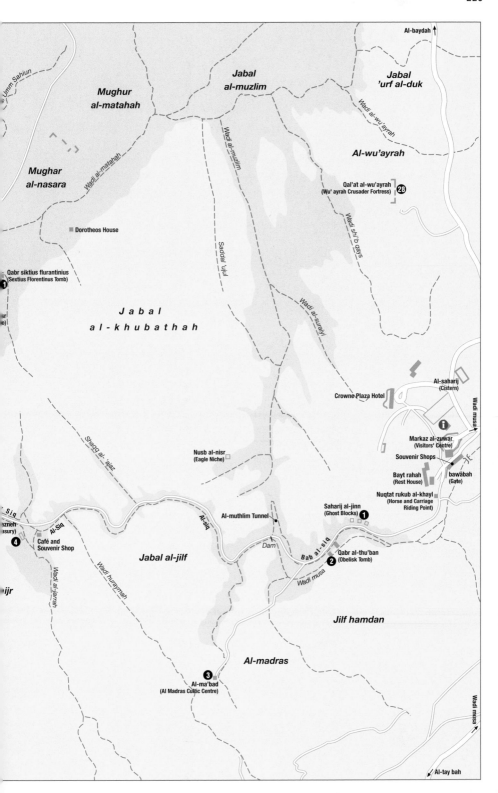

PETRA

There are not many places in the world where landscape and human civilisation have combined to such spectacular effect, but Petra in south Jordan is one of them.

Petra  (Al-batra') is not just Jordan's greatest tourist attraction, it's one of the world's "must-sees". Uniquely, it combines spectacular ancient ruins with sensational natural scenery. In 1985, it officially became a Unesco World Heritage Site, and in 2007, the site was voted worldwide as one of the "New Seven Wonders".

From sunrise to sunset, a steady stream of tourists tread the millennia-old footpaths, yet the numbers never manage to diminish the majesty of the place or its mystery. Though Petra was first and foremost a thriving Nabataean city, the magnificent funerary monuments and prolific references to gods, animals and mythological beings combined with the looming rockscapes and continual shifts of light and shade create an almost supernatural aura.

The city is also exceptionally well preserved. All but abandoned by the late 8th century, the architectural and artistic details of the monuments appear amazingly fresh. In many places, the carving is almost as sharp as it must have been 2,000 years ago.

Though Petra has helped shed much light on the relatively sophisticated and cosmopolitan culture of the Nabataeans, whose powerful kingdom-confederation stretched from the Red Sea all the way to the Euphrates, much remains shrouded in mystery. Exactly

when, why and how the kingdom went into decline, for example, is still unclear, though archaeologists believe that Petra still holds many secrets that are just waiting to be revealed. With a reputed 80 percent of the city still unexcavated, that's very likely.

VISITING PETRA TODAY

All visits to Petra begin and end at Wadi musa, the modern town that has grown up to serve Petra's tourism industry and where all transport, hotels and restaurants can be found.

Main Attractions
The Siq
The Treasury
Royal Tombs
High Place of Sacrifice

Map on page 224

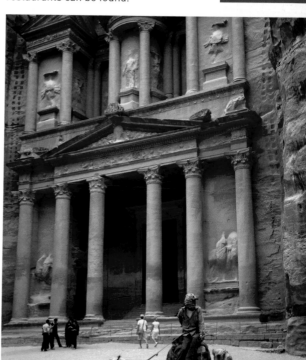

The Treasury (Al-khazneh).

The site of Petra itself is composed of nearly 850 registered monuments spread over an area of almost 100 sq km (38 sq miles). It would take weeks to visit all sites, dotted as they are on rock faces, mountain tops and at the bottom of wadis. A good idea is to decide how much time and inclination you have. All the main attractions can be seen fairly comfortably in two days, but see the box below for suggested itineraries if you're short of time. Don't forget to bring sunscreen, water and a hat.

Petra's Ticket Office (Maktab al-tadhakir; daily, summer 6am–6pm; winter 6am–4pm; tel: 03-215 7093; www.visit petra.jo; charge), currently residing in a temporary home among the souvenir shops near the gate.

PETRA BY NIGHT

For the Petra by Night experience (Mon, Wed, Thur 8.30–10.30pm; charge; tickets available from the visitor centre or some hotels), visitors are led from the main gate down a candlelit Siq to sit cross-legged in front of the Treasury. Here, a Bedouin musician and storyteller

Swirling colours of the sandstone.

perform. Rather like with Egypt's sound and light shows, traveller reaction is split: some are put off by the crowds (up to 800 in the high season) and disappointed by the performances, seeing the experience as little more than a money-spinner (tickets cost JD17; children under 10 free); others relish the chance of seeing Petra by moonlight and the Siq and Treasury lit by over 1,000 candles. For those seeking silence and solitude in which to contemplate the ruins, the best advice is to hang back from the crowds and make your own way through Petra; there's plenty of time before the entertainment starts.

PETRA'S HISTORY

Petra is best known for its dramatic tomb and temple facades that the Nabataean Arab inhabitants carved into the soft Nubian sandstone some 2,000 years ago. Since the city was "rediscovered" for the west in 1812 by Swiss explorer Johann Ludwig Burckhardt (see page 241), Western and Arab scholarship has identified over 800 monuments in the Petra area; all

⊙ ITINERARY IDEAS

Half day

Head for Petra's most famous monuments: the *Siq* and Treasury, followed by the High Place of Sacrifice and Obelisk. Later, head for the Royal Tombs and Colonnaded Street before stopping for a leisurely lunch at one of the eateries on the site, the upmarket Basin Restaurant or the good-value Nabaten Tent Restaurant.

Full day

After a refreshing lunch following the above itinerary, explore the city centre then head for the Snake Monument (Jabal al-tha'abin). After a cup of tea with the Bedouin, head for the Monastery before photographing the Royal Tombs at sunset. If you still have the energy, return to see Petra by moonlight as part of the Petra by Night experience.

but a few dozen were carved directly into the red-hued cliff-faces.

A closer look at the monuments, however, quickly reveals their hybrid, trans-Mediterranean nature. Petra was a dynamic, peaceful meeting place of people and ideas from the four corners of the earth; a timeless point of convergence of trade and commerce, communication and cultural exchanges from the leading Occidental and Oriental civilisations of the Mediterranean basin. Hellenistic and Egyptian architectural influences blend in with traditional Arab/Semitic local traditions, creating what we now refer to as Nabataean architecture. The Nabataeans also used a combination of languages, mainly their own Nabataean script, but also Greek, Aramaic and Latin languages, which were common among trading cultures in the 300 years before and after the time of Christ.

This cross-fertilisation of ideas that characterises Nabataean architecture and culture reflects the single most important force that gave rise to Nabataean civilisation: international trade. Historical knowledge of the birth of Nabataea is hazy. Most scholars accept that the Nabataeans were a semi-nomadic people from the northern Arabian Peninsula who migrated to southern Jordan in the 6th and 5th centuries BC to the lands of the former biblical kingdom of Edom. They were particularly successful in this semi-arid climate due to their exceptional ability to harness scarce water resources and make maximum use of camels for transport.

By the 4th century BC, Petra was establishing itself as a centre of Nabataean culture, first and foremost as a commercial entrepôt of a people whose economic base in southern Jordan relied on income from regional trade in bitumen, aromatics, salt, copper and agricultural goods.

The importance of trade to the Nabataeans explains their developed sense of diplomacy; it compelled them to resolve disputes with neighbours without warfare, so that security could be maintained and trade continued. As a result, Nabataean traders, professionals and public figures interacted

---

⊘ Fact

Even as recently as the late 1960s, Petra was seldom visited. An expanding tourist industry has since crept up around what is one of the most dramatic and engaging sites of the Middle East, bringing the mixed blessing of home comforts and easy access.

⊘ PETRA'S HIGHLIGHTS

It is advisable to start as early as you can to avoid the heat of the day and the crowds, and to get the best light for photos.

The Siq: Arguably the most spectacular entrance to any ancient site via a sheer chasm. Though many visitors hurry through (or trot by on carriages or donkeys), there's plenty of interest on the way. Around 15 minutes' easy walk from the visitor centre.

The Treasury: Petra's most visited (and photographed) monument; the first glimpse of this spectacular building spotlighted by the early morning sun as you emerge from the deep shade of the canyon is an unforgettable experience. Around 30 minutes' easy walk from the visitor centre. Carriages are now allowed to transport passengers the whole way.

The Royal Tombs or Theatre: Though long since emptied, the tombs (and theatre opposite) are atmospheric and stunningly set, commanding beautiful views of the wadis below. Around 20 minutes' easy walk from the Treasury to the Royal Tombs or Theatre. At sunset, the tombs turn several shades of pink.

High Place of Sacrifice and Obelisk: Get off the main beat and head heavenwards along the processional way for spectacular views above Petra. Around 45 minutes' moderately testing walk from the Treasury.

Petra City Centre: Many visitors don't make it here, but it's well worth continuing to the heart and soul of the Nabataean city. Around 30 minutes' easy walk from the Treasury, or 45 minutes' moderately challenging walk from the Obelisk to the Petra Archaeology Museum.

Monastery: Another iconic monument and as spectacular as its much-photographed facade suggests. Around 40 minutes' moderately challenging walk up 800 steps from the museum. The walk is best attempted in the afternoon, when the route is shady; be sure to avoid the midday heat.

Little Petra: Lying 8km (5 miles) northwest of Petra, you can walk from the town, hike from the monastery, drive or take a taxi here. Much less visited than its bigger sister, but just as interesting.

The Theatre.

The Obelisk Tomb in the Bab al-siq area.

regularly with nearby civilisations, and in so doing, absorbed elements of foreign culture into their own. Examples of this that can still be seen today include Roman Corinthian capitals, Hellenistic pedimented temple facades, Egyptian obelisk funerary monuments, Assyrian cultic high places, to name but a few. At the peak of its fortunes in the 1st centuries BC and AD, Petra was renowned for its sophisticated system of justice, humane monarchy and technological and commercial prowess.

After the Emperor Trajan formally annexed Petra and the Nabataean Kingdom into the Roman Empire in AD 106, Nabataean trade and culture continued to flourish for several hundred years after. But Petra seems to have declined gradually after the 4th century AD, and was dealt the coup de grâce, reduced to a shadow of its former urban splendour, after a series of devastating earthquakes between the 6th and the 8th centuries AD.

WALKING TOUR OF PETRA

Ruins and remains of Petra's remarkable past lie everywhere. To get the most out of your visit, keep a sharp eye out. Even around the visitor centre (Markaz al-zuwwar) and Ticket Office (Maktab al-tadhakir) lie remains: small graves and chambers cut into the ground; a large Nabataean tomb, today converted into a bar, stands next to the resthouse, and across from the Crowne Plaza Hotel, there is a large water reservoir which once fed the city centre through a rock-cut channel.

THE SIQ

From the visitor centre, the route descends into the site of Petra through the **Bab al-siq** area, passing three **jinn** ("ghost") **blocks** ❶ (saharij al-jinn), early Nabataean tombs, on the right, and the stately **Obelisk Tomb** ❷ (Qabr al-thu'ban) with its four obelisks on the left.

Facing it, on the other side of the path, is a large Greek/Nabataean bilingual funerary inscription. Just before reaching the dam, it's possible to walk up into the hills to the south to the **Al Madras Cultic Centre** ❸ (Al-ma'bad), with its altars, inscriptions, rock-cut monuments, water installations and many niches.

Today, as in Nabataean times, the dam at the entrance of the *Siq* prevents winter floodwaters from damaging the *Siq* and the city centre by diverting water through the Al Muthlim tunnel. The traces of the monumental arch just beyond the dam mark the start of the main route into Petra through the 1.25km (0.75-mile) -long *Siq* – a natural fissure in the mountain, which the Nabataeans developed into a stately entrance to their capital city. Look out for the remains of the paved Nabataean/Roman road, two water channels, and innumerable religious niches, stone god-blocks and inscriptions.

THE TREASURY

Suddenly, the *Siq* opens to the drama of the iconic **Treasury** ❹ (known locally as Al–khazneh), Petra's most famous monument. Its name reflects the loca egend that the urn on top of the monument held the pharaoh's treasure. This monumental tomb was probably built for the Nabataean King Aretas III in the Ist century BC. Its facade still shows a variety of classical and Nabataean architectural elements, including statues of gods, animals and mythological figures. The Outer Siq leads from here past the stalls of the local sand artists towards the theatre and the city centre, also passing several large tombs and *tricilinia* (singular: *triclinium*, a funerary banqueting hall with benches along three sides).

THE THEATRE

On the left just before the theatre are the 44 tombs that make up the eerie **Street of Facades** (Shari' al-wajhat). The 7,000-seat **Theatre ❺** (Al-masrah) was first constructed by the Nabataeans, probably in the early Ist century AD, but was refurbished by the Romans soon after their conquest in AD 106. The Romans evidently had little regard for the Nabataean tombs, which they sliced through to expand their beloved theatre.

ROYAL TOMBS

From the refreshment stands beyond the theatre, a restored Nabataean staircase ascends to the **Royal Tombs** (Al-maqabir al-malakiyah). Consisting of a dozen large burial chambers, they are thought to have housed the remains of Nabataean kings. The stairs lead to the most striking one, the **Urn Tomb ❻** (Qabr al-jarrah), with its subterranean vaults and its large internal chamber that was converted into a Byzantine church in AD 446–47. The southernmost of the Royal Tombs is the very well preserved **Tomb of Unayshu ❼** (Madfan 'nishu), a minister who served the Nabataean kings. North of the Urn Tomb is the heavily eroded but very colourful **Silk Tomb ❽** (Qabr al-harir), set back in a recess.

Beyond it is the equally eroded but somewhat busy-looking **Corinthian Tomb ❾** (Qabr al-kuranthi), which combines Nabataean and classical architectural styles, including a replica of the Treasury in its upper storey. Immediately north of it lies the huge, three-storey **Palace Tomb ❿** (Qabr al-qasr), with parts of its upper storey

Start as early as possible to avoid the heat and crowds.

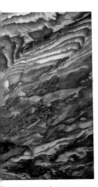

See the sandstone change colour at sunrise and sunset.

Colonnaded street and Royal Tombs.

constructed rather than carved. Just north of the Palace Tomb is a large Cistern into which flowed the water that came from the pool found today near the Petra Forum Hotel.

SEXTIUS FLORENTINUS TOMB

North of the pool lies the **Sextius Florentinus Tomb** ⑪ (Qabr siktius flurantinius), built around AD 130 for the Roman governor of the province of Arabia (note the faint Latin inscription and imperial eagle on the facade). A sacred processional way of staircases and corridors started from here and wound its way up to several religious High Places on the summit of the mountain.

NYMPHAEUM

As you walk from the theatre towards the city centre, a few minutes after passing the refreshment stands, you will see on your right the remains of the **Nymphaeum** ⑫, the public water fountain dedicated to the mythological nymphs who lived near rivers and water sources. Here, you can pick up the remains of the ancient colonnaded

street that was built around AD 106 along the lines of an earlier Nabataean gravel-surfaced roadway lined with buildings, probably shops. The street was used well into the 6th century, from when the existing street-side shops date.

THE GREAT TEMPLE

The street leads directly to the Arched Gate that formed the formal entrance into ancient Petra's most important temple precinct. Before you reach the Arched Gate, note a staircase leading south from the street towards an open area that scholars have called the "markets" of Petra. Also on the hill overlooking the street from the south is the collapsed **Great Temple** ⑬ (Al-ma'bad al-kabir), one of the few structures in Petra that were free-standing rather than carved into the rock.

Some scholars think this temple might in fact have served as the city's forum or *agora*, the heart of its business and administrative dealings, but recent excavations have failed to confirm this theory. The 7,000 sq metre

(75,300 sq ft) temple complex, guarded from the front by four 40-metre (130ft) -high columns (two of which remain intact in spite of the powerful earthquake that destroyed most of the temple), includes an upper and lower *temenos* (sanctuary) and a temple.

Further excavations unexpectedly revealed a small theatre – perhaps used for religious plays. The original colonnade was used to form an intercolumnar wall. This has led scholars to speculate that the site was originally home to a small shrine, although no supporting evidence has been found. Artefacts such as pottery shards dating from the early Nabataean era through to the Islamic period have further compounded the mystery surrounding the purpose and function of this enormous monument.

BYZANTINE CHURCH

The slopes north and south of the colonnaded street are covered with broken pottery shards, worked stones, wall lines and architectural elements that indicate the presence of many unexcavated structures – most probably public buildings that once formed part of the city centre. Overlooking the colonnaded street from the north side of the *wadi* are two excavated structures. A triple-apsed **Byzantine Church** ⑭ (Al-kanisah al-bizantiyah), discovered in 1993, has very fine and well-preserved mosaic floors. The elaborate decoration flies in the face of traditional assumptions about the fate of Petra during the 5th and 6th centuries: that the city had by then set into a steady period of decline.

Recent excavations here have uncovered dozens of papyrus scrolls, the only known written documents of Nabataean history in Petra. The scrolls, almost parallel in historical importance to the Dead Sea scrolls, were sadly badly damaged in a fire that also destroyed parts of the church. Nonetheless, researchers in 1998 completed the daunting task of unrolling and reading the singed scrolls, most of which document land ownership and dispute settlements. These scrolls have helped illuminate what is

Path to the Monastery.

otherwise a blank page in Petra's history. Today, they are stored under strict environmental control at the American Centre for Oriental Research in Amman, while the Jordanian Department of Antiquities works to provide a permanent storage and display area.

TEMPLE OF THE WINGED LIONS

Near the church and almost parallel with the Arched Gate is the **Temple of the Winged Lions** Ⓖ (M'bad al-asad al-mojannah), first built around AD 27 and dedicated to a consort of the supreme Nabataean male deity, Dushara. The **Arched Gate** Ⓖ (Al-bawwabah) – a common, three-entrance Graeco-Roman structure – had wooden doors that gave on to the *temenos* of the still-standing Qasr al-Bint temple, the city's leading sanctuary. Note the small carved panels flanking the central doorway of the Arched Gate, with their human busts, soldiers, animals and geometric designs, and the capitals lying on the ground, which bear animal head decorations. The **Baths of Petra**

The Monastery.

Ⓖ (Al-hammamat), still not accessible to visitors for safety reasons, stand immediately above and south of the gate. Opening on to the corner of the *temenos*, they may well have been used in association with religious rites conducted in the *temenos*.

The 200-metre (656ft) -long *temenos*, parallel to the *wadi*, originally included a low platform, shallow steps, a long double row of benches along its South Wall, and fine stone paving, all dating from the early 1st century AD.

QASR AL-BINT TEMPLE

The 23-metre (75ft) -high **Qasr al-Bint Temple** Ⓖ (Ma'bad qasr al-bint, or Qasr Bint Faroun, "Palace of Pharaoh's daughter) is Petra's most impressively constructed – as opposed to carved – structure, and dates from just before or after the time of Christ. Its open-air altar was used for public religious ceremonies. The temple faces north towards the Shara Mountains, which gave rise to the name of the leading Nabataean god, Dushara ("He of Shara"). The external walls were once

decorated with painted stucco, plaster panels, a Doric frieze, rosette medallions and bust reliefs, some of whose remains can still be seen. The temple was destroyed in the late 3rd century AD, perhaps when the forces of Queen Zenobia of Palmyra marched south to Egypt.

AL-HABIS

The small mountain overlooking Qasr al-Bint from the west is **Al-habis**. Head up to the processional route leading to the **Habis High Place** ⑲ (Habis al-makan al-'ali), about 250 metres/yards west. This is the easiest High Place to reach for visitors who cannot make more demanding climbs on foot. Like most High Places, this one consists of benches, a water basin or tank, an altar, an approach staircase and a dramatic, perch-like setting overlooking a *wadi*, in this case the Wadi al-siyagh (the site of a massive Nabataean rock quarry and the important Wadi al-siyagh spring).

On the east face of Al-habis (facing Qasr al-Bint) are two interesting monuments that are easy to reach.

The large **Unfinished Tomb** ⑳ shows how the Nabataeans carved from the top down; the adjacent **Columbarium** ㉑, a former Nabataean tomb retooled with hundreds of small niches, was used either to hold cremation urns or to raise pigeons and doves.

A small, 12th-century **Crusader Fortress** (Qal'at al-shawbak) on the summit of Al-habis can be reached easily in five minutes along a pathway and stairs from the south. The aerial view into central Petra is well worth the short climb to the fort's keep. The fort was a subsidiary lookout post for the bigger Crusader Fortress at al-wu'ayrah (located near the Crowne Plaza Hotel in Wadi musa).

UMM AL-BAIYARAH

Overlooking Al-habis from the southwest is the towering massif of **Umm al-baiyarah** ("Mother of Cisterns"), whose east face sports a variety of Nabataean tomb styles. The trek to the summit along an ancient processional way is demanding and requires a guide, but provides breathtaking panoramas of

Lion Monument in Wadi farasah.

Altar at the High Place of Sacrifice.

the entire Petra region. The summit retains the excavated remains of a small Edomite village from the 7th century BC Old Testament period, with impressive rock-cut water channels and Cisterns. The Nabataeans also used the summit and built a small temple and other structures along its east rim.

THE MONASTERY

The 45-minute ascent from the museum area to the **Monastery** ㉒ (known locally as Al-dayr) is best made in the afternoon, when much of the route is in shade. On the way up, you can visit several interesting monuments amidst stunning scenery: the **Lion Triclinium** (ma'idat akl al-asad); the **Wadi kharubah Biclinium** (room with two benches); the **Qattar al-dayr** natural rock ledge and water source, which the Nabataeans used as a sanctuary; and the **Hermitage** (Al-sawma'ah), a perch-like chamber with many carved crosses.

At the summit of the mountain is the open plain where the Nabataeans carved Al-dayr. This mid-1st century

The Soldier Tomb.

AD Nabatean temple or royal tom boasts Petra's largest facade (45 50 metres/130 by 164ft) and som impressive classical Nabataean cap tals. Like Qasr al-Bint, it also has a open-air altar (just north of the cour yard, near the steps to the urn on top the tomb, now blocked off). The nam Al-dayr ("the monastery") derives fro the crosses scratched in its rear wall

The adjacent plateau has many oth monuments, including tombs, wat works, *tricilinia*, decorated niches a a relief of two men with camels.

THE HIGH PLACE OF SACRIFICE

Petra's most important and perhap oldest major cultic facility is the **Hig Place of Sacrifice** ㉓ (Al-madhbah a 'ali), located on top of Jabal (Moun al-madhbah, 200 metres (650ft) abov the theatre. For those who have th time, the three-hour circular trip the High Place is recommended, complement their walk through th city centre. Such a trip is best made the early morning.

The route up via the Wadi al-mata-ah starts near the theatre, and follows the Nabataean processional way that passes by two huge stone-carved obelisks (probably representations of deities) just before reaching the High Place. The remains of the fort you have to walk through to reach the High Place are probably those of a Nabataean defensive/lookout facility, or perhaps the stately entrance to the High Place of Sacrifice itself.

The Nabataeans may have inherited the High Place of Sacrifice from the Edomites. This important religious facility comprised two adjacent altars and associated cultic installations, an open central court with a small raised platform for offerings, and shallow benches around three sides, and a nearby pool, water channels and drains probably used for animal sacrifices.

WADI FARASAH

From the High Place, you can return to the city centre via the **Wadi farasah**, with its collection of fine Nabataean monuments. You can see Nabataean inscriptions (near ground-level) in the rocks to your right just after starting down from the High Place. The first major monument you come upon is the **Lion Monument** ㉔ (Manhutat al-asad al-mojannah), a 5-metre (16ft)-long, rock-carved cultic fountain; a few metres away is a small stone-cut altar. The water that emerged from the lion's mouth reached the city centre in a water channel that ran parallel with the staircase from the Lion Monument that winds down to the Wadi farasah.

The first monument in the *wadi* is the **Garden Temple Complex** ㉕ (Ma'bad al-hadiqah). It includes a small shrine, and an associated terrace complex above the temple that contained a once-arched room and a large plastered Cistern. Water reached the city centre from here through a distribution system of Cisterns, channels and ceramic pipes.

The next complex in Wadi farasah is the **Roman Soldier Tomb** ㉖ (Qabr aljundi al-rumani) and its *triclinium*. Note the three statues in Roman military dress in niches on the tomb facade.

⊙ Fact

Rain – causing flash flooding in some of the wadis – still presents danger in Petra, so some areas are off-limits in winter. If hiking off the main tourist routes, always keep an eye on the weather, particularly from late October to March, and beware the narrower valleys and wadis. If in doubt, engage a guide.

Young Bedouins near Petra.

Bedouin silver jewellery on sale at Petra.

The Bduul tribe inhabit Petra.

The *triclinium* sports Petra's most spectacular interior today, due to the weathering of the rock. Further down Wadi farasah on your right is the **Renaissance Tomb** (Qabr al-nahdah), with its delicate facade of Nabataean capitals and six urns, and then the **Broken Pediment Tomb** (Qabr al-muthallath al-maksur), perched on a raised recess.

The Wadi farasah trail towards the city centre passes through an area full of rock-cut tombs and houses, crosses the low remains of a small gate within the South City Wall, and finally meanders through the area of **Al-katutah**, which is thought to have been used as the town rubbish dump in the 2nd century AD (that's why there is so much broken pottery on the ground).

The path then passes the rocky summit of Al-zantur before reaching **Faroun's (Pharaoh's) Pillar** (Khaznat fer'awn), one of two pillars which marked the entrance to a Nabataean temple that lies unexcavated in the hillside. It is possible that this structure was located next to a road that entered Petra from the south and that brought camels and goods to the so-called "markets" above the colonnaded street. Recent excavations in this region have uncovered domestic and cultic structures, including a Byzantine church, dating from the 1st to the 6th century AD.

OUTER PETRA SIGHTS

From this area south of the city centre, those still with the energy and inclination can head off on foot or horseback to visit two distant sites, each requiring over two hours to reach. The Nabataean suburb of **Wadi sabrah** still shows the remains of a small theatre, several major buildings, a possible baths, a water catchment system, Cisterns, tombs, niches and other remains from the Nabataean and Roman periods.

At the highest summit in the Petra region – 1,350 metres (4,430ft) above sea level – is the 14th-century **shrine of Nebi Harun** (Mazar al-nabi Harun, the Prophet Aaron), which enjoys a marvellous view of the region. The white dome of the shrine can be seen from most areas in and around Petra.

On the opposite, north side of the city centre, visitors can also explore some slightly out of the way districts of Petra such as **Mughar al-nasara** (the "Christian" or "Nazarene caves", so called because of the crosses that are carved into some tomb walls). This unspoilt area boasts many tombs, Cisterns and altars, traces of the ancient northern entrance to Petra, a rare *triclinium* adorned with four shields and two Medusa heads and some of Petra's most bizarre and colourful natural rock formations. The more adventurous and fit can exit Petra from Mughar al-nasara by walking for about an hour to the north and then east around Jabal al-khubathah and parallel to the rock-cut water channel that linked the pools near the Crowne Plaza Hotel and the Palace Tomb.

A kilometre (0.5 miles) north of Mughar al-Nasara is the new Bduul village at **Umm Sayhun** (see page 236), near an ancient quarry, cultic altars, tomb

and hydraulic installations. And 15 minutes by foot west of Mughar al-nasara, on the other side of Wadu umm sayhun, is **Conway Tower** (Burj qunuway). This 25 metre (82ft) -diameter tower fortified the northwest corner of the Nabataean town walls and overlooks the entire region.

Two other outlying districts well worth visiting are located immediately west of Mughar al-nasara. **Wadi Turkumaniyah** has the very important **Turkmaniyya Tomb** (Qabr al-Turkumaniyah), on whose upper facade is the longest known Nabataean inscription. It mentions the facilities that a proper Nabataean tomb complex should have: tomb, *triclinium*, Cistern, courtyard, portico, gardens, houses, terraces and other facilities (most of which can be seen at the Roman Soldier Tomb or the Tomb of Unayshu). West of Turkumaniyah is **Jabal al-mu'aysirah**, a rarely visited area full of tombs, water works, cultic installations and processional ways.

AROUND PETRA

Within half an hour's drive from Petra are several interesting archaeological sites that fill in important historical gaps in the past 10,000 years of human civilisation in the Middle East. Three of these sites are located alongside the paved road that heads north from the visitor centre and past the Crowne Plaza Hotel.

Wu'ayrah Crusader Fortress ㉘ (Qal'at al-wu'ayrah), west of the road about a kilometre (0.5 miles) north of the hotel, was built in the early 12th century and abandoned when Salah' ad Din (Saladin) defeated the Crusaders in Jordan in 1189. The Crusaders called this region La Vallée de Moïse (the Valley of Moses), a name that retains a link to the present Arabic name of the town of **Wadi musa** (which also means the Valley of Moses). The dramatic entrance bridge over a precipitous moat (not for the fainthearted) leads into a roughly rectangular fortress, still sporting some of its defensive walls, towers, vaults, Cisterns and internal structures, including a possible church.

LITTLE PETRA

Known locally as Al-siq al-barid or **Little Petra**, this site lies 10 minutes

Painted House, Little Petra.

by car to the north. It was a prosperous "suburb" of Petra located at the junction of ancient caravan routes that linked Petra with the Wadi 'arabah/Dead Sea region, Gaza, the Palestine coast, Egypt and the Mediterranean basin. Several immense Cisterns carved into the rocks are still used today by local livestockers.

The name Siq al-barid comes from the miniature *siq* (fissure) that gives access to a splendid collection of tombs, temples, *triclinia*, houses, Cisterns, water channels, niches, cultic installations, staircases and other structures. One small *biclinium* (room with two benches) still has the remains of 1st-century fresco paintings with floral motifs, birds, and classical mythological figures, including Pan and Eros.

Five minutes to the southwest (by rough dirt track) is the Neolithic village of **Al-baydah**. This early farming and livestock settlement still retains standing walls, staircases, hearths, grinding stones, plastered floors, doorways and cultic installations

dating from 7000–6500 BC, a period of transition for humans from nomadic hunter-gatherers to year-round settled farmers. Neolithic fans can also visit a similar excavated site at **Basta**, half an hour to the southeast.

UDHRUH AND AL-DAJNIYAH

Fifteen minutes by car east of Petra is the important ancient site at **Udhruh**, whose spring and strategic location were the main reasons for its almost uninterrupted settlement since the Iron Age, approximately 3,000 years ago. The principal remains above ground today are the external walls and towers of a Roman legionary fortress, though the site was also important in the Nabataean and early Islamic eras.

Another Roman fortress can be visited at **Al-dajniyah**, a 10-minute drive over a desert track southwest of the junction of the Desert Highway and the east–west road to Shawbak and Petra. Its standing fortifications and water system are particularly impressive. Like most of the forts along the southeastern frontier of the Roman Empire, it was probably built in the 2nd century AD, and abandoned during the decline of Roman power in this area between the 5th and 6th centuries.

AL-TAYBAH

A more recent historical period – the late Ottoman era of the end of the 19th/early 20th century – is well represented at **Al-taybah**, a 10-minute drive south of Petra. This traditional Jordanian village has been renovated into a pleasant tourist village equipped with modern amenities but still retaining the buildings and atmosphere of early 20th-century Jordan. Similar traditional village architecture is visible throughout the Petra area; a good easily accessible example is **Khirbet Nawafleh**, on the north side of Wadi musa town.

Bedouin hawk souvenirs and coffee at Petra.

BURCKHARDT

It was with some reticence that a young Swiss explorer summed up his visit to Jordan, on 22 August 1812: "It appears very probable," he pronounced, "that the ruins in Wady Mousa are those of ancient Petra."

Johann Ludwig Burckhardt was the first Westerner for 600 years to see the capital of the ancient Nabataeans. Burckhardt was born in Lausanne in 1784, the son of a wealthy merchant. After attending university in Germany, he spent two years in London. With no work and dwindling finances, he eventually had a fruitful introduction to a certain Sir Joseph Banks, a member of the Association for Promoting the Discovery of the Interior Parts of Africa. The association had hit on the idea of exploring caravan routes as a means of finding the source of the River Niger. Undeterred by the death or disappearance of everyone so far sent on this mission, Burckhardt offered his services and was accepted.

After a crash course in Arabic at Cambridge University, he set off in March 1809 for Syria, where he perfected his Arabic and adopted the clothes and manners of his chosen alias, Ibrahim ibn Abdullah, a Moorish trader. Once master of the local dialect, he began travelling with the Bedouin. Burckhardt explored large areas of Syria and Lebanon, taking copious notes as he went, but always secretly since discovery could have cost him his life. During interludes in Aleppo, he studied Islam, wrote a treatise on Bedouin customs, a classification of the Bedouin tribes on the Syrian borders, and various notes on the geography of the region.

In spring 1812, Ibrahim ibn Abdullah finally left Syria for Cairo. En route he visited Jarash, Amman and Al-karak, where he was delayed for 20 days by the sheikh, who demanded protection money. At Al-tafulah, he detached himself from this "treacherous friend", and continued southward with a Bedouin guide called Hamid.

After leaving Shawbak, Burckhardt wanted to deviate from the route agreed with his Bedouin guide in order to see some ruins in the valley of Wadi musa that the local people had spoken of with admiration. Knowing that this would arouse suspicion, he feigned a vow to sacrifice a goat at the shrine of Harun (Aaron) at the end of the valley. With a local guide and a goat for the sacrifice, he made his way through the ruins towards Jabal Harun (Mount Aaron), concealing his interest in the monuments lest he gave himself away. Entering the Treasury, he passed by the Theatre and observed the Royal Tombs, noting everything in his journal.

The sun was setting as Burckhardt and his guide reached Jabal Harun and the guide became increasingly agitated at the lateness of the hour, so Burckhardt reluctantly agreed to sacrifice the goat on the spot. The next day, he resumed his journey south, but regretted not going to the top of the mountain. As he wrote: "a traveller ought, if possible, to see everything with his own eyes." He added, with characteristic modesty, "Whether or not I have discovered the remains of the capital of Arabia Petraea, I leave (it) to the decision of Greek scholars." The Greek scholars confirmed that he had.

Johann Ludwig Burckhardt (1784–1817).

Seven-pinnacled mountain of Jabal al-mazmar.

Umm Fruth Rock Bridge.

WADI RUM

Wadi Rum is one of Earth's most spectacular topographies. It also has long historical associations: pilgrims, traders, herdsmen and caravans have journeyed here for millennia; few have been untouched by it.

From the heights of Ras al-naqab, the land falls away abruptly to the south to the Quweirah plain, an expanse of pinkish sandy desert some 600 metres (1,970ft) below. Pinnacles and spires of rock thrust upwards from the desert floor, stacked one behind another into a distant haze. Coming from the north, this is the first view of the vast tract of southeastern Jordan known as Wadi Rum. The desert, the space, the sky and the silence are colossal, inspiring T.E. Lawrence in Seven Pillars of Wisdom to pen perhaps the most evocative description of Rum: "vast, echoing and godlike."

The area takes its name from the largest and grandest of a whole network of *wadis* (valleys), which for millennia offered the easiest passage through the area to the nomadic Bedouin and trading caravans en route to or from the Arabian peninsula. "Rum" itself is believed to derive from the ancient Semitic word *irum*, meaning "high" or "heights", a probable reference to the enormous crags that erupted from the sands millions of years ago.

Rum is also a window through which one can view the history of the earth itself, for the stratification of some 600 million years has been identified here. Keep an eye for traces of earliest life in

the shape of animals and plants fossilised in the cliffs.

Keep an eye out for living wildlife too. It may look inhospitable and barren, but a surprising number and variety of life makes its home here, ranging from dozens of bird species to the elegant but elusive ibex and dainty Arabian sand cat. There are also several hundred species of wild plants and herbs that have been used for millennia in traditional Bedouin medicine.

Around 6,500 Bedouin, mainly of the Howeitat tribe, are thought to live

Main Attractions

Visitor centre
Nabataean Temple and
  inscriptions
Lawrence's House and
  Red Sands
Ayn abu aineh
Lawrence's Spring
Rock bridges

Map on page 250

Camel and 4WD are the best modes of transport.

⊘ **Tip**

To be sure of what they're getting (particularly in the busy high season), many travellers prefer to book camps and guides at Wadi Rum in advance. Consider carefully how much time you will have, exactly what you want to see and your budget, and get all details confirmed by email. One of the best camps is run by Eid Hamdan, who also provides delicious traditional meals and can organise jeep tours, camel treks, hikes and rock climbing (tel: 00962 777 545 119; email: eid_hamdane@yahoo.com).

here (1,500 in Wadi Rum; 5,000 in Al-disi), though many are now settled or semi-settled in the villages around Wadi Rum. With 105,000 visitors in 2016, tourism is a lucrative business and many Bedouin today serve as guides or run the camps of the area.

In 2011, Wadi Rum Protected Area was declared by Unesco as a World Heritage Site.

VISITING WADI RUM

From the Desert Highway, a turn-off located about 10km (6 miles) south of the little town of Al-quwayrah and 42km (26 miles) north of Al-'aqabah heads east across the desert to Wadi Rum. After about 18km (11 miles) of increasingly spectacular scenery, you reach the **visitor centre** (daily, summer 7.30am–7.30pm, winter 8am–4pm; tel: 03-209 0600; www.wadirum.jo). From here, admission to the Wadi Rum Protected Area is strictly controlled and all vehicles must have authorisation from the visitor centre. Though you are permitted to drive your own 4WD or walk alone in Wadi

Rum, it is not recommended as it's very easy to get disorientated and the area in places requires skilled driving.

At the centre is the Guides Office, shops selling decent-quality local crafts and jewellery, an excellent Interpretation Hall (daily, summer 8am–7pm, winter 8am–4pm; charge), an auditorium showing a nine-minute film introducing Wadi Rum, its history and geology, and a restaurant.

For trips into Wadi Rum, there are really two options: if you have prebooked a guide/driver or accommodation at a camp, the guide/driver or camp manager will meet you here. If you haven't and wish either to take a tour or overnight in a camp, then the visitor centre can allot you a driver (drivers have formed a co-operative and work by rota) and recommend a camp. All the drivers and guides are official and regulated, prices are posted clearly on boards, and 50 per cent of profits are ploughed back into the co-op.

Trips are available by 4WD, horse or camel or a mixture of several, and can

⊘ GUIDES IN WADI RUM

Though many visitors content themselves with a visit to the visitor centre and a brief foray into the desert, an excursion deeper into Wadi Rum is well worthwhile, on foot, by camel or by 4WD. Though many sites are well-trodden on the tourist trail, nothing detracts from the sheer size, scale and majesty of Wadi Rum. If you can, spend at least a day and a night here. Prices are per vehicle (with driver), so forming a group can keep costs down. Be wary of unofficial guides or touts operating outside Wadi Rum (including Petra); many visitors lured by cut-price offers end up sorely disappointed.

Attayak Ali (tel: 0795 899723; www.bedouinroads.com) is considered one of the best climbing and adventure guides.

Eid Ali (tel: 0776 924937; www.wadirumdiscovery.com) specialises in longer stays for hiking and scrambling and also offers bivouac camping. Jeep tours also available.

Attayak Aouda (tel: 0795 834736; www.rumguides.com) has also been highly recommended as a climbing guide in Wadi Rum.

Mazied Attayak (tel: 0777 304501; www.mzied.com) offer

jeep tours into the Wadi Rum Protected Area, as well as trekking and scrambling with local Bedouin guides, and trekking and camping with camels.

Sabbah Eid (tel: 03-201 6238) has also been recommended as an official climbing guide.

Salem Goblan (tel: 0795 319996) specialises in camel treks as well as trekking and scrambling accompanied by local Bedouin guides.

Mohammed Hammad (tel: 0777 359856; www.bedouinguides.com) is currently the only guide offering technical climbing here. He has climbed with a number of professional foreign guides (mainly French – and he has also climbed with them in France).

Attayak Hammed (tel: 0779 934985; www.wildbedouinlife.com) offers reputable jeep and camel tours.

Mohammad Hussein (tel: 0777 472074; www.wadirumadventures.com) can arrange, on request, hikes, jeep tours and camel rides deep into the desert.

Muhammad Moutlaq (tel: 0777 424837) offers jeep and camel tours.

last anything from an hour's excursion to a six-day trip (or more) by camel to Al-'aqabah à la T.E. Lawrence, with all meals and camping equipment included. There's a wide choice of sleeping options also: from air-conditioned tent-cabins to a mattress and blanket under the stars; from "party camps" complete with DJs at weekends, to desert-silent camps amid the dunes. Sleeping under a starry sky in the deep desert of Wadi Rum is for most travellers a highlight of their trip to Jordan.

The centre can also advise on organised activities, such as hiking, canyoning and rock climbing. More recently, hot-air balloon trips and microlight flights have started being offered (ask at Beit Ali Lodge, which also rents out quad bikes and sand yachts).

The best time to visit Wadi Rum is spring (March and April) and autumn (October to November). Winter can be bitterly cold at night (bring coats, gloves and hats) and summer breathtakingly hot.

THE HISTORY OF RUM

Today, Wadi Rum lies in the territory of the Howeitat, one of the largest Bedouin tribes in Jordan, who claim descent both from the Prophet Muhammad and from the Nabataeans. They are no longer fully nomadic as they live in villages in winter, but in the long, parched summers many still move around with their flocks and tents in search of pasture.

But early humans in their most primitive Paleolithic form were in southern Jordan at least 400,000 years ago. Water was plentiful from the springs in Wadi Rum, and they lived by hunting the abundant wildlife with stone-tipped weapons, and by gathering fruits and roots in a savannah-like terrain dotted with trees. Very slowly, through the Paleolithic millennia, the inhabitants' pattern of life evolved from one of almost perpetual motion to a nomadic lifestyle in which temporary camps were re-inhabited periodically, probably on a seasonal basis.

From 9000 BC on, Neolithic families and groups began to introduce

> **⊙ Fact**
>
> There are numerous fossil traces of marine creatures which once lived in the shallow tidal waters that recurrently inundated much of Jordan in the Paleozoic and Mesozoic eras.

Exploring Wadi Rum by camel.

agriculture and started raising domestic animals. Increasingly, in the Chalcolithic period (4500–3300 BC), semi-permanent seasonal agricultural settlements were established throughout the complex network of *wadis*. Other groups opted for a more pastoral way of life, and continued their nomadic life in search of pasture for their flocks and herds. They ranged over a huge territory, in winter often penetrating deep into the Arabian peninsula. Some became traders, and travelled north, south, east and west, exchanging items of value with the more acquisitive sedentary groups.

The Nabataeans may have started visiting Rum in the 6th century BC, but there is no concrete evidence of their presence until the late 4th century BC, when they controlled all the lucrative trade routes through their territory in southern Jordan: frankincense and myrrh from Arabia Felix (modern-day Yemen), spices from India and purple cloth from Phoenicia. Through an astute combination

of trade and trade protection, the Nabataeans grew immensely wealthy. Though their main centre was at Petra, they also had settlements in the Hejaz at Madain Saleh in modern-day Saudi Arabia, in Sinai and the Negev in today's Israel, and here in Wadi Rum.

The Nabataeans were not just talented traders; more importantly, these erstwhile nomads had acquired a mastery of water management that enabled them to create settlements on a scale far larger than many of their contemporaries. To provide for their settlement in Wadi Rum, for example, they built an aqueduct from the most abundant spring, 'Ayn al-shallalah, to a reservoir in the valley below. The Nabataeans also extensively used wells and water channels to irrigate and water their fields and settlements.

They also constructed three great dams, the largest at Bir Ram al-'atuq, just south of the road from Al-quwayrah, about 6km (4 miles) west of the Rum Al-disi junction; another on the

Sudanese man training camels for racing.

est face of Jabal abu judaydah; and a ird just east of Jabal mahraj. Towards e end of his reign, the last Nabataean ng, Rabbel II (AD 71–106), also built a mple in Rum, dedicated to the godss Allat.

HE GEOLOGY OF RUM

he valley floors lie some 900–1,000 etres (2,950–3,280ft) above sea vel, and the great sandstone crags se sheer a further 500–750 metres ,640–2,460ft). Jabal ram, at 1,754 etres (5,755ft) above sea level nd today a popular destination for imbers), is the highest peak in the rea and the second highest in Joran; the magnificent Jabal umm alshirin, with its 20 domes which gave se to its name "Mother of 20", just cross the *wadi*, qualifies as the third ighest, a metre less than Jabal ram.

The cataclysm which 30 million ears ago created the Great Rift Valy – running from southern Turkey rough Syria, the Jordan Valley, the ead Sea, Wadi 'arabah, the Red Sea nd into East Africa (see page 192) – so forced up the great layers of rock ere, the deposits of a wide range of eological periods. As the rocks seted, they were rearranged into the trange and complex formations that e see today, in a pattern of crissossing fault lines. Interestingly, most nes run NNE–SSW, roughly parallel the Wadi 'arabah rift, but these are aversed by counter-faults running E–SW, NW–SE, E–W and N–S.

The rocks were thrown up higher in e west, nearest the Rift Valley, and l the strata tilt down eastwards. In e western areas, the granite rises bove the *wadi* floor beneath a man- e of younger sandstones, and sevral **springs,** including the famous awrence spring near the Wadi Rum esthouse, are found here, particu- rly along the east face of Jabal ram. hese springs were created by winr rainfall penetrating the porous sandstone until hitting the sloping layer of impermeable granite, whence the water seeped down into the open and formed pools and waterfalls sur- rounded by lush foliage.

CONSERVATION AND WILDLIFE

In the late 1980s, Jordan's Royal Soci- ety for the Conservation of Nature (RSCN; www.rscn.org.jo; see page 105) declared the establishment of sev- eral new wildlife reserves, including a 510 sq km (197 sq miles) one at Rum. Constructing an enclosure in this area measuring 75 sq km (29 sq miles), the society then transferred into it some of the Arabian oryx at Shaumari near Azraq (see page 274).

Officially protected since 1988, the management of the park was taken over in 2004 by ASEZ – the Al-'aqabah Special Economic Zone – which seeks both to conserve the natural environ- ment of Wadi Rum and the wildlife that inhabits it, and to assist the social and economic needs of the Bedouin who make their home here. Realising that the conservation and

Wadi Rum contains several hundred species of wild plants and herbs.

management of Wadi Rum is impossible without the cooperation (and knowledge) of the Bedouin, it aims to promote tourism to their benefit – they are permitted to work as guides and manage the tourist camps both inside and outside the reserve.

Although Wadi Rum sadly does not boast the wildlife it had even a few decades ago, there is still plenty of life around. Sit silent and still for a while at sunset or sunrise, and animals and birds often appear from nowhere. Hyrax, hares, fennec foxes, jackals, hedgehogs, jerboas and gerbils come out at dusk, as does the Arabian sand cat, an elusive nocturnal hunter. Nubian ibex and gazelle, once abundant, now survive in residual herds. Meanwhile, some animals continue to be reintroduced. In 2009, and again in 2012, 20 Arabian oryx were released. Having successfully bred, their off-spring were released at the beginning of 2013.

Marvel at the huge rock formations.

More easily seen is the birdlife frequenting Rum, including desert larks, crested larks, pale rock sparrows and

bright pink male Sinai rosefinche along with their somewhat dowdi wives. Look out also for birds of pre catching the thermals above th rocky outcrops.

A TOUR OF WADI RUM

From the rear terrace of the visit centre, there's a terrific view due sou onto the great sandy avenue of Wa Rum itself. In front lies the enormou seven-pinnacled mountain of **Jabal a mazmar**, recently spuriously rename "The Seven Pillars of Wisdom" in ho our of Lawrence – though not actual mentioned by him. Cashing in on th European (and particularly Britis fascination with the 19th-century arm British officer (see page 57) and i tourism potential, references to Lav rence today are everywhere.

About 6km (4 miles) before the vis tor centre, a sign points off the roa to the **Bayt Ali Lodge**, a well-run ar comfortable resthouse and restaura lying outside the Wadi Rum Protecte Area but set amidst a comparab grand desert landscape.

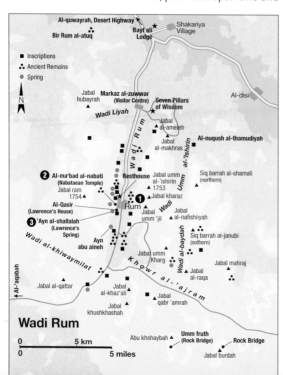

WADI RUM VILLAGE

About 7km (4.25 miles) beyond the visitor centre, in the heart of Wadi Rum itself, is **Rum village ❶**, a small settlement of mostly breeze-block houses that has mushroomed since tourism to the area began in the 1980s. The village is centred on a small **fort,** one of a string built in 1933 by Glubb Pasha (see page 65) as an outpost of the Desert Patrol (now the Bedouin Police).

On the village outskirts is the **Resthouse**, which looks across the sandy *wadi* to the great wall of Jabal umm al-'ishirin. It offers accommodation, including tents, and a restaurant.

NABATAEAN TEMPLE AND INSCRIPTIONS

Around 300 metres/yards due west of the resthouse is a path leading to the scant remains of a **Nabataean Temple ❷** (Al-ma'bad al-nabati), which were discovered in 1933 and excavated in 1997. Nearby, on the rock face, are some **Nabataean inscriptions** that date to the 2nd century AD. Behind the temple lie the remains of what are believed to be **baths** and if so, rank as the oldest baths in Jordan.

LAWRENCE'S HOUSE AND RED SANDS

Just south of the temple lie the rather underwhelming remains of a house where Lawrence is said to have stayed during his participation in the Arab Revolt. The **Lawrence House** (Al-Qasir) actually lies on an ancient Nabataean water Cistern and various inscriptions can be found nearby. There are also good views of the red sands from here, particularly at sunset.

AYN ABU AINEH AND THUMUDIC INSCRIPTIONS

Though sometimes passed off by unscrupulous guides as Lawrence's Spring, the **Ayn abu aineh** is easier to reach (lying around 2.5km/1.5 miles due south of Lawrence's House and navigable by 4WD) but less scenic though no less historical. Piped from the mountain into a large tank, the spring has watered animals for millennia, and behind the tank are a series of boulders containing

Red sand dune.

Well-preserved rock inscriptions can be seen at the Al-nafishiiyah and Al-ameleh sites.

Many tour guides are Bedouin who have lived in Rum all their lives.

good **Thumudic inscriptions**, perhaps by bored herdsmen waiting for their charges to quench their thirst.

LAWRENCE'S SPRING ('AYN AL-SHALLALAH)

About 6km (3.5 miles) east of Ayn abu aineh at the base of the mountain-side lies an entry to the Wadi Shallalah. A path climbs the boulders to the **'Ayn al-shallalah spring and pool ❸**, around a 20-minute walk one way from the temple.

Several springs in Wadi Rum have Nabataean rock-cut channels to divert the water into Cisterns, forming useful waterholes for thirsty caravans. T.E. Lawrence found one along with some Nabataean inscriptions when he bathed in the pool of 'Ayn al-shallalah, and it has been named after him almost ever since.

AL-NAFISHIIYAH AND AL-AMELEH INSCRIPTIONS

Around 4km (2.5 miles) due north of Ayn al-shallalah, at the base of Jabal al-nafishiiyah, are the **Al-nafishiiyah**

inscriptions, where a large number of well-preserved Thumudic inscriptions can be seen etched into the rock face. Further etchings can be seen at the **Al-ameleh inscriptions** site around 8km (5 miles) north of Al-nafishiiyah; these are also well-preserved, vibrant and charming.

ROCK BRIDGES

Exposure to rain and wind has sculpted Wadi Rum's sandstone into weird and wonderful shapes that look at times like giant mushrooms, organ-pipes or dripping candle wax. In some places, this process of erosion has created unbroken arches of rock over a canyon. One such place is **Jabal burdah** to the far south-east of the Protected Area (with care you can scramble to the top); others include the **Umm Fruth Rock Bridge** around 7km (4.25 miles) due west, which can also be climbed; the bridge known as **Little Rock Bridge** (Rakhabat al Wadak locally) lying around 4km (2.5 miles) south of Lawrence's spring; and the arch at **Jabal Kharaz**, in a remote area some 27km (17 miles) north of Rum village.

The Little Rock Bridge.

📷 THE BEDOUIN INHERITANCE

The romantic notion of camel-riding nomads may be a far cry from the Bedouin of today, but their deeply valued traditions and culture endure.

Whether kings or coffee-sellers, the very great majority of Jordanians boast Bedouin ancestry and many of their customs and way of thinking today stem directly from Bedouin traditions. Less than a century ago, Jordan's towns were little more than villages inhabited by recently settled or semi-settled Bedouin who also interacted regularly with those still leading a fully nomadic existence. In exchange for provisions, visiting Bedouin would sell animals and animal produce. Even today, you'll see Bedouin tents dotted all over Jordan. Young men in their 20s recall childhoods herding goats or living under goat-hair awnings.

Bedouin society is perceived as honourable and its way of life as an ideal. Even in fashionable parts of Amman, its influences still pervade everything, from jewellery and clothing to weddings and food.

HIERARCHY AND TERRITORY

The social organisation of Bedouin society centres on the tribe. In exchange for absolute allegiance, members receive protection, patronage and connections. The head of the tribe, the "sheikh", is drawn from the leading family and is the arbiter of disputes, the official greeter of guests and the tribe's representative to outsiders.

The major tribes of Jordan include the Beni Khaled in the north, Beni Sakhr in the centre and the al Howeitat in the south. All grazing land in the Badia belongs to the government and is theoretically available to all, but undrawn tribal boundaries established over hundreds of years latently separate tribes and their territories.

Bedouin man and his mother drinking tea at a camp in Rum. Coffee is also drunk from small, handleless cups.

Bedouin rugs, camel bags and saddle blankets make great souvenirs. Some of their patterns haven't changed since biblical times.

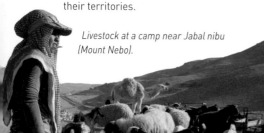

Livestock at a camp near Jabal nibu (Mount Nebo).

Living in goat-hair tents doesn't mean the Bedouin don't have access to mobile phones and the internet.

The Camel Corps

Perhaps the greatest move at integrating the Bedouin into modern society has been made by the army. As fighting and feuds were always a major part in the lives of tribesmen, it was perhaps natural that their warring nature and skills should be put to good use in the defence of the realm. Thus the army has often offered training and opportunities to Bedouin who have otherwise missed out on education.

The value of having Bedouin as the backbone of the army, especially in the rugged "Hajaneh" Camel Corps, is acknowledged by Jordan's urban majority, many of whom also harbour a latent romantic fondness for the perceived simplicity of desert life. The search for work and opportunity as well as the perceived draws of the city and what's seen as an easier life, is seeing a further migration of Bedouin to the towns.

...net connection in the Bedouin village of Rum. Not all ...uin are nomadic; some are semi-nomadic, while ...s live in villages.

...uin jewellery. The designs for necklaces, headpieces ...mulets often incorporate Islamic symbols or Koranic ...s to bring good luck.

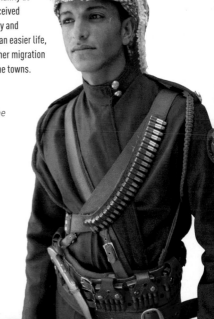

Member of the Royal Guard.

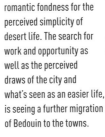

One of Al-'aqabah's marinas.

The golden sand and clear waters of Al-ʿaqabah.

AL-'AQABAH

The warm waters of Al-'aqabah are a perennial draw for Jordanians and tourists alike, and beneath the pleasure boats, swimmers and water-sport enthusiasts, a serene world teems with marine life.

As Jordan's only outlet to the sea, the port city of **Al-'aqabah** evokes a feeling of freedom and a promise of fun and relaxation to most Jordanians, who flock to their country's only real beach resort whenever possible. It is known for its clean, sandy beaches and agreeable climate, especially in the spring, autumn and winter. When the temperature in Amman is a chilly 0–10°C (32°–52°F), the temperature in Al-'aqabah can be a pleasant 25°C (77°F).

Other visitors, especially the growing bands of Italian, German, British, East European and Russian tourists, come for the offshore attractions. For like its Israeli counterpart, Eilat, a pebble's-throw across the bay, and Egypt's Sharm el-Sheikh, Al-'aqabah offers world-class scuba-diving on the preserved coral reefs of the Red Sea (see page 268).

Al-'aqabah is situated on the tip of the Gulf of Aqaba, enclosed by barren, pink- and mauve-tinted mountains rich in phosphates. To the south, a string of dark-golden beaches stretch about 27km (17 miles) along the length of Jordan's coast to the Saudi Arabian border.

AL-'AQABAH'S STRATEGIC VALUE

Despite its resort feel today, Al-'aqabah's chief importance has always been as a commercial port. Jordan's most strategically important city has also been crucial to other countries in the region: it served as a lifeline to Iraq throughout the eight-year Iran–Iraq War, which paralysed the Iraqi port of Basra, and was the main point of entry for goods moving into Iraq. As the number and variety of ships docking at the port and the massive truck park on Al-'aqabah's approach road testify, the city is still the major hub of sea-to-land transport routes in Jordan and beyond. Ferries departing

Main Attractions

Ayla
Al-'aqabah Fort
Al-'aqabah Church
Al-'aqabah passegiata
Red Sea diving and
  snorkelling

Map on page 261

Water-seller in traditional costume.

from Al-'aqabah also provide an important passenger link to other countries, including Egypt.

To first-time visitors, Al-'aqabah's proximity to the Israeli city of Eilat is astonishing. Indeed, at night the lights of the two cities seem to merge into one twinkling curve, and with the opening of the Wadi 'arabah border crossing between Jordan and Israel, visitors to either country can easily visit the neighbouring resorts. Al-'aqabah also vividly demonstrates Jordan's position in the thick of the Arab world: from here, one can gaze simultaneously on four countries: Israel, Egypt, Saudi Arabia and Jordan.

AL-'AQABAH'S HISTORY

Al-'aqabah's history goes back at least to biblical times. According to the Old Testament, King Solomon built a naval base at Ezion Geber, which is thought to lie some 3km (1.8 miles) north of modern Al-'aqabah, next to the Jordanian-Israeli border.

On the public beach when night brings cooler temperatures.

From Ezion Geber, the Old Testament king traded with the rulers of what is now Somalia, and oversaw trade with the old Kingdom of Sheba (Yemen) and Abyssinia (Ethiopia).

The Romans (who arrived in AD 106) ruled the region from Bosra in Syria and used the town as one of their main trading stations en route to the sea. In the early 4th century, the port city came under the rule of the Byzantine Empire and was ruled on their behalf by the Ghassanides, Christian Arab tribes originating from south Arabia.

Ayla (as Al-'aqabah was then called) came under Islamic rule in 630–631, when the spread of Islam from the Hejaz reached north to the peoples of the Red Sea.

Twelfth-century Crusaders wrested it from the Muslims and built a fort some 7km (4.25 miles) offshore on Far'un Island – then called the Ile de Graye. When Saladin launched his counter-crusade against Western Christendom, he also captured Ayla and the former Crusader castle there became known as Saladin's Castle. In 1182, the Crusader and arch-enemy of Saladin, Reynald de Chatillon

onquered the Ile de Graye, but success was short-lived – it was retaken he following year.

With the rise of the Mamluke sultans n Egypt, Al-'aqabah (as they renamed t) came under Mamluke Egyptian rule. Al-'aqabah Fort, now one of the main andmarks of Al-'aqabah, was built in he 14th century by Qansah Ghouri, one f the last sultans of the Mamluke era.

After the Mamlukes came the Ottomans who controlled Al-'aqabah for ome 400 years. During this time, the entre of commercial power shifted o Baghdad and Al-'aqabah slowly leclined to a relatively unimportant ishing town.

Al-'aqabah's fortunes revived in the early 20th century. It became of key mportance during the Arab Revolt, when Lawrence and the Arab forces prised the city from the Ottomans n 1917 and used it to receive crucial arms shipments from Egypt.

MODERN AL-'AQABAH

The last few decades have seen what was, until relatively recently, a sleepy fishing village completely transformed. The huge port facilities were built in the 1960s and 1970s just south of the city centre, fuelling Jordan's economy as they still do today. For many years, while tourism flourished in neighbouring Israel and Egypt, it took a distant second place to heavy industry in Al-'aqabah. Through the late 1990s, it became clear that Al-'aqabah was underperforming: its most beautiful beaches lay completely undeveloped, and the town had only a very few tourist-class hotels.

In 2000, the city and its immediate surroundings were re-created as the **Al-'aqabah Special Economic Zone**, or ASEZ, which offered a wide range of tax breaks for business and the waiving of all kinds of customs duties on imports. As an experiment in attracting investment to what was ultimately a failing region, this has been hugely successful: Al-'aqabah has been transformed by a rush of local and foreign investment into its infrastructure, new development and tourism-related projects.

Sunset over the Gulf of Aqaba.

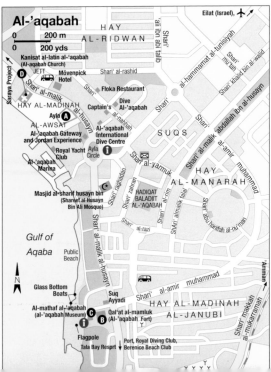

The city centre has also been revamped, with new street furniture and public works of art being installed, and the widespread planting of palm trees. The population has also grown as the town attracts migration from around. Shopping malls sprouting across town are indicators of consumer confidence despite the current economic climate, and diverse projects that include the new American University at Al-'aqabah campus show the breadth, scale and ambition of the city's rejuvenation.

But it is on a rash of grand schemes focused on leisure and tourism that Al-'aqabah has pinned its future above all. Al-'aqabah is styling itself as a kind of Eilat, but on a larger scale. The **Tala Bay Resort** occupies a beautiful sweep of golden sand 15km (9 miles) south of the city. The first phase of the project is already complete – a cluster of luxury residential properties arrayed around a marina, the new beach and luxury hotels alongside.

West of the city centre and set slightly back from the beach, is the

vast, US$2.5 billion **Saraya Projec** (www.sarayaaqaba.com), comprising series of marinas carved out a shor distance inland. The lagoons wil again, be surrounded by upmarke properties, including hotels, shop and restaurants, a golf course, wate park and even a university. Als planned is the **Ayla Oasis** (www.aylao sis.com) near the Israeli border; th first stage should be completed i 2018, as should the regeneration c various spots downtown.

Such schemes could have threat ened to kill Al-'aqabah's golden goose its coral, a large and still untappe source of tourism revenue. And ye in an exceptional display of long-term vision, the ASEZ authorities have bee compelled by law to employ an envi ronmental commissioner to examin the ecological impact of such hug construction projects. In a move tha is rare in the Middle East, the city ha imposed a string of tough restriction on beachfront development, includin a ban on new construction within 10 metres (300ft) of the high-tide mark.

Al-'aqabah Fort.

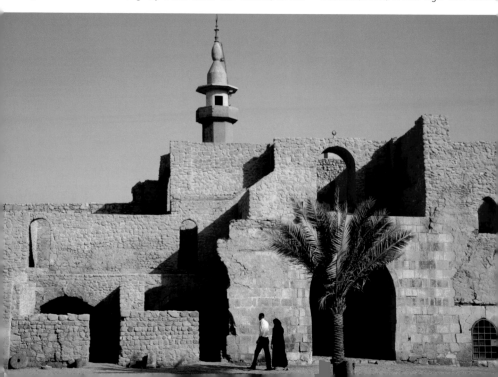

Al-'aqabah is embarking on an all-out bid to become Jordan's most important city after Amman, as well as a major economic powerhouse in its own right, attracting tourism and private investment from all across the world. Yet for all its go-getting business enthusiasm, Al-'aqabah remains, at heart, one of Jordan's more conservative cities, and still retains a small-town appeal and relaxed and friendly atmosphere. It's a great place to chill out after sightseeing or hot dusty days in Wadi rum.

Al-'aqabah also retains strong links to Saudi Arabia, its southern neighbour, as well as to the rest of the Arab world. Western tourism to Al-'aqabah is matched, or superseded for the time being at least, by tourism from Arab countries. Private hotel beaches cater mostly to the Westerners, while Al-'aqabah's public beaches are almost the exclusive preserve of the Arabs. This juxtaposition between scantily clad European sun-worshippers and modestly dressed Arab family groups on holiday is a curiously incongruous but harmonious one.

AL-'AQABAH'S SIGHTS

The remains of **Ayla** Ⓐ, Al-'aqabah's medieval forebear, can be visited, although it's worth bearing in mind that what can be seen today is probably a fraction of what once stood. The majority of Ayla's remains presumably extend far eastwards, buried under 20th-century Al-'aqabah. The excavations, begun in 1987, lie opposite the Mövenpick Hotel in the centre of town. Signs in Arabic and English take visitors on a guided tour of the once high-walled city. Historically, Ayla was located on important trade routes, and even Chinese ships were known to dock here. Evidence of Egyptian, Syrian and Moroccan presence has all been found.

At the southeastern end of Al-'aqabah's corniche don't miss the Mamluke-built **Al-'aqabah Fort** Ⓑ (Qal'at al-mamluk; off Shari' al-malik al-husayn; Sat–Thur 8am–5pm, Fri 10am–4pm; charge). Built between

The town is a particularly good place to buy beads and silver jewellery.

Fantastic shopping at the market stalls and suqs.

Souvenir bottles filled with sand from the desert are arranged into patterns and words.

1510 and 1517, it served as a *khan* (caravanserai for Hajj pilgrims travelling to Mecca and Medina) before it was occupied by the Ottomans. The Hashemite coat of arms over the entrance was added after the Turks were ousted from Al-'aqabah during World War I. Sherif Husayn ben Ali, the leader of the Arab Revolt, resided here.

Just below the fort, in an attractively restored complex that also includes the **Department of Antiquities** and the **tourist office**, is the **Al-'aqabah Museum** Ⓒ (Al-mathaf al-'aqabah; daily 8am–noon, 5pm–9pm; charge with fort), dedicated to the history of Al-'aqabah and the archaeology of Ayla. The exhibits, well-displayed and with good information panels, include lovely Islamic 8th-century stone carvings, a Byzantine cross lintel and collection of lamps, a beautifully carved Roman milestone from the Trajan Road, a crucible and moulds showing evidence of ancient copper metallurgy and a good collection of small

Spices in the suq.

Abbasid ivory panels. Opposite the entrance to the fort is the **Suq Ayyadi** (daily 8am–noon, 5–9pm), which sells good-quality arts and crafts from charitable projects across Jordan.

Although Ayla was known to flourish during the Nabataean, Roman and Byzantine periods, antiquities of the pre-Islamic period remained lost until mid-1998, when archaeologists unearthed what may prove to be one of the oldest churches on earth. In front of the JETT bus station, the mud-brick **Al-'aqabah Church** Ⓓ (Kanisat al-latin al-'aqabah) is believed to date from the late 3rd century, making it slightly more ancient than the Church of the Holy Sepulchre in Jerusalem and the Church of the Nativity in Bethlehem, both dating from the 4th century. Most of the early churches in Jordan are thought to date from the late 5th or early 6th century.

The building measures 28 by 24 metres (92 by 79ft), and its walls stand about 4 metres (13ft) tall around most of the perimeter. Trapped under the rubble of the earthquake that destroyed the church in AD 363 were several artefacts that convinced archaeologists that this had indeed been an early church: of the 100 or more coins found on the floor, none dated later than AD 360, and a high concentration of oil lamps were identified as chandeliers common to early churches. A nearby cemetery containing a grave marked by a cross further bolstered the theory that the structure was a church.

After the earthquake of AD 363, the church was filled with sand and never touched again. As early churches tended to metamorphose through long periods of use and reuse, archaeologists expect the Al-'aqabah Church to shed new light on the "model" 4th-century church structure – that is, if present development plans don't consume this ancient monument first.

AL-'AQABAH'S *PASSEGGIATA*

Al-'aqabah's not insignificant historical attractions aside, one of the town's greatest pleasures is its lively street life. In such a torrid climate, the days can be relatively quiet, the mood in the town soporific. But after dark, Al-'aqabah comes alive, and this is a great time to discover its soul. The main central boulevard of Shari' al-hammamat al-tunisiyah is lined with shops and cafés, with a long, slender strip of palm trees occupying the central reservation. This is a pleasant place to come for the evening's *passeggiata* (promenade) as the locals do, with many of the shops open late, and people gathering under the trees to chat and gossip or eat ice creams.

Opposite a modern fountain is Shari'al-nahhah, which boasts good restaurants, as well as coffee houses, fast-food joints and internet cafés; while on the other side of Shari' al-hammamat al-tunisiyah is a dense web of alleys, market stalls and **suqs** comprising the main commercial centre of Al-'aqabah. It's packed with budget eateries, spice stalls and jewellers and is a fascinating place to wander. Look out for the newly renovated and gleaming-white **mosque**, a project completed by King Abdullah in 2011.

At the corniche end of Shari' al-hammamat al-tunisiyah, off a large roundabout, is the **Al-'aqabah Gateway** complex, a modern shopping mall centred on a replica Arab dhow moored on a (currently dry) artificial lagoon.

South of here, down to the Al-'aqabah Fort, is Al-'aqabah's **public beach**, another fascinating spot for people watching, busy from late afternoon until late into the night. Between the cornice and the beach, look out for the little **allotments** between the palm trees containing tiny vegetable gardens. Note that the beach is not the place for stripping off to bathe, however: the main clientele are extended Arab family groups, with women often sitting in the shallows chatting while fully clothed, kids splashing happily

The public beach.

and men tending sizzling barbecues while watching precariously rigged-up TVs. Stretched along this beach are a succession of impromptu cafés, offering tea, coffee and *argileh* – an attractive spot to watch the sun go down. It's also here that you can find many of the **glass-bottom boats** and their captains touting for business. A few also offer **speedboats** that take you for a tour around the bay. Along the beach, down from the Al-'aqabah Fort, is the conspicuous giant **Flag-pole**, marking a spot known as the Great Arab Revolt Plaza. It commemorates the ousting of the Ottomans from Al-'aqabah by King Feisal and T.E. Lawrence during the Great Arab Revolt (the flag of which it flies). Measuring 132 metres (433ft) high, it's one of the tallest freestanding flagpoles in the world.

DIVING, SNORKELLING AND BOAT TRIPS

The main appeal of Al-'aqabah for most travellers lies in its offshore coral reefs. Deep water lies close to

the Gulf coast, creating a fascinating marine environment where divers may encounter a wide variety of species, including the largest fish in the world, the whale shark. The marked diurnal tidal range also supports an interesting array of shore life that can be investigated at low tide, with rocks carpeted in creatures such as limpets, chitons and periwinkles that have adapted to survive the constant to and fro, from submerged world to air and strong sunlight.

For recommended dive schools, see page 269.

One dive school, the Royal Diving Club, lies 15km (9 miles) out of town, 4km (2.5 miles) from the Saudi border. It offers scuba diving lessons in a pool and on a number of nearby reefs. There is also a restaurant, good three-star accommodation and a daily minibus service that transports people to the centre from Al-'aqabah's main hotels.

Independent private sailing is not allowed in Al-'aqabah for security reasons, but some dive companies

Glass-bottom boats.

⊘ GLASS-BOTTOM BOATS

Jostling for space on Amman's public beach are Al-'aqabah's glass-bottom boats, their captains touting for business from dawn to dusk to anyone who so much glances their way. Some travellers are disappointed by the lack of marine life seen from the boats, but the key is to hire a boat for two to three hours (ideally in a group to split the cost) and head to one of the reefs. Even better, bring snorkelling gear and fishing tackle. The current charge is around JD10-15 for 20 minutes, JD30-35 for an hour or JD120 for three hours, though you will need to negotiate hard. Bring cameras too: in the evening, you should get some great shots of Al-'aqabah and the beaches as the sun sets on the town.

an organise trips. A new cruise company based in Al-'aqabah Marina with a good reputation is **Sindbad** (www.sindbadjo.com; tel: 03-205 0077), which offers boat trips and cruises round the Gulf of Aqaba, including snorkelling trips with barbeques. It also owns the beautiful brand-new private beach club, **Berenice Beach Club** (tel: 03-205 0077; www.berenice.com.jo; charge), located on the South Beach just north of Tala Bay around 15km (9 miles) from downtown, the first of its kind in Al-'aqabah. Open to all, it offers access to its 300-metre (1,000ft) beach, three pools and bars, all facilities including a gym, beach volleyball, kid's zone and diving centre. Water sports offered include windsurfing, kitesurfing, parasailing, water-skiing, wake and kneeboarding, as well as banana boats. There's a shuttle bus connecting the club to downtown Al-'aqabah.

AL-'AQABAH'S SEAFOOD

As you might expect, Al-'aqabah has several excellent seafood restaurants, offering a range of familiar dishes as well as a local speciality, *sayadiya*, a tasty concoction of spiced red mullet served on a bed of flavoured rice.

One of the most romantic restaurants in town is the Mövenpick Hotel's Red Sea Grill, an open-air, candlelit spot overlooking the beach. Vying with it for the title of Al-'aqabah's finest is the outpost of Romero of Amman within the **Royal Yacht Club** (located on the marina behind the Al-'aqabah Gateway complex); this is a high-class restaurant, with excellent fish dishes and a range of pizzas and pastas.

Other options include Al-'aqabah's best-known eatery, Ali Baba, on Shari' al-hammamat al-tunisiyah, which serves a full range of Arabic specialities along with *masgoof* (grilled fish) and an unusual fish curry. Two other specialist fish and seafood restaurants are Captain's and, considered the best in town for quality, the well-known Floka, opposite each other on Shari' al-nahhah.

Scuba divers head for the coral reefs.

📷 THE RED SEA – A WORLD APART

The Red Sea is known as one of the richest marine kingdoms in the world. Al-'aqabah's small but special stretch remains little spoilt, clean and easily accessible.

Almost any spot along Jordan's 27km (16.5-mile) -long Red Sea coastline offers an escape into an underwater world teeming with colour and life. Al-'aqabah's calm waters are conducive to diving all year around. Even those who don't want to do more than snorkel in the shallows will find a wealth of marine life.

The most colourful dives are to be had along the southern extremities of Al-'aqabah. A thriving world of corals, sponges and sea fans thrives as little as 5 metres (15ft) below the surface.

Al-'aqabah boasts not just a huge variety and number of fish (including Red Sea favourites such as parrot fish, damsel fish, turtles and moray eels), but also good wrecks and a few rarer treats too, such as little seahorses and the very occasional whale shark, the largest fish in the world. This perfectly harmless fish, reaching 15 metres (45ft) in length, is attracted by plankton in the northern shallows and, at certain times of the year, its mating call can be heard when diving or snorkelling around Al-'aqabah.

Butterfly fish amongst the coral. Rarely does the w drop below 20°C (68°F) and in summer it is 26°C (7 or above.

Lionfish.

Close encounter with the rare whale shark, which visits these waters from June to August.

Al-'aqabah is an ideal place to learn to scuba dive.

Diving

Diving centres in Al-'aqabah recognise well over a dozen dive sites, and favourites within the diving community include excursions to the *Cedar Pride* and the *Gorgonian I*. The *Cedar Pride* was a Lebanese transport ship, which, following a fire in the port, was deliberately sunk in 1985 to foster coral growth. It now lies pitched on its side in 27 metres (89ft) of water. Although the corals are still in their relative infancy, the ship's body is well colonised and patronised by many numbers and varieties of fish.

The profusion of hard and soft corals and brilliant reef fish has earned *Gorgonian I* a reputation as one of the finest dive sites in the Gulf of Aqaba, and it is suitable for both novice and experienced divers.

For those wishing to learn to dive, Al-'aqabah, with its generally calm waters, good visibility and easily accessible sites, is a good place to learn. The Aqaba International Dive Centre (tel: 03-203 1213; www.aqabadivingcenter.com), Dive Aqaba (tel: 03-210 8883; www.diveaqaba.com) and the Royal Diving Club (tel: 03-201 7035 are all accredited, well-established and have good reputations.

ghly 100 metres/yards from the shore, the sea floor
ɔs steeply towards a profusion of delicate coral and
ine life.

/ moray eel.

Mild currents allow good visibility from May until February.

Camels are bred and raised by the Bedouin in the stony desert of the Badia.

EAST TO THE BADIA

The area between Amman and Azraq is defined by a looping road linking the remarkable "desert castles". At the easternmost limit of this route is the Shaumari Wildlife Reserve, and beyond that, the area known as the Badia.

⊙ Main Attractions

Qasr al-hallabat
Qasr al-azraq
Qasr al-tubah
Qusayr 'amrah
Qasr al-haranah
Qasr al-mushta
Jawah
Dayr ahl al-kahf
Qasr usaykhim
Qasr burqu'

Map on page 276

East of Amman and Al-zarqa', the steep, green hills that encircle the capital abruptly fall away to a flat and stark desert that stretches to the country's easternmost border with Iraq. A vast territory that appears to be one desert is, in fact, three. A landscape littered with limestone pellets gives way to one strewn with black basalt stones, which in turn gives way to the encroaching sands of Wadi Sarahan, which stretches into Saudi Arabia.

At the confluence of the three types of desert stands the much reduced Azraq oasis, its pools filled by a complex network of aquifers fed mainly from the Jabal Druze area of southern Syria (the passage of water taking up to 50 years). Surrounding the oasis is the Qa' al-Azraq, about 60 sq km (23 sq miles) of silt, beneath which lies such a concentration of salt that hundreds of tons each year are collected for both industrial and domestic use.

The ring of intriguing desert castles that rise from the flat and barren earth is the area's main attraction for visitors. Settlement is limited, though Bedouin still eke out a living here, their survival a testament to their timeless resourcefulness and endurance.

HISTORY OF THE EASTERN DESERT

Several hundred million years ago, the area, like most of present-day Jordan, lay beneath the sea, which withdrew and re-inundated the land several times. The last inundation probably receded in the Eocene period about 50 million years ago. Around 1 million years ago, in the Pleistocene era, the broad shallow basin in which Azraq stands today was a huge inland lake measuring about 4,000 sq km (1,500 sq miles). As the waters slowly receded the basin became a fertile plain with large swamps and pools and luxuriant vegetation at its centre.

The otherworldly landscape of the Badia.

Until only a few decades ago, the desert teemed with wildlife. Gazelle, wild ass, ostrich and the magnificent white Arabian oryx roamed freely, preyed upon by wolf, hyena and man – the Bedouin. Azraq was a paradise of birds and animals, great and small, living in or around its waters or arriving from the desert to drink. Some 12,000 to 40,000 years ago, rhinoceros and hartebeest also inhabited its marshes. Stones found in a ruined Roman wall, carved with ostrich, snake, fish, hoopoe and wild ass, are graphic testimonies to the abundance of wildlife 2,000 years ago. "Each stone or blade of it," wrote T.E. Lawrence in *The Seven Pillars of Wisdom*, "was radiant with half-memory of the luminous silky Eden, which had passed so long ago."

Today, there is little wildlife, and most lie protected in reserves. The culprit is not climatic change but man, who has cut down trees, overgrazed pasture, pumped out water for cities, and hunted with automatic weapons and 4WD vehicles.

THE DESERT CASTLES

The climate has changed little since Roman times. Undaunted by the desert, they built a string of forts here – the *limes arabicus* – along the boundaries of their Arabian province. The main fort-builders were Septimius Severus (AD 193–211) and, 100 years later, Diocletian (284–305). These frontier posts survived into the Byzantine era, some falling into disrepair, others restored for service until the Islamic Arab conquest in 636.

From the mid-7th to the mid-8th centuries, when the Omayyad caliphs were establishing their court and centre of Islam in Damascus, a scattering of settlements were built in the Jordanian desert. Each had a different function: fort, hunting lodge, trading-post, farm, caravanserai or meeting hall. Common to all was a sophisticated management of water, and

the establishment of an agricultural base. All were probably also intended, whether by the caliph or his local ruler, to keep an eye on the Bedouin tribes on whose loyalty the Omayyads depended.

No desert asceticism applied here. The buildings included bathhouses, spacious courtyards and great halls for entertainment, adorned with columns and carvings, mosaics and frescoes. They were served by sophisticated hydraulic and heating systems, so that the stresses of a hard day's hunting or diplomacy could be soothed by fountains, pools and hot baths.

Sometime around the year 750, when the Omayyads were ousted by the Abbasids and the Islamic capital moved to Baghdad, many of these settlements in the Jordanian desert fell into disuse and ruin. The abandoned buildings became temporary encampments for Bedouin who lit fires in the decorated halls for heat or to cook food before moving on to new territory.

In 1896, Alois Musil, an Arabist from Prague, was told by Bedouin of richly decorated buildings deep in the desert.

The Badia's version of a petrol station.

🔍 NATURE RESERVES

Shaumari Wildlife Reserve was the first nature reserve to be created by Jordan's Royal Society for the Conservation of Nature (RSCN).

Shaumari was created in 1975 on 22 sq km (8.5 sq miles) of desert. It was designated as a breeding centre for species that had become extinct or endangered in Jordan, prior to their release into the wild. The RSCN's vital work continues, despite funding difficulties. Shaumari Wildlife Reserve lies south of Azraq, off the main road to Saudi Arabia.

Specially targeted was the Arabian oryx *(Oryx leucoryx)*, extinct in Jordan since the 1920s. As early as 1962, the Fauna Preservation Society and the World Wildlife Fund had launched "Operation Oryx" in Arizona, with a World Survival Herd of nine animals donated by Aden, Kuwait, Britain and Saudi Arabia. When numbers grew, sub-groups were established. The RSCN proposed that Jordan should be the first country to reintroduce the oryx into the Arabian desert, and in 1978, four pairs were sent to Shaumari. The ruler of Qatar donated a male and two females, and from these 11 animals the Jordanian herd multiplied.

In 1983, when the herd numbered over 30, they were released into the greater area of the reserve. Though zoo-bred, their behaviour showed that they had not lost their wild instincts. They quickly split into smaller herds and established a hierarchy. In 2011, seven further head of oryx were introduced

Sand gazelles at Shaumari Wildlife Reserve.

from Saudi Arabia and in June 2012 another eight, in the hope of diversifying the gene pool. Other rehabilitation projects have also been undertaken, notably with the Arabian ostrich and onegar (Syrian wild ass), and in 2012, twenty sand gazelle were imported from Saudi Arabia. A clinic has been established too, specialising in the care of oryx, gazelle and confiscated animals illegally taken by locals. Currently, the Arabian oryx number around 200, the sand gazelle around 20 and the wild ass around 17, though the animals are successfully breeding.

The **Azraq Wetland Reserve**, 12 sq km (4.5 sq miles) of marsh, mudflats and pools, was designated soon after Shaumari. It lies near Al-azraq al-janubi; visitors should check in first at the RSCN Lodge, 600 metres/yards towards Amman from the junction in Al-azraq al-janubi, up a paved road on the left.

About 300 bird species were recorded here in the 1970s – migrants, residents and seasonal visitors – but since then, marshes and birds alike have diminished dramatically as water levels have fallen.

During the past 30 years, the reserve has suffered from over-pumping to supply Amman and other cities with water, leading to the drying up of large areas of the marshland. In 1993, the RSCN signed an agreement with the government by which 1.5 million–2.5 million cubic meters of water were to be pumped back into the wetland. This water is not sufficient to restore the wetland to its former status, but it has managed to restore around 6 percent of the original marshland area. A project to manage the reed bed, using water buffaloes in a grazing scheme, has been introduced.

Despite the rehabilitation efforts and the reintroduction of endemic species, water fluctuation, in terms of both quantity and quality, continues to have profound effects on the wetland's ecosystem.

Nonetheless, a visit is hugely rewarding, especially during the spring and autumn migration periods when a large variety of birds can be seen, from swallows to eagles. A faint echo of Lawrence's "luminous, silky Eden" can be heard in the susurrus of wind in reeds, punctuated by the piping of birds, and the hoarse trumpetings of the marsh frogs.

See page 103 for more information on both reserves.

Two years later he returned, and within a few days found two of these palaces, Qasr at-Tuba and Qusayr 'amrah. In the following months and years, several more were discovered. Though not quite "palaces" (the meaning of the Arabic word *qasr*), nor castles (as they are called in English), they are nonetheless exceptional examples of Islamic domestic architecture in its earliest days, taking inspiration from Byzantine and Persian art, but also showing the beginnings of an unique and original style and personality.

VISITING THE DESERT CASTLES

Today, with tarmac roads in place of the ancient desert tracks, some of the Omayyad Palaces (as well as Qasr al-azraq) can be seen in an easy day trip from Amman. The roads form a neat circuit, with Azraq at the eastern end. Two other impressive structures, Qasr al-mushta and Qasr al-tubah, lie outside this circuit, but are well worth a visit if you have the time. The former can be found near Queen Alia Airport, while the latter lies off the Desert Highway east of Al-qatranah. Qasr al-tubah is the most inaccessible and you'll need a four-wheel-drive vehicle to get there.

The suggested route runs clockwise from Amman, but it can easily be done anticlockwise too. To break up the "castle bashing", stop-offs at the Azraq Wetland Reserve (see page 274) and Shaumari Wildlife Reserve (see page 274), home of the famous Arabian oryx, are highly recommended on the way. If you want to spend more than a day in the area, there is accommodation at Azraq.

QASR AL-HALLABAT

Take the road north out of Amman towards Al-zarqa', and after about 22km (13.5 miles), turn right at the sign to the Syrian and Iraqi borders. After another 12km (7.5 miles), take the right turn to Al-zarqa' and the Iraqi border; 7km (4.25

miles) further on, at a junction with a right turn to Azraq, continue straight ahead towards Al-mafraq. After 6km (3.5 miles), a small blue sign points right towards **Qasr al-hallabat** ①. About 8km (5 miles) further on, another blue sign points right to the castle itself.

This large desert complex started life as a Roman fort, but was converted into a luxurious country estate by the Omayyads.

The original small fort was built around AD 111–114 to guard Trajan's new road to the south, the Via Nova Traiana; a Latin inscription mentions an extension in the early 3rd century; and another in Greek records a Byzantine restoration in 529.

Between 709 and 743, the Omayyads as good as demolished the earlier structures to make way for their complex, a series of buildings that included a castle, mosque and bathhouse, all of which can be seen today. There was also a large reservoir, various Cisterns and a walled agricultural enclosure.

The castle was thereby transformed into a palatial residence and lavishly

Tip

If navigating around castles seems a bit daunting, or you're short of time or cash, consider taking a tour from Amman or Ma'daba. A number of hotels run tours of the main castles (JD20–25 per person; one day) including the Mariam in Ma'daba, and Cliff and Palace hotels in Amman.

Azraq wetlands.

decorated with frescoes, carved stucco and lively mosaics of animals, birds, fruits and geometric designs – now removed for safe keeping. Although this is a limestone area, many of the stones are basalt, and several carry sections of a long Greek inscription, including one, an edict of the Emperor Anastasius I (AD 491–518) reorganising the province of Arabia. As the inscriptions were plastered over, they were evidently reused purely for their architectural value. It is believed they might have been imported to Hallabat by the Omayyads from the ancient basalt city of Um al-jimal, located some 30km (18 miles) to the north (see page 185).

The mosque stands immediately to the east of the castle, some of its walls still stand at their full height. The doorway in the North Wall, facing the remains of the *mihrab* (niche indicating the direction of prayer) has an attractive cusped arch.

HAMMAM AL-SARH

The bathhouse, known as **Hammam al-sarh**, lies 2km (1.2 miles) to the east of the castle beside the main road. It a finely built limestone complex orig nally finished with marble, mosaic and frescoes. The rectangular audi ence hall, now identifiable only by a outline of walls, once had three para lel tunnel-vaults, and an alcove with small room on either side, complet with latrines. A doorway in the nort corner leads into the changing roo (*apodyterium*) of the bathhouse, whic doubled as a cool room (*frigidarium* This opens into the room of mediu heat (*tepidarium*) with a tunnel-vaulte recess, and finally into the domed h room (*calidarium*), which has two sen icircular recesses covered with sem domes. Beyond this was the furnac which sent hot air under the raise floor of the calidarium. This complex very similar in design to that of Qusay 'amrah (see page 279).

Beside the baths stands a wate storage tank into which water wa poured after it was hauled up fro the well, measuring 18 metres (59f deep. Water was raised by a pulle system operated by donkeys or horse

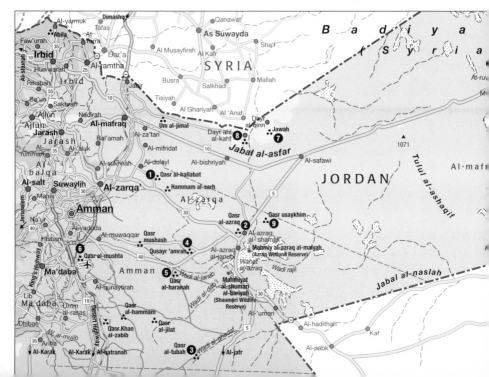

eading a circle. A *mihrab* nearby indi-
tes the remains of a late-Ottoman
en-air mosque.

ASR AL-AZRAQ

he road running southeast from
ammam al-sarh turns right and
ter 3km (2 miles) joins the main
-zarqa'–Azraq road. After 55km (34
iles), it reaches a junction at Al-
raq al-janubi (south), one of the two
.lages of the Azraq complex, passing
e RSCN lodge just before the junc-
on. Turning left, the tree-lined road
 the resthouse can be seen on the
ft after 2km (1.25 miles). Al-azraq
-shamali (north) is another 2.5km
.5 miles) further on and, 500 metres/
rds ahead is the great black basalt
asr al-azraq ❷ (Azraq castle).
Azraq's abundant waters have made
 an attractive location since time
memorial. Paleolithic campsites
ve been found in the marshes, with
nt tools fashioned by early Stone
ge inhabitants 100,000 years ago.
e importance of the oasis was lost
either on the Bedouin who roamed

the desert, or the traders who passed
through. Azraq stood at the head of
Wadi Sirhan, the main caravan route
between the Arabian Peninsula and
Mesopotamia and Syria.

The first fort here may have been
built by Septimius Severus (AD
193–211), forming one of the eastern
defences of the *limes arabicus*. The
earliest inscription relating to the castle is in fact a dedication to Diocletian
and Maximian, who ruled as co-emper-
ors from AD 286 to 305. Diocletian also
built a new road to Azraq, the Strata
Diocletiana, to improve the lines of
communication between the regions
of Syria and southern Arabia.

The fort remained in use under the
Byzantines, and was an occasional
base for the Omayyads, useful both
for hunting and for meetings with
the desert tribes. After the fall of the
Omayyads, it fell into disrepair and had
to be rebuilt in 1237 by the Ayyubid governor, Azz al-Din Aybak, as recorded in
an Arabic inscription above the main
entrance. It was probably then that
the little mosque in the middle of the

Qasr al-hallabat.

East to the Badia

0   50 km

0   50 miles

courtyard was built. How far the castle was remodelled is unclear. Plenty of Roman-cut stones were available, and several Roman doors (one weighing an incredible three tons) were reused exactly in the Roman fashion. They are still there, and still turning on their stone hinges. The Mamlukes and Ottomans also occupied Qasr al-azraq.

Later, it was dubbed "the blue fort on its rock" by T.E. Lawrence, who used it as a base in the winter of 1917–18; his office lay above the entrance gatehouse. Holed up here, Lawrence learned "the full disadvantages of imprisonment within such gloomy ancient unmortared places." As the rain came in and the men shivered, "past and present flowed over us like an uneddying river. We dreamed ourselves into the spirit of the place; sieges and feasting, raids, murders, love-singing in the night."

Today, the castle is less intact than during Lawrence's day due to a severe earthquake in 1927. The shell of an upper storey remains in parts, as well as handsome arched stables with

stone mangers and tethering blocks on the north side. The ancient well lies on the east side.

QASR AL-TUBAH

The splendid **Qasr al-tubah** ❸, in Wadi al-ghadaf, is one of the least accessible Omayyad Palaces. There is a choice of three routes there, but they all demand a 4WD, high-clearance vehicle, a guide and possibly a compass. The route with the least rough driving runs 55km (34 miles) south of Azraq, along the road that passes the turning to Shaumari. A track to the right leads to the palace.

More difficult is a track from Qasr al-kharaneh leading almost due south to Tuba (47km/29 miles). Criss-crossed by other tracks, the route can be difficult to make out. The third route runs 70km (43 miles) east from Al-qatranah on the Desert Highway, half on paved road, half on rough tracks.

Qasr al-tubah, the first palace rediscovered by Alois Musil in 1898, is a great architectural skeleton, half lost in the desert sand. It was probably designed as a caravanserai on the trade route

Bedouin encampment in the Azraq area.

between Amman and the west, and Wadi Sirhan and southern Arabia. Wandering in its silent courts, surrounded by the limitless and haunting desert, it is not hard to imagine the men, horses and camels that once thronged these ruins. It is thought Qasr al-tubah was constructed in 743–44, at the end of the decadent Caliph Walid II's reign, but remained unfinished at his death.

The complex consists of two symmetrical enclosures, together forming almost a double square each, with suites of inter-connecting rooms around a central courtyard. A round tower was set at each corner, and semicircular towers at intervals along the sides. In the north corner, the buildings remain nearly intact, including a magnificent barrel-vaulted hall. Also surviving is most of the lower part of the west wall. The rest is a broken line of tumbled wall and foundations. The walls were originally built of three courses of stone, above which were laid sun-dried mud bricks. Stone also framed the door arches, and Musil originally found some finely carved stone door jambs and lintels. Sadly, all these have long since disappeared.

For water, the inhabitants relied on nearby pools, three huge wells, and the remains of round buildings where donkeys or horses operated a pulley system to raise the water.

QUSAYR 'AMRAH

The main road from Azraq to Amman divides into two, nearly 9km (5.5 miles) from Azraq. Take the left-hand fork and after another 17.5km (11 miles), you will pass the harmonious-looking stone-built **Qusayr 'amrah** ❹ on the right. You may find that you share the castle with others. In 1985, the castle was declared a Unesco World Heritage Site hailed as a "masterpiece of human creative genius" as well as "an outstanding example of a type of building, architectural or technological ensemble or landscape which illustrates a significant stage in human history".

The castle stands in Wadi Butm, a shallow watercourse (dry most of the year), named after the *butm* (wild pistachio trees, *Pistachia atlantica)* which

Qusayr 'amrah.

The vivid frescoes inside Qusayr 'amrah.

The wall and ceiling frescoes are Qusayr 'amrah's famous principal attraction.

were once numerous here. Qusayr is the diminutive of *qasr*, and this "little palace" is the remains of a larger complex that was built in 711, under Caliph Walid I, which probably also included a fort, some agricultural enclosures and living quarters.

Today, the remains of an audience hall can be seen with three barrel vaults, and an alcove flanked by two small rooms, as well as a three-roomed bathhouse, including a domed *calidarium* with under-floor heating. All the walls and ceilings are covered with vivid frescoes, Amra's famous principal attraction.

Restored in 1971–73 by experts from the Madrid National Archaeological Museum (Mathaf al-aathar), and again today by an Italian team of restorers (from the Roman *Istituto Superiore per la Conservazione ed il Restauro*, and the *Ministero per i Beni e le Attività Culturali* in conjuction with the Jordanian Department of Antiquities and World Monument Fund), their former colour, life and charm has been largely restored after the centuries of neglect,

smoke from Bedouin fires and local defacement from graffiti.

Their interest lies not just in their style (in fact rather mixed), nor for the joyous naturalism, but for what they reveal of the brilliant eclecticism of early Arab/Islamic art (which drew from both Byzantine and Persian sources), and for the very fact that they exist at all. It was under Caliph Yazid II (720–24) that the first edict was issued ordering the destruction of images. Though these frescoes would almost still have been wet from the application, mercifully they were overlooked. In fact, destruction of images was not generally rigorously imposed in secular buildings.

Here at Amrah, the painters were uninhibited in their depictions of human and mythological life: the mosaics show hunting scenes; athletes in training; the goddesses of poetry, philosophy and history; musicians and dancers; women and children bathers (notable in varying states of undress). Six figures are believed to represent rulers conquered by Walid I: the Byzantine emperor, the Visigothic king of Spain, the Sassanian

king and the Negus of Abyssinia (all with inscriptions); and two without inscriptions who may represent the emperor of China and the Turkish khan. In addition, there are dainty gazelles, monkeys and birds, and a delightful guitar-strumming bear; and pastiches of the working life of various craftsmen.

Most interesting of all is the fresco in the dome of the *caldarium*. It is the earliest known representation of the night sky portrayed in the round instead of on a flat surface. The Great and Little Bears, Andromeda, Cassiopeia, Sagittarius, Scorpio, Orion and others are all depicted. But the artist who worked on the ceiling appears to have copied them from a drawing. Transposing them from right to left, he altered the relationships of the constellations one to another.

QASR AL-HARANAH

About 16km (10 miles) west of Amrah, immediately left of the main road, stands **Qasr al-haranah** ⑤, the most complete of the Omayyad castles and the most castle-like in appearance.

This great four-square, two-storey structure has round towers on each corner and semicircular ones in each wall, except on the South Wall, where the entrance is situated. It is built of large undressed stones, with layers of smaller stones between them, and with a decorative line of bricks in an open herringbone pattern running all round the building near the top. Originally it was plastered, but most of this plaster has now dropped off.

Small holes at intervals in the walls look like arrow-slits, but inside it is clear that they would not have given the archers insufficient field of fire; some would also have needed 3-metre (9ft) giants to reach them. In fact, they probably served for ventilation and light rather than for battle.

The entrance leads past large stables or store rooms on either side, and into a central courtyard, beneath which was a Cistern. Suites of rooms are arranged in the traditional Arab pattern of a large rectangular room, with two smaller square rooms on each long side. Two handsome stone stairways lead to the

Truck driver having a coffee break in the Badia.

upper floor, where several rooms still retain some of their original decoration of arches and vaults, semi-domes and corbelling, and plasterwork medallions, all reminiscent of Sassanian buildings. Above a door in one of the large rooms on the upper floor, a small painted Kufic inscription records the date in AD 710 when the castle was built.

The function of Qasr al-haranah remains uncertain. Its large stable area might, at first glance, suggest a caravanserai. But though the site lies near an old trade route, it is not actually on one; and with no evident springs, or other means of storing water, the one Cistern (Al-saharij) would not have been sufficient to supply a regular traffic of traders. Therefore, it may have served simply as an occasional meeting place for the Omayyad authorities and the Bedouin tribes, like a kind of old conference centre.

Around 37km (23 miles) west of Haranah is the village of **Al-muwaqqar**, once the site of a considerable Omayyad settlement, which has now all but disappeared. Remains survive, however, of a large ancie reservoir which is still used to this d

Between Al-haranah and A muwaqqar, but some distance north the main road along an unmarked tra lies **Qasr mushash**, a very large but v ruined Omayyad agricultural estate, w little to show today for its past glory.

QASR AL-MUSHTA

The largest and most richly decorat of Jordan's Omayyad Palaces was **Qa al-mushta** , which lies today close Queen Alia airport. To get there, tu off the highway towards the airpo and then take a right just past the A Hotel. It lies on the right of the peri eter road, after 11km (7 miles).

The palace takes the form of a gr square, walled enclosure with rou towers at the corners and five semic cular towers on each side, except on t south face, where a monumental ga way stood marking the centre. Arou this gateway were the finest of Musl ta's carvings, but in 1903, the Ottom Sultan Abdul Hamid II gave them Kaiser Wilhelm II. They now reside

An Arabian oryx.

the Pergamon Museum in Berlin. A few delicate carvings still bear witness to the palace's original artistry and glory.

The interior of the palace was never completed and most of it consists of outlines of walls and foundations around a large courtyard. North of this lie the remains of the royal audience hall and residence, probably constructed by Walid II, the extravagant and hated caliph who built Qasr al-tubah around 743–44. The audience hall is basilical in form and has a trefoil apse that was once covered by a dome. On either side are barrel-vaulted halls. While stone was used for the outer walls, the whole of this inner palace was built of bricks made of burnt mud.

THE BADIA

The term Badia describes the arid and semi-arid region in the east of Jordan. It covers a whopping 80 percent of the total landmass of the country. Roughly speaking, it can be split into three sections. The northern Badia is the land that lies to the east of the Amman–Al-mafraq road, including the "pan-handle" bordering Syria and Iraq. This area is characterised by low rolling hills covered in black basalt boulders and silty mudflats known as qa'a. The central Badia stretches east of the Desert Highway, roughly between Amman and Al-karak, and lies closest to the urban sprawl of the capital. The third region, the vast southern Badia, extends over all of southern Jordan east of the Desert Highway, below Al-karak and south of the Ras al-naqab escarpment. Here, the desert plains give way to the spectacular mountain landscape and sand dunes of Wadi rum.

HISTORY OF THE BADIA

The northern Badia has not always been the harsh and arid place it appears today, as testified by the many ancient carvings depicting lions, cattle and hunting scenes. Unique to the area are the ancient "desert kites", kilometres of basalt walls that were used to direct herds of wild animals – gazelle, antelope and ostrich – to a restricted killing ground. Hundreds of these weathered structures lie all over the Badia; look out for them.

The Badia is populated mostly by those of Bedouin descent.

⊘ THE BADIA BEDOUIN

When the Middle East's national boundaries were redrawn after World War I, huge areas of the Syrian and northern Arabian deserts were carved up and split between Syria, Jordan, Iraq and Saudi Arabia, with scant regard to existing tribal boundaries. The effect on the local Bedouin with their ancient ties to the land, on their culture and traditions, was devastating. As a result, many felt compelled to follow a more sedentary lifestyle, well away from the strategic "straight lines" borders. Today, less than 5 percent of Jordan's population lives in the bleak land of the Badia, mostly settled or semi-nomadic people of Bedouin descent. Life remains challenging, with extremes of temperature, unreliable water supply and unyielding terrain to cope with.

One of the main developments in the history of the northern Badia came with the construction of the IPC (Iraq Petroleum Company) pipeline between Kirkuk and Haifa in the 1930s. The pumping stations known as H4 and H5 became the centre of the settlements of Al-ruwayshid and Al-safawi respectively, which flourish to this day. In 1992 Prince Hassan, working with British institutions, set up the Jordan Badia Research Development Project (JBRDP). Its remit was to study over 70 major factors in the Badia such as biodiversity, desertification, reverse migration and tourism potential.

JAWAH

Seldom visited, the impressive fort at **Jawah ❼**, overlooking Wadi rajil, is the best-preserved 4thmillennium BC town yet discovered anywhere in the world. Very little is known about this "lost city of the Black Desert" or the people who built, occupied and abandoned it – all within the space of a few decades.

Remains of houses and several preserved gates can be found inside the huge surrounding basalt wall, which is split between upper and lower towns, but it is the water supply system which is the most impressive aspect. A series of canals directed rainwater into large circular reservoirs, visible to the west of the upper town and still used today by local people. Why Jawah is located in such a bleak, basalt-strewn, waterless place is still a mystery, though the commanding views to the east and south, including to the entrance of the strategically important Wadi Sirhan, may provide a clue: it was on the natural route into the heart of central Arabia.

Some time later, perhaps around the 2nd millennium BC, the abandoned ruins received a reprise when a "Citadel" was built in the middle of the upper town. Some experts believe that it may have served as an overnight stop on a trade route that linked the Arabian Gulf to Palmyra in the north, and the Nabataean trade to the south. To reach it requires a 4WD and local guide for the 7km (4.25 miles) from **Dayr al-qinn** village.

Qasr burqu'.

DAYR AHL AL-KAHF

Many of the more ancient villages in this area boast ruins of Roman forts nearby, often built as part of the Strata Diocletiana highway in the 3rd century. They served as a series of defences which included Qasr al-azraq) to protect Roman interests from the problematic Arab raiders from the east. One of the more important was at **Dayr ahl al-kahf ⑧** (The Monastery of the Caves), a village lying 13km (8 miles) north of Al-bishriyah on the Al-mafraq-safawi road. The large basalt fort has remains of three-storey towers, stables, a pool and church, with some fine examples of roofing techniques of the time. Inscriptions indicate it was built in AD 306, with extensions added later.

QASR USAYKHIM

Another dramatic hilltop Roman fort is at **Qasr usaykhim ⑨**, lying some 16km (10 miles) northeast of Azraq. Again, a 4WD is needed to reach the white limestone hill, with the black basalt fort perched on top. This commanding position could easily monitor all trade in and out of Wadi Sirhan, and like many of these outposts, conceivably dates from Nabataean times.

QASR BURQU'

The impressive but isolated fort of **Qasr burqu' ⑩** is situated about 20km (13 miles) to the north of Muqat on the main road into Iraq. Though a regular car can reach the fort with difficulty, a 4WD is a much safer bet. You'll need to engage a local guide to find the fort.

Mainly dating from the 3rd century, the basalt-built fort lies on the southeastern shore of a small lake that attracts migratory birds. The construction of the dam secured a water supply for passing traders and possibly a later monastic community. Remains include a solid basalt tower, several rooms with inscriptions and a Cistern, and are well worth an exploration. Both the drive and the desert setting of the fort are spectacular and worth the trip alone. If you need a guide, ask at Azraq Wetland Reserve. With advance notice, they can also organise a 4WD.

⊘ Fact

In the boulder-strewn Badia region, impassable even to 4WDs, the Hajaneh still use camels to patrol the Syrian and Iraqi borders. This Bedouin corp of the Jordanian Army track smugglers and illegal immigrants. At their base near Al-safawi they have a force of some 500 camels.

Roman fort of Qasr usaykhim.

⊘ THE BADIA PROJECT

The area chosen for the JBRDP research area is based at Safawi, covers around 11,000 sq km (4,250 sq miles) and contains a population of 16,000 in 35 villages and half a million head of livestock.

The work is being undertaken with the help of the UK's Royal Geographical Society and the University of Durham, and is already yielding results: the use of vaccines on livestock has improved productivity, and agricultural plans for the rich, silty volcanic ash soil are concentrating on less water-demanding plants. Water-harvesting programmes as practised by the Nabataeans are being formulated to make best use of the little rainfall, through reduced evaporation, and tapping into the massive subterranean supplies held in aquifers.

Meanwhile, areas along the borders are now providing safe havens for the gazelle and oryx population, as well as for the fox, hare and wolf, all vital to the development of eco-tourism. With many of Jordan's 6,000 or so archaeological sites straining under the pressure of too many visitors, diverting some to the Badia in the form of nature reserves could be beneficial to both. Although tourism already exists in the Badia, most tours focus on Wadi Rum and Azraq, with few nights spent here.

A young Jordanian cyclist.

JORDAN

TRAVEL TIPS

TRANSPORT

GETTING THERE

By air

Jordan's national airline, Royal Jordanian (www.rj.com), flies direct to Amman from numerous destinations in Europe, the Middle East, North America, India and Southeast Asia. RJ has offices in cities around the world, including almost every European capital. For bookings in Amman, tel: 06-510 0000.

Royal Jordanian offices abroad include the following:

Bahrain: Ground Floor, Chamber of Commerce Building, King Faisal Highway, Manama
Tel: 973-1722 9293
Email: bahtbrj@rj.com
Cairo: 6, Zamalek Sporting Club Building, 26 July Street, Mohandeseen
Tel: 20-2 33036057
Email: caitbrj@rj.com
Chicago: O'Hare International Airport, Terminal 5, Mezzanine level, office PL311
Tel: 01-212-949 0060
Email: nycterjchitbrj@rj.com
Damascus: 29 Ayyar Street
Tel: 963-11 232 2014
Email: damtbrj@rj.com
Detroit: 6 Parklane Boulevard, Suite 122, Dearborn, Michigan 48126
Tel: 01-212-949 0060
Email: dtttbrj@rj.com
Dubai: Business Avenue Building, Al-Etihad Road, PO Box 4534, Dubai
Tel: 971-4 294 4322
Email: dxbtbrj@rj.com
Istanbul: Cumhuriyet Cad. Safir Apt. No. 361/1, K:2 Harbiye, Istanbul
Tel: 90-2123 688138
Email: isttbrj@rj.com
Karachi: Hotel Metropole, Mereweather Road, Karachi 75520
Tel: 21-566 0458/8/440
Email: khitbrj@rj.com
London: 8 floor, Vantage London, Great West Rd, Brentford TW8AG

Email: lontbrj@rj.com
Montreal: P.E. Trudeau Airport, 975 boul. Romeo-Vachon Nord, Suite 441, Dorval (Quebec) H4Y 1H1
Tel: 631 2403
Email: abdelmajid.elhoussamiyultbrj@rj.com
New York: 355 Lexington Ave, fl. 14, New York, NY 10017
Tel: 212-949 0060
Email: nyctbrj@rj.com
Riyadh: Abraj Attawuneya, King Fahd Rd, Olaya, Riyadh 11462
Tel: 966-1 218 0850
Email: ruhtorj@rj.com
Sydney: Level 9. 338 Pitt St, Sydney, NSW 2000
Tel: 1300 855 057
Email: royaljordanian@worldaviation.com.au

Other airlines operating flights to Jordan are: Aegean Airlines, Air Algerie, Air France, Air Ukraine, Air Yemen, Aeroflot, Alitalia, Arabia Airlines, Austrian Airlines, British Airways, Egypt Air, Emirates Airlines, Etihad Airlines, Delta, Gulf Air, Iberia, Iraq Airways, Jazera Airlines, Jordan Aviation, KLM, Kuwait Airways, Libyan Airlines, Lufthansa, Middle East Airlines, Oman Air, Palestinian Airlines, Qatar Airlines, Royal Wings (a subsidiary of Royal Jordanian), Qantas, Saudi Airlines, Sudan Airways, Tarom, Tunis Air, Turkish Airlines, United Airlines and Yemen Airways.

By train, bus, boat and service taxi

By train from Syria

The famous Ottoman-built Hejaz railway (www.jhr.gov.jo), which famously ran between Damascus and Medina (Saudi Arabia) but which was sabotaged by Lawrence and his fellow guerrillas during the Arab Revolt, has been partly repaired over the last years and now runs passenger services. Unfortunately, it's for pre-booked groups only, though scheduled

passenger services may be offered in the future. It was closed at the time of writing due to the civil war in Syria, though it should resume in the future.

By bus or service taxi to/from Syria

At the time of writing, public transport to Syria had stopped due to the civil war in the country. When the situation settles, the following services should resume.

Currently the future of Karnak (the Syrian state-run company) is in question. However, private Syrian and Jordanian bus companies and minibuses ply the route between Damascus and Amman throughout the day, but particularly in the mornings and afternoons. One-way tickets cost around US$15, and the journey takes between five and seven hours depending on the time it takes to complete formalities at the border crossing. Jordan Express Tourist Transport (JETT; Al-malek al-husayn St, Shumaysani; International Terminal nr Abdali Bus Station; tel: 06-566 4141; www.jett.com.jo) runs a twice-daily service (JD15). When the borders reopen, visas for Jordan and Syria should be available (see page 295).

Service taxis (pronounced *servees*) are shared taxis that operate like buses and run throughout the day. They leave from Baramke Garage in Damascus and from Abdali bus station in Amman. The trip is much faster than going by bus (three to four hours), though you will have to wait for the car to fill before leaving. Alternatively, you can charter the whole car. The fare is around US$15 or JD15 per person. In theory, they run 24 hours a day, but you'll have less of a wait if you travel during the day (particularly morning).

Before the war, Royal Jordanian (www.rj.com) flew daily to Damascus on very reasonably priced flights. Flights should resume in the future.

You must obtain a visa for Syria before travelling, preferably from a Syrian embassy or consulate in your own country, or at the embassy in Cairo, Ankara or Istanbul. The Syrian embassy in Amman only handles visa applications from foreign residents (expats). You may be asked whether you have ever visited Occupied Palestine – the answer should be "no".

If your stated occupation is writer or journalist, your visa application will take considerably longer to be processed as it has to be vetted by the Ministry of Information in Damascus.

You will be denied a visa or entry into Syria if your passport carries any Israeli stamp or an Egyptian or Jordanian stamp from the border crossings with Israel. Therefore, if you plan to visit Syria from Jordan, do not enter Jordan from Wadi 'arabah or the Sheikh Husayn Bridge (Jisr al-shikh husayn). You may, however, enter from the King Hussein/Allenby Bridge (with a valid visa to Jordan) so long as you politely, but firmly, ask not to have your passport stamped.

By bus or boat to/from Egypt

A daily long-distance bus, run by Jordan Express Tourist Transport (JETT terminal, runs between Amman and Cairo at 1pm taking about 19 hours to reach Cairo (tel: 06-566 4141; www.jett.com.jo; email: info@jett.com.jo).

It is faster to travel by boat. From Egypt, take a bus from Cairo to Nuwayba on Egypt's Red Sea coast; buses leave from Cairo main bus station and take about six hours to reach Nuwayba. From there, the daily catamaran (crossing one hour) or the daily conventional ferry (crossing three–four hours) sail to Al-'aqaba. The one-way fare is over $70 for the ferry or around $85 for the fast catamaran.

From Al-'aqaba, two ferry services (one–three hours; $60–75 depending on speed) regularly run daily services from the Passenger Terminal (tel: 03-201 9849; www.abmaritime.com.jo), around 15–20 minutes' drive south of Al-'aqaba.

If you want to continue your journey from Al-'aqaba, there are service taxis to Amman and Petra, costing around JD35-90.

Royal Jordanian and Egypt Air have **daily flights** between Amman and Cairo. You can obtain a visa for Egypt upon arrival.

By bus to/from Saudi Arabia

Note that obtaining a tourist visa for Saudi is notoriously difficult. For details, contact the nearest Saudi embassy.

JETT runs a bus service from Amman to Jeddah three times a week (journey around 22 hours), as well as to Riyadh, Saudi's capital, and Dammam in the Eastern Provinces. Land crossings in Jordan are found at Ad Durra in the far south, Al Umari in the east (southeast of Azraq) and Al-mudawwarah, also in the east.

By bus, taxi or plane to/from Israel and the Palestinian Territories

From Amman

From Amman, JETT runs a daily 7am service to the King Hussein/Allenby Bridge crossing (Jisr al-malik husayn; one hour; JD10) from the Abdali bus station. Arrive at least 30 minutes prior to departure to buy your ticket. They can also collect passengers from hotels. The fare is more expensive than service taxis, which cost no more than JD5 at any time of the morning, or the public bus that leaves from Tabarbour bus station and charges JD3. However, apart from comfort, the important advantage of the JETT bus is that it guarantees you a rapid crossing and, moreover, it secures a place on the only means of transport allowed across the bridge itself, namely a bus that shuttles between the Jordanian and Israeli checkpoints.

If you take a taxi, it will drop you at the Jordanian checkpoint, where you must wait for a place on the next shuttle bus. The fare is JD10 and the last bus leaves the Jordanian checkpoint half an hour before the bridge closes. The bridge is normally open for departures from Jordan Sun–Thur 8am–10pm (arrival is recommended by 7pm) and Fri–Sat 8am–1pm (arrival is recommended around 10am), with reduced hours on Jewish or Muslim holidays. Opening hours can be unpredictable during periods of political uncertainty: it's best to ask your hotel or travel agent to check.

If you manage to make the journey over the bridge (called Allenby on the west side of the river), you can share a service taxi (called *sherout*) to Jerusalem for a rate advertised on a board inside the checkpoint building. There are also less frequent buses to Jericho and from there to Jerusalem.

It is advisable to make advanced reservations for accommodation in Jerusalem, especially in the Christmas and Easter periods.

Royal Jordanian flies daily from Amman to Tel Aviv with fares starting at JD260 one way.

The Wadi 'arabah border can be reached from Al-'aqaba in service taxis.

From Israel

From Israel, bus services operated by the Israeli state company **Egged** (tel: 03-694 8888; www.egged.co.il) can take you to Beit Shean and Eilat. From there you can take a shared taxi (*sherout*) to the border crossings. **Mazada Tours** in Israel (tel: 03-544 4454; www.mazada.co.il; email: mazada@mazada.co.il) runs a bus tour service from Tel Aviv to Jordan, with prices starting at $400.

In East Jerusalem, service taxis leave from just opposite Damascus Gate (Bab Al Amoud) for the **King Hussein (Allenby) Bridge** (Sun–Thur 8am–8pm for arrivals and 8am–2pm for departures; Fri–Sat 8am–1pm) and fill up from 7.30am onwards. Reserve a seat at the nearby office or ask your hotel to call the taxi company and organise for you to be picked up from your hotel at a pre-arranged time. Try to book in advance and ensure that they take you all the way to the checkpoint. It's a good idea to start your trip early as the bridge crossing can take time, especially during high season (it can take anything from 15 minutes to two hours). The fare is around 50 Israeli shekels per person if the seven-seat taxi is full; if not, you can charter the whole taxi (around 200 shekels).

The trip takes 40 minutes to the bridge checkpoint on the Israeli-occupied side. From there, buses shuttle between the Jordanian and Israeli checkpoints. Travellers are not allowed to walk, drive their own vehicle or hitch.

Once you are on the Jordanian side you must pass through passport control where your bags will be checked by customs officers. For Amman, service taxis at the nearby rank can drop you at Abdali bus station or South bus station (JD10; 45 minutes). You can also catch the cheaper public minibus that will drive you straight to Abdali.

As well as the King Hussein (Allenby) Bridge, there are two other border crossings between Jordan and Israel: the **Sheikh Hussein Bridge** (Jisr al-shikh husayn) at the north of the Jordan Valley, between the Jordanian town of Irbid and the Israeli town of Beit Shean, Sun–Thu 8am–10pm, Fri–Sat 9am–8pm), and the **Wadi 'arabah** border crossing between Al-'aqabah and Eilat in the south (open Sun–Thur 6.30am–8pm and Fri–Sat 8am–8pm. Closed on Islamic New Year day and Yom Kippur).

You can reach the Sheikh Hussein Bridge from Irbid in a service or private taxi. On the Israeli side you will have to take a taxi or *sherout* to Beit Shean, from where Egged (tel: 03-694 8888; www.egged.co.il) runs buses.

Visas for most nationalities can be obtained at this border and prior permits are not needed except for restricted nationalities.

The Israeli exit visa costs 179 shekels at the King Hussein/Allenby Bridge crossing, and less at the other borders, payable in shekels, dollars or Iraqi dinars.

Note that on exiting, your passport will be stamped automatically on both sides of the border. If you plan to travel to Syria, Iran, Lebanon, Libya, Saudi Arabia or Yemen (and in theory Bahrain, Oman, Qatar, and the UAE also) and have an Israeli stamp in your passport, you may well be denied entry. Many travellers get round this by asking Israeli immigration to stamp a loose piece of paper instead, but beware unexplained periods of time in your passport – say between entry and exit visas. Another solution is to put Israel last on your itinerary.

By car

To bring your car into Jordan you will need an international driving licence (*carnet de passage en douane*) and insurance, both of which should be obtained before leaving home. You may also have to pay for a local third-party car insurance (usually very reasonable), or you may prefer to buy local comprehensive insurance (price varies according to the make of the car). Your car is free of import duty for up to one year unless you decide to sell it to tax-paying residents, when you will have to pay duty.

From Syria

When the border is open again, following the civil war, you can drive to Dir'a and cross into Al-ramatha in Jordan. The two crossing points, Dir'a–Ramtha and Nasib–Jaber, are open 24 hours a day.

From Egypt

Drive to Nuwayba and take the Egyptian or Jordanian ferry to Al-'aqabah, which leaves daily at midnight (but timetables change often; check before travelling). You can buy tickets at the port office in Nuwayba and you must pay for each passenger as well as the car ($90 per person, $190 per vehicle). The ferry journey should take three to four hours but it can take much longer, depending on traffic and weather conditions.

From Israel and the Palestinian Territories

Only private vehicles are permitted passage between Jordan and Israel (though note that private vehicles are not allowed over the King Hussein/Allenby Bridge (Jisr al-malik husayn) border). Rental cars are not allowed to pass. If you want to drive a rented car in Jordan, arrive first by bus or plane and rent when there.

GETTING AROUND

On arrival

Though Jordan officially has two international airports, Queen Alia Airport, its principal gateway and hub, and King Hussein Airport (also known as Al-'aqabah Airport) in the far south, 10km (6 miles) north of the town of Al-'aqabah, the latter is really only used for international flights by European charter airlines, particularly from Germany, Poland and Hungary.

Getting from the airport to Amman

Queen Alia Airport (tel: 06-445 3000 or 06-500 2777; www.qaiairport.com), 32km (20 miles) south of Amman, is served by the Airport Express Bus (tel: 06-489 1073; outside Arrivals Hall, Terminal 2), which connects it to the North Bus Station via the 4th, 5th, 6th and 7th Circles. It runs daily on the hour from 6.30am to midnight.

A service also runs every 30 minutes from 6am–midnight to Abdali bus station (45 minutes depending on traffic) and costs JD3 and JD 0.50 per piece of luggage. Tickets must be purchased before departure. Buses leave from outside the Arrivals Hall in Terminal 2.

Private taxis (as opposed to service – shared – taxis) are yellow and are plentiful. The journey to downtown Amman takes 30–40 minutes depending on traffic and costs around JD20–30 depending on distance, but ensure the metre is used.

Terminal 1 is Royal Jordanian's hub; Terminal 2 is used by other international airlines. Both contain ATMs, foreign exchange bureaux, car hire agencies, cafés, a post office and left luggage facilities.

At the end of 2012, Jordan's much-anticipated new terminal opened. Designed by renowned British architect Norman Foster and partners, the spectacular and iconic building takes its inspiration from the Bedouin tent and appears to billow above the desert, despite its composition: over 127 concrete domes each weighing up to 600 tonnes. The new terminal has almost triple the old terminal's capacity.

Getting from Al-'aqabah to Amman

JETT (King Hussein St, Corniche, near Mövenpick Resort; tel: 03-201 5222) runs six buses daily (JD9; 4–4.5 hours).

A cheaper (but slower) public minibus service (JD5.5; 5–5.5 hours) leaves from the main bus station near the police station to Amman's South Station. Buses only depart when full and make multiple stops along the route according to passenger demand.

Royal Jordanian (Ash Sharief al-Hussein St; tel: 03-201 4474; www. rj.com) flies daily to Amman (from JD50). Their subsidiary, Royal Wings (www.royalwings.com.jo), flies daily to Amman. Flying time is about 45 minutes.

Jordan Aviation (tel: 06-550 1760 in Amman; 03-201 7766 in Al-'aqabah; www.jordanaviation.jo) also offers regular flights between Al-'aqabah and Amman (around JD50; 45 minutes).

Public transport

There are four types of public transport in Jordan: the large, "tourist" buses run by JETT, Trust and other companies, which are comfortable, air-conditioned and reliable; the public minibuses, which are cheap and run all over the country; the white "service taxis" that are shared and run much like little buses, covering fixed routes, but stopping on request and only leaving when full; and the yellow taxis that are not for sharing.

By bus

JETT runs daily services from Amman to Al-'aqabah (see page 290). JETT also travels daily to the King Hussein/Allenby Bridge (Jisr al-malik husayn), to the Dead Sea, and to Petra.

There are three main **bus stations** in Amman: Abdali Bus Station in Jabal Amman, Wahdat Bus Station (also known as the South Bus Station for its location in the southern suburbs of Amman) and Tabarbour (also known as the North Bus Station), the main station for northern destinations. Smaller bus stations include the Muhajireen Bus Station on Muhajireen Street, south of the 2nd Circle.

Buses from the Wahdat station go to Al-'aqabah, Ma'daba, Petra, Ma'an, Wadi musa, Al-karak and Hammamat Ma'in. If you want to go to Azraq, you must first get a bus to Al-zarqa'. From Muhajireen Station, buses run to Wadi as-Sir, and minibuses to South Shuna, Ma'daba and – indirectly – to the Dead Sea. Fares are cheap and rarely exceed JD5.

Taxis

The yellow private taxis are a fast (depending on the city's notorious traffic) and fairly cheap way of getting around Amman. They are abundant in most parts of the city and can be flagged down. They are obliged by law to use their meter, which starts at JD0.25. Most rides cost between JD2–3 depending on distance. Beware of taxis lurking in ranks

⊘ Service taxis

Service taxis run all over Amman and are a very cheap way of getting around. Similar to minibuses, service taxis post their destination outside. This is usually in Arabic but you can always shout out your destination at a passing service taxi. If it's going there, it will stop and pick you up.

outside big hotels or tourist attractions: they often don't use their meter and can ask a greatly inflated flat rate. Walk a short distance away from your hotel and hail one.

Jordanian women never sit in the front of a taxi next to the driver (just as they don't sit next to male passengers in buses), so it's wise for women travellers to follow suit and sit in the back to avoid "misunderstandings".

Cars with drivers

Most hotels offer cars with drivers for a whole or half day for between JD40–60 for the day, though it's worth trying to negotiate, particularly in the smaller hotels. Alternatively, if you find a city taxi driver you like, ask him to quote a day rate. Most are delighted to have the work.

Driving in Jordan

Jordan has an excellent infrastructure of well-maintained roads. Good motorways connect many parts of the country.

Driving in Jordan is fairly hazardous and is not for the faint-hearted, however. Drivers across the country very rarely indicate or use mirrors. Some, particularly in the country, don't check the road properly before pulling out, and many pull out anyway. The unwritten rule is that the largest vehicle gets priority, followed by whoever pushes hardest, and use of the horn is unremitting.

A particular problem for travellers is the paucity of road signs, particularly in the north and east of the country (the south, from Petra to Al-'aqabah and Wadi Rum, is well signposted). Many car hire companies offer sat navs which can help greatly, though the transliteration of Arabic names can cause confusion.

Beware of driving at night. Some cars have broken headlights or park unmarked to the side of the road. Wandering animals are also a hazard. If you hit one, you will be expected to compensate the owner on the spot. In the towns and villages, beware pedestrians who often cross without due attention. In the event of an accident, the driver is automatically held responsible whatever the circumstances. Pay attention on the motorways too, where trucks belting to Iraq or Saudi Arabia overtake one another

dangerously. Nonetheless, if you can keep your nerve, it's surprising how quickly you get accustomed to driving in Jordan.

Unmarked speed ramps are found throughout the country and fines for speeding are common on certain stretches of highway, particularly in the south. Speed limits are 50km/h (30mph) in built-up areas, and 90–110km/h (55–67mph) on multi-lane highways (usually indicated). Wearing a seatbelt is compulsory but not enforced so very few Jordanians do. Petrol stations are fairly abundant in towns and along some highways, but beware long stretches between towns, such as on the Dead Sea Highway, where there are few.

If you drive in the desert, ensure that your car has the right type of tyres (tyre pressure should be slightly lowered for desert conditions), and always take a container with extra petrol/gas and plenty of water.

Car hire

Car hire in Jordan is relatively expensive in comparison to the rest of the Middle East, and to a lesser extent Europe and the US, but there are plenty of companies competing in Amman and at the airport – less so in Al-'aqabah –who are often open to negotiation, particularly in the low season or for longer rentals. Prices range from around JD25–35 per day for a small to medium-size car with unlimited mileage but can drop with negotiation.

Apart from the well-known international car hire companies such as Avis (tel: 06-4451133; www.avis. com.jo; email: queenaliaairportheadquar teroffice@avis.com.jo), Europcar (tel: 06-5504031; www.europcar.jo) and Budget (tel: 0796969490; www.budget jordan.com email: infobudget@budget jordango.com.jo), there are plenty of local companies which can often offer more competitive rates and an accommodating service, but choose carefully. One that is particularly recommended is Montecarlo Car Rental (Building No 23, Northern Gate, University of Jordan; tel. 06-533 5155; www.montecar.com), run by the efficient, reliable and helpful Ayman Zayed, whose family business boasts 20 years' experience and a fleet of 90 cars. You can also hire a car with driver (US$30/40 per day inside/outside Amman plus the car hire).

A

Accommodation

Choosing a hotel

There is a good range of hotels in Jordan's capital, Amman, and at the main tourist sites such as Petra, where options range from family-run hostels or guesthouses to five-star luxury resorts. Outside these places, options can be more limited, though there is usually at least one two- or three-star hotel to be found.

Non-graded hotels (those without stars) are best avoided in Jordan. Rooms are very basic and grubby; sheets and pillowcases are not provided and any "extras", including showers in the communal bathrooms or air conditioning in summer (or heaters in winter), usually cost extra. One- to two-star establishments usually provide sheets, breakfast, a fan or sometimes a/c, and a certain level of cleanliness plus free access to communal showers. Three-star places usually offer rooms with better furnishings, including TV, a/c (or heater – a must in winter), mini-bar, phone and private bathrooms. Four-star hotels are often older five stars, and five-star ones generally want for nothing and also have their own pools and or beaches, gardens, spas, sport facilities, car hire offices, bookshops, craft shops, several restaurants and bars.

For those on a budget, some one- and two-star hotels offer dorm rooms, or triples or quads. In summer, many also allow travellers to sleep in beds lining the roof.

A speciality of Jordan's wildlife reserves are the RSCN-run lodges or resthouses, often eco-designed and attractively set in protected habitats. Accommodation varies from simple cabins to tents or tented bungalows, and though they seem expensive for their simplicity, a very high percentage of proceeds go back to the community they support. For an escape from the cities or ruin trails, a night in one is unmissable.

Almost all hotels are open to some negotiation over prices, especially during the low season (October–March) and for longer occupancies; smaller hotels are particularly flexible. It is always worth asking. All hotels charge an additional 16 percent sales tax so check if this is included in the price quoted. The busiest (and most expensive) seasons are from September to October, Christmas and New Year, and from March to mid-May. It is essential to make reservations during this time.

If you are a foreign resident in Jordan, enquire about rates for residents. Many hotels offer two different rates: one for Jordanians and one for foreigners, but might consider charging foreign residents the same rate as Jordanian residents (as occurs in entrance fees to some museums).

Prices quoted below may vary according to season. The resthouses listed below provide adequate and clean accommodation for the budget traveller, and tend to be very popular, so book ahead.

Campsites

The only site that could qualify as a fully serviced campsite is the beautiful **Rummana campsite,** located in the **Dana Nature Reserve**. It has 20 large, well-maintained tents (each equipped with mattresses and blankets), two bathrooms (with four showers in each), and a communal, Bedouin-style tent. Gas cookers are available to rent. It is open for visitors from March to October. See www.rscn.org.jo for rates/booking. A single/double/triple/quadruple tent costs from 60JD (plus 8 percent tax); this includes breakfast.

Camping is also possible in the grounds of some of the other reserves. Some have permanent installations such as the "tented bungalows" (canvas bungalows on wooden platforms) at 'Ajlun Forest Reserve.

Camping is permitted elsewhere in Jordan, though the lack of seclusion or access to water and the often litter-strewn sites can limit options. One place that is popular with fully independent campers is the desert landscapes of Wadi Rum. Overnighting in one of the Bedouin campsites in Wadi Rum is a highlight for many travellers. Facilities are basic: usually shared showers, a campfire or stove-cooked meal and a mattress in a (hot) tent or under the stars, but a night in the desert is a memorable experience.

The odd Bedouin-style camp can be found elsewhere, such as on the outskirts of Wadi musa near Petra.

Admission charges

In 2015, the government introduced the Jordan Pass (www.jordan-pass.jo), which enables tourists to visit various archaeological sites and museums in the Kingdom at a price of JD70 (around $99). The pass is a sightseeing package that covers entries to over 40 of Jordan's attractions, including Petra, Jarash and Wadi Rum. The pass also waves a tourist entry visa fee, if you purchase it before arriving in Jordan and stay a minimum three nights (four days). For children under 12, the admission is free to all sites covered by the Jordan Pass. Foreign students are usually not granted discounts (even with an international student card) unless studying in Jordan itself. Some museums are free.

Budgeting for your trip

Jordan is one of the most expensive Middle Eastern countries (though cheaper than Israel). In recent times, the cost of living has increased considerably and this has had a knock-on effect on the tourist industry. However, it's still possible to get by on around JD40 a day if you are ready to survive on street food and stay in basic budget hotels. Very basic accommodation starts at about JD10 (or even JD5, but don't expect sheets, let alone clean sheets, and access even to communal showers is sometimes charged as an extra). It is easy to eat cheaply and reasonably healthily for as little as JD5–10.

Mid-range to expensive accommodation starts at JD40 and can go up to as much as JD150 or more. Much more than that will get you into one of Jordan's increasing number of luxury hotels.

Eating out is relatively inexpensive (at least by European standards); lunch or dinner in a basic restaurant costs around JD5, a more substantial meal in a more upmarket establishment between JD10 and 15, while JD20–30 and above will buy a meal in quite a smart restaurant. Tea, coffee, water and street food (falafel, for example) cost around JD0.5–1, and a local beer about JD4–5.

Transport within cities is cheap (especially public buses and service taxis). A journey around Amman should not cost more than JD2 or 3.

Business travellers

Avoid making appointments on Friday and Saturday (the Muslim weekend), and carry lots of business cards. After greetings, this is often the first thing that is exchanged. Dressing smartly is important since appearance (including the quality of clothes) is seen as a reflection of success. Men should wear a suit and tie for business meetings while women are best advised to show cultural awareness – such as by avoiding short, tight-fitting skirts, blouses buttoned down low and so

on. In business circles, English is widely spoken.

Be sure to obtain a Business Visa from Jordanian Consulate in your country before travel; a letter from your employer stating the purpose of your trip will be requested.

Most of Jordan's top hotels have fully equipped conference facilities. Large, world-class events are usually held in the King Hussein Bin Talal Conference Centre (www.3.hilton.com) on the Dead Sea or the Zara Expo (www.zaraholding.com/zara-expo) in Amman.

Amman Chamber of Industry (ACI)
Tel: 06-464 3001
www.aci.org.jo
Jordan Chamber of Commerce (JCC)
Tel: 06-566 5492
www.jocc.org.jo; www.jordan-business.net

Children

Children in the Middle East are seen as a blessing from God and the principal purpose in life, and travellers with children are usually welcomed with delight. Jordanians love children and take them everywhere and you will often see them about at parties and in restaurants until late in the evening. Crime against children committed by strangers is unheard of.

Most restaurants can cater to children's needs and increasingly have play areas for children, particularly in Amman. Some hotels have playrooms and can also arrange babysitting. Almost all hotels of three-stars and up have baby cots.

Babies up to two years of age travel free on planes, and those up to age 12 travel for half price.

Climate

Jordan enjoys almost year-round sunshine and blue skies. Rain falls only from late autumn to mid-spring. In recent years, the annual rainfall has declined steadily. Al-'aqabah, the south and the desert have negligible rainfall.

What to wear

Comfortable walking shoes are a must. In the cold months (November–March), bring warm

and waterproof clothing. Even in the summer, the temperature can drop significantly after sundown and you will need something to keep yourself warm in the evenings.

A pair of decent sunglasses are essential, even in winter, as is suntan lotion and sunblock. Insect repellent is also useful.

In the summer, cotton clothes are a much better choice than synthetic materials, and a hat is highly recommended, particularly for the days spent under the scorching sun exploring the extensive ruins at places like Petra, Jarash and Umm qays.

Even if you're not planning to swim in the Red Sea or Dead Sea, you may wish you'd brought a swimsuit to take advantage of hotel pools or for trekking in the gorges of Wadi al-mujib.

Jordan is a conservative country as far as dress code is concerned. Women should avoid wearing tight clothes, sleeveless blouses, shorts, mini-skirts, and any see-through materials. As a rule of thumb, the more respectfully you dress, the more respectfully you will be treated. Some single women like to don wedding rings to prevent "misunderstandings" arising.

When to go

The best time to visit Jordan is in the spring (March–May), when the winter rains have turned the country green and brought out the wild flowers. In places, even the desert is a mass of colourful blooms. Also pleasant is autumn, September–October, when the hot summer has given way to milder weather that is perfect for outside dining and café culture. In winter (December–February),

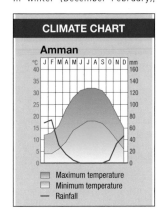

CLIMATE CHART

Amman

- ▢ Maximum temperature
- ▢ Minimum temperature
- — Rainfall

Jordan can be decidedly chilly, with rain and even snow in Amman and Petra, but there will be far fewer tourists (except during Christmas and New Year). Weather remains warm and pleasant year-round at Al-'aqabah and the Dead Sea.

Average temperatures: January: Amman 7°C (45°F), Irbid 9°C (47°F), Al-'aqabah 16°C (61°F); July: Amman 25°C (76°F), Irbid 25°C (76°F) and Al-'aqabah 31°C (88°F).

Crime and safety

It is advised to exercise a high degree of caution in Jordan due to the threat of terrorist attacks. Monitor the media and check the government website and other sources of information about possible new security risks. The ongoing conflicts in Iraq and Syria have the potential to cause instability in Jordan. At the time of writing, the Jordanian government advised that the border crossings from Jordan to Syria and Iraq remain closed. It is also advised against all but essential travel to within 3km (1.8 miles) of the entire Syrian border, and to within 6km (3.7 miles) of the Syrian border between routes 15 and 35. There is also a heightened risk of terrorism against aviation.

Jordan is a relatively safe country to travel in but the usual travel precautions apply: keep your money in a hotel safe if available and keep an eye on your belongings in public places. Women are best advised to avoid places where they're likely to find themselves alone (such as wandering around remote ruins). If in doubt, find a companion to go with you or ask to be accompanied. A good tip if concerned is to confide your worry to a local, who will feel obliged to look after you.

If you run into serious trouble and need legal advice or representation, contact your embassy, which may be able to recommend local lawyers. The vast majority of lawyers and doctors speak English. In case of a car accident, leave all vehicles involved exactly as they are, call the police (dial 196; 911 in an emergency), wait for them to arrive, and obtain a police report (essential for your car hire company and insurance claims).

The country is surrounded on all sides by neighbours with turbulent pasts and presents. This, along with the intake of refugees, has resulted in Jordan becoming a victim of terrorism. A number of terrorist-related incidents occurred in 2016 (some serious) and they are likely to continue until the conflict is solved. In the past, tourists have been targeted in Jordan. In March 2008, a German tourist was wounded when walking in downtown Amman. In July 2008, a man opened fire on a tourist bus in the capital. In September 2006, a man opened fire on a group of tourists who were visiting the Roman Theatre (Al-muddaraj al-rumani) in Downtown Amman; four months later a Dutch tourist was wounded. In November 2005, three Al Qaeda suicide bombers from Iraq hit three major hotels in Amman killing 60 people and injuring almost a hundred. Nonetheless, such incidents remain relatively rare, and the Jordanian security services, considered one of the most effective and active in the region, remain alert and have successfully foiled an unknown number of terrorism threats since – minor and major. There is no reason to be unduly alarmed, though it pays to be vigilant at all times.

Because of simmering local political tensions, demonstrations occur frequently at university campuses, town centres, and near the Palestinian refugee camps. It is advisable to stay away from these, as they can turn violent. Remain alert to trouble or problems when close to the borders of Israel, Iraq and Syria.

Customs

Exempt from duty are: personal effects such as cameras, clothes, and digital equipment for personal use, plus up to 200 cigarettes, 1 litre of spirits and 2 litres of wine and 200 grams (7oz) of tobacco.

Both departing and arriving passengers can buy duty-free items at Matar al-malika 'alya'. The Mall duty-free shop is open from 8am to midnight.

Cars and electrical equipment, from household goods to personal computers, are subject to duty in Jordan, and this can be very high. If you are bringing in taxable goods that you will take with you when you leave, such as a laptop computer, ask the customs officials to enter details in your passport to avoid paying tax. Upon exit you will be asked to show that your goods were tax exempted.

Unlike most Arab countries, Jordan does not censor foreign publications. That said, sexually explicit material is not welcome and may be confiscated.

D

Disabled travellers

Facilities for the disabled are found in five-star hotels and some four-star establishments, as well as a few upmarket restaurants in Amman. Outside these places, facilities are rare, public transport is challenging and town streets are notoriously obstacle-ridden. Nonetheless, Jordanians are always delighted to help and nothing proves too much trouble. Disabled visitors to Petra can travel to the main sites by horse-driven carriages. Royal Jordanian (along with other airlines that fly to Jordan) can provide wheelchair service with prior notice.

E

Electricity

Jordan operates on a current of 220–240V. Most places use two-pin European-style plugs but a few use British-style three-pin plugs. You can find adaptors as well as transformers for American electrical goods in electrical stores.

Embassies

The following diplomatic missions are in Amman. Egypt also has a consulate in Al-'aqabah. Other diplomatic missions are listed in the monthly *Your Guide to Amman*, available free at hotels and travel agents in Amman.

American Embassy
Tel: 06-590 6000
www.jo.usembassy.gov
Sun–Thur 8am–4.30pm; closed public holidays.
Australian Embassy
Tel: 06-580 7000
41 Kayed Al-Armoti St, Abdoun Al-Janoubi

www.jordan.embassy.gov.au
Email: amman.austremb@dfat.gov.au
Sun–Thur 8am–4pm; closed public holidays.
British Embassy
Tel:06-590 9200
www.gov.uk/government/world/organisations/british-embassy-amman
Sun–Wed 8am–3.30pm, Thur 8am–3pm.
Canadian Embassy
Tel: 06-590 1500
http://www.canadainternational.gc.ca/jordan-jordanie/contact-contactez.aspx
Sun–Wed 8am–4.30pm, Thur 8am–1.30pm.
Egyptian Embassy
7 Mohamed Bedir St, Abdoun
Tel: 06-592 9809
Email: eg.emb_amman@mfa.gov.eg
Sun–Thur 9am–3pm; closed public holidays.
Syrian Embassy
Prince Hashem Bin Al-Hussein St, Abdoun
Tel: 06-592 0684
Sun–Thur 8.30am–2pm.

Emergencies

Telephone numbers
Emergency: 191
Police: 191
Ambulance: 193

Entry requirements

All passports require an entry visa. Most nationalities currently pay JD40 for a single-entry visa, or JD180 for a multiple. Visas can be obtained in advance from the Jordanian embassy in your home country, or a single-entry visa valid for one month can be obtained for JD40 upon arrival at any border entry or airport. However, note that you still cannot obtain an entry visa at the King Hussein (Allenby) Bridge if you are entering from the West Bank, because Jordan does not recognise this to be a border. If you want to enter Jordan from the bridge, you must have a valid visa already stamped in your passport (it doesn't need to be a multi-entry visa if you are re-entering). If you are returning to Jordan (such as after a trip to Jerusalem), you don't need a new visa so long as your old visa is still valid and you re-enter at this point.

Single-entry visas obtained in Jordanian consulates are valid for two months from the date of issue.

You will need to register at the nearest police station if you stay for more than one month in Jordan. Multiple-entry visas are valid for six months; tourist visas issued upon arrival allow a stay of up to one month (which can be extended before the first visa expires). Upon expiry, this period can be extended for another two months. Beyond that date, you should exit and re-enter the country or undergo the complicated immigration procedures. If your visa has not been renewed properly by the time you leave Jordan, you will have to pay a fine at the border.

The Jordanian government has waived visa fees for all non-restricted nationalities coming through Jordanian tourist operators. The visa fee is waived on the condition that travellers spend a minimum of two consecutive nights in Jordan. Non-restricted nationalities include most European countries, the USA, Canada, Mexico, South Africa, Australia and New Zealand.

For information on visa requirements to neighbouring countries, including Egypt, Israel and the Palestinian Territories, Saudi Arabia and Syria, see the Transport chapter.

Al-'aqabah visas
As part of the free-trade agreement operating within the Al-'aqabah Special Economic Zone (ASEZ; www.aqabazone.com), one-month visas to enter Jordan are issued free on arrival at Al-'aqabah port, Al-'aqabah international airport, the overland crossing from Saudi Arabia, and even from Amman's Queen Alia Airport. If arriving in Amman, be sure to tell the officers that you are going to Al-'aqabah, and ask for an ASEZ visa.

Note that these visas come with no obligation to stay inside the ASEZ area; they grant you free movement around the whole country. You must, however, report to the ASEZ Authority (Visa Directorate in Al-'aqabah within two working days of arrival. There you will need to fill out a form and get it officially stamped. If you do not, you will be liable to pay the JD40 visa fee upon departure. ASEZ visas can only be extended beyond their initial one month at the ASEZ offices. If you will be elsewhere when your ASEZ visa runs out, request a normal JD40 entry visa at immigration when you arrive at Al-'aqabah, since these can

be extended at any police station in Jordan.

Animal quarantine
There is no animal quarantine in Jordan, nor any regulations currently about bringing pets into the country. At the very most you may be asked for a certificate of health for the animal.

Etiquette

Dress
Conservative dress is advisable for both men and women, especially in downtown Amman and outside the cities. Muslim Jordanian women cover their arms, legs and hair. Although Western women are not expected to do the same, revealing clothing is considered inappropriate. Shorts are very rarely worn by either sex, and would be out of place in downtown or rural areas. Topless sunbathing is prohibited. Two-piece swimsuits are acceptable in touristy areas such as large hotel pools, although one-piece swimsuits are preferred.

Greetings and physical contact
When people are introduced, shaking hands is the norm among men. Women who know each other usually greet each other by several pecks on the cheek. Many women prefer to avoid touching a man (including a handshake) whom they do not know well; don't extend a hand unless the woman does; a hand on the chest, a smile or nod suffices. Older men or devout Muslims will often avoid touching a woman at all if she is not directly related to them and will place a hand on the chest instead. Public displays of affection between members of the same sex are common, especially among men, who sometimes walk down the street hand in hand (though gay travellers should note that homophobia is rife and homosexuality is still strictly taboo), but displays between a man and a woman are frowned upon and in conservative areas considered taboo.

Hospitality
Jordanians, like other Middle Easterners, are famous for their hospitableness and will jump at the slightest opportunity to invite you home for tea, lunch or dinner. If you can't attend, place your right hand

Avoid unwanted attention by dressing conservatively.

culinary choice is greatly reduced, except in very touristy areas such as Petra.

Meanwhile, in line with current Middle Eastern obsession with fast food, American chains have arrived in full force, with a McDonald's or Burger King around almost every corner.

Like the cuisine, the type of restaurant varies widely: from ornate dining rooms served by waiters in black tie to tiny hole-in-the-wall joints serving the Arabic equivalent of fast food: falafel in flat bread. In between are buzzing fish restaurants, where the day's catch is displayed at the door, grills where the smell of meat sizzling on hot coals reaches you long before you're seated, and simple diners where there are no menus and the day's speciality is slapped down on plastic plates in front of you.

Vegetarians won't feel shortchanged with Arabic food. Many of the meze are vegetable-based, including the ubiquitous hummus and baba ghanoush, and a spread of meze can be eaten either as starters or as a main.

During the hot summer months (usually May to October), many restaurants move their main dining area to their outdoor terraces and gardens; eating out is one of the great joys of dining in Jordan. Note that Jordanians tend to eat late, with lunch at around 2pm and dinner rarely before 9pm. However, restaurants open earlier: at 12.30pm or earlier for lunch and around 7.30pm for dinner.

During Ramadan, when those fasting refrain from eating during daylight hours, many restaurants close for the whole month. Those that remain open serve food only after sunset when the fast is broken. Some of these put on special postfast feasts.

Be aware that all the hotel restaurants and many larger establishments add on a 10 percent service charge and a 16 percent sales tax to bills, which can considerably increase the cost of a meal.

Jordan, and particularly Amman's, dining scene is constantly changing – and no more so than during the economic downturn, when some establishments have been forced to close – so it's a good idea to check current recommendations on the ground. Hotel managers or

over your heart and politely make your excuses.

Hands and feet

When entering the home (and when visiting mosques), it's customary to leave shoes at the door. Avoid pointing the soles of your feet at anyone as this is an insult. Remember to accept food or drink and to eat with the right hand only (the left is used for personal hygiene) and keep the left tucked firmly to your side or behind your back.

During Ramadan, as a sign of respect to those observing the fast, visitors are expected to refrain from smoking, eating and drinking in public during daylight hours.

Food and drink

Where to eat

In general, Arabs eat out less that people in the West; an invitation to eat at home is one of the most important means of social interaction and

huge pride is attached to homecooking. When Jordanians do go out to eat, they expect at least the same high standard of cooking that they would enjoy at home. Amman therefore has plenty of restaurants that serve fine Arabic food. Many of the restaurants are Lebanese, considered by many as the haute cuisine of the Arab world.

After a week or two with meze, falafel or kebabs for lunch and dinner (and sometimes breakfast too), some travellers crave other cuisines. In the past, Amman has been criticised for its lack of culinary diversity. In fact, the city's tastes have broadened considerably in recent years. This is in part due to demand from the large expat population, as well as the considerable demand from well-heeled, welltravelled young Ammanis. Now restaurants in Jordan offer cuisine as diverse as Armenian, Thai, Mexican and Vietnamese. Many of these international restaurants number among Amman's best and most famous restaurants and are worth sampling if you're craving a culinary change. Outside Amman, the receptionists are often a great source of information, particularly in the larger hotels. Taxi drivers are also good, particularly for the best local food. Unfortunately, there is no regularly updated listings magazine or book.

Arabic fast food

Anyone on walkabout throughout the city should keep their eyes open for chains such as Al Kalha, Al Jabri or any SAJ restaurants. The Arab version of fast food, they serve fresh and delicious *shawarmah* and all kinds of *muqabalat* (traditional starters). There's usually at least one in almost every city neighbourhood and you can usually eat in or take away. Taxi drivers know them by heart, if you suddenly find yourself peckish.

Alcohol

Most of the larger restaurants (including those inside the larger hotels) serve alcohol, particularly those used to catering to tourists. The smaller restaurants usually do not. During Ramadan, when alcohol sales and drinking are banned, most do not.

Jordan has its own beer, the rather refreshing Amstel, brewed locally under licence. Wine is generally imported from the Palestinian Territories and Israel, Tunisia, Cyprus and France. Some of the best Palestinian wines come from the Domaine de Latroun. Look out in particular for the sauvignons, pinots, and the caregnano grape varieties. Alcohol can be purchased at many grocers and supermarkets. Safeway stocks the widest selection of foreign wines.

H

Health and medical care

Vaccinations

If you come from a country infected by epidemic diseases such as cholera and yellow fever, you will have to show a certificate of vaccination. It is advisable to be vaccinated against diphtheria, hepatitis (gamma globulin), polio, tetanus and typhoid.

Food and drink

The four-star hotels and upwards generally have their own water filtering systems and their tap water is safe to drink. Elsewhere you should drink bottled water, which is widely available and, outside hotels, cheap.

All the usual travel advice applies: wash thoroughly any fruit and vegetables that you buy, avoid suspect salads and ice cream.

Sun

The temperature in summer months can reach over 40°C (104°F). Suncream, sunblock, sunglasses and a sun hat are essential accessories against the heat of the sun. Also drink plenty of water to avoid dehydration.

Medical services

All treatment including emergency treatment must be paid for before leaving the medical centre. A certificate of treatment will then be issued to enable you to claim back the expenses from your insurance. Travel insurance is essential.

Generally speaking, Jordan has good medical care, and there is a clinic in every town and village as well as plenty of pharmacies staffed by qualified and knowledgeable staff. Amman is home to a large number of hospitals and high-quality specialists. Hospital beds are categorised into three classes and prices are fixed for all.

Contact your embassy for a list of recommended hospitals and doctors. To find a doctor or pharmacist that is open outside normal hours consult the free monthly *Your Guide to Amman*, which lists doctors and chemists on night duty and hospitals.

The *Jordan Times* publishes a daily list of doctors and chemists on night duty in Amman. There's a good 24-hour chemist near Al-Khalid (Rawhi; tel: 06-464 4454). In an emergency, contact your hotel and embassy.

Reputable hospitals in Amman include the following:

Hussein Medical Centre
Wadi Seer
Tel: 06-585 6856
Italian Hospital
Al-Muhajreen
Tel: 06-510 1010
Jordan Hospital
Queen Noor Street
Tel: 06-560 8080/30
Palestine Queen Alia
(near Marriott Hotel)
Tel: 06-560 7071
Philadelphia Hospital
8th Circle, Prince Rashid Dist
Tel: 06-585 4801/9

I

Internet

The government's tolerance towards online news and comment

⊙ Jordan's festivals and events

Jordan Rally (www.jordanrally.com; usually April; Dead Sea area). Organised by the FIA World Rally Championship, it attracts international competitors for the 1,008km (614-mile) run.
Dead Sea Ultra Marathon (www.deadseamarathon.com; usually April; Amman to Dead Sea). The 50km (30-mile) race attracts competitors from around the world.
Independence Day (25 May; across Jordan). Marked usually by local festivities such as military parades in Amman and music or dance displays.
Jarash Festival (www.jerashfestval.jo; July; Jarash ruins). Jordan's most famous cultural festival attracts major international acts, including dance, music, poetry, opera and theatre.

Global Village (www.globalvillagejo.com; July and August; Amman). An annual carnival that stages musical and theatrical performances, a fun fair, themed pavilions and a large food court.
Summer Theatre (July and August; various). During the summer months, theatre and musical performances are held in Amman's Roman Theatre (Al-muddaraj al-rumani) and Al-udi'un, as well as in other towns including Al-salt, Fuheis and Jarash.
Jordan Running Adventure Races (November; Petra to the Dead Sea via Wadi Rum) offers two routes of either 80km (49 miles) or 190km (116 miles).

See also Public Holidays, page 299.

has from the start been greater than towards traditional news journalism, including print and broadcast news media. One of the results is that Jordanians can obtain information from the internet that would be considered taboo or simply go unreported in the printed press. As a result, internet cafés have boomed and there are now thousands of cybercafés across Jordan. Initially proliferating in Amman, they have now sprouted up in other cities and towns throughout the country. Wireless access is increasingly available in hotels also. Even three- and two-star hotels often have it, particularly those catering to tourists.

Prices vary. Wireless or business centre access in the big hotels can be expensive, but the cafés usually offer per hour rates from around JD1 an hour.

L

LGBTQ travel

Although homosexuality is not rigorously persecuted, and Jordan's approach to it is a lot more relaxed than that of some of its Muslim neighbours, it is still illegal under the country's law. Public displays of affection between homosexual couples can result in fines and prison sentences, similar to those convicted of possession or trafficking of narcotics. It is not uncommon, however, to see two men or women holding hands, wrapping their arms around one another or even greeting each other with a kiss as a way of expressing their friendship.

There are no gay organisations or fully gay venues in Amman, though some cafés and bars in Amman have garnered a reputation for being "gay friendly", including Books@café near Rainbow St. Most of gay Jordan centres on the virtual community created by the internet.

Lost property

Lost property should be reported to the police, and a police report obtained, as this will be required by your insurance company. If you lose your passport, contact your embassy.

M

Maps

Basic tourist maps of towns are often available in hotels. Better but fairly outdated maps in Arabic and English are produced by the **Royal Jordanian Geographic Centre** (www.rjgc.gov.jo), and are available in some bookshops in Amman and elsewhere. These include *the Road Map of the Hashemite Kingdom of Jordan*, as well as the town or site maps of: Amman, Jarash, Petra, Wadi Rum and Al-'aqabah. The RJGC also prints a *Map of Jordan* in Arabic, English, French, German and Italian. Foreign maps of Jordan are hard to come by in Jordan, so it is better to purchase your map before travelling.

One of the most frequently updated maps is Bartholomew's map of Israel with Jordan, although it omits the eastern tip of Jordan bordering Iraq. In addition to this, Cartographia (www.cartographiaonline.com) and ITMB Publishing (www.itmb.com) publish decent maps of Jordan.

In Britain, the famous travel bookshop Stanfords (12–14 Long Acre, London WC2E 9LP Tel: 020 7836 1321; www.stanfords.co.uk) sells most of the maps above.

Media

Newspapers and magazines

Jordan has a large number of newspapers in circulation in proportion to its population. The two biggest are the centrist *Al Dustour* (The Constitution) and *Al Ra'i* (The Opinion), while *Al Arab Al Yawm* (The Arab Today) and *Al Ghad* (Tomorrow) are more free-thinking. There are various other dailies and a host of weeklies.

There are two main English-language papers: the *Jordan Times* (www.jordantimes.com), a daily that covers events in Jordan and the region fairly comprehensively and reproduces more analytical pieces from the international press.

Many Amman news agencies and some hotels also stock a good selection of foreign newspapers and magazines in English, French, German, Italian, Spanish and Arabic. Imported publications are expensive.

Radio and television

Most hotels of three stars and up have satellite TV in the rooms; hotels of lower grades will often show satellite TV in the communal areas. Jordanian television's Channel 1 is pretty turgid, with news of the King's official engagements, slightly banal talk shows and plenty of melodramatic soaps and dramas. There are some US shows and TV movies, as well as English news nightly at 10pm. Most of the satellite channels are Arab, with a scattering of European channels too, but the US news channel CNN is widely available along with one or two US light entertainment or movie networks. The BBC's international channels – BBC World and BBC Prime – can sometimes be found on satellites in the bigger hotels.

With the recent deregulation, a clutch of new radio stations have started up in Amman, mostly playing Western pop music. Mood 92FM concentrates on classic rock and 1970s/80s pop, while Play 99.6FM has more current chart music. Radio Jordan's English station is on 855kHz medium wave all over Jordan, and also 96.3FM in Amman and 99.7FM in Al-'aqabah, but it broadcasts little other than pop music and brief English news bulletins at 7am, 2pm, 7pm and 10pm. Otherwise, Amman has no shortage of Arabic pop stations: the best are Radio Sawa, with a 24-hour English-language service (98.1FM), Radio Fann (104.2FM) and MBC (106.7FM).

BBC World Service broadcasts 24 hours a day on 103.1FM, and on short wave at 6.195, 9.410, 11.760, 12.095, 15.565, 15.575 and 17.640MHz at various times of day.

Money

Jordan's currency is called the Jordanian Dinar (JD), which is pegged to the dollar, and it is divided into 1,000 fils or 100 piastres (or *'irsh*). It appears in paper notes of JD50, 20, 10, 5 and 1. Coins come in denominations of JD1 and 0.5, and 250, 100, 50, 25, 10 and 5 fils.

At the time of going to press, the following rates apply:

1US$ = 0.70 JD
1£ = 0.904 JD
1 euro = 0.79 JD
1AU$ = 0.537 JD
100Yen = 0.637 JD

You can change foreign cash or travellers' cheques in banks, money changers and some hotels. Moneychangers usually offer the best rates (followed by banks, then hotels), but shop around among several before handing your cash over. Authorised moneychangers can be found in all the major cities and sometimes smaller towns too (usually near the town market). There are no foreign currency restrictions.

When changing travellers' cheques, you will be charged a commission. This varies from place to place but should be no more than around JD5. Amex is the most widely accepted brand. Don't forget to bring your cheques' sales receipt with you when changing. If you find you can get a good rate of exchange outside the country, buy in advance, as you can import as much Jordanian currency as you like.

Credit cards are accepted in most hotels, restaurants, airline offices, tour agencies and the larger shops. Among those commonly accepted are Visa, MasterCard and American Express.

Cash is preferred by smaller shops and in all the suqs (markets). Note that only cash (Jordanian dinar) is accepted as payment for entry visas at the airport (JD240/120 for single/multiple entry).

You can also use your card to draw cash (up to JD500 only and depending on your bank's own limits) at any bank linked with your credit or debit card network, in theory for no charge, but check.

ATMs (Automatic Teller Machines) are found throughout Amman and in all the cities, and increasingly in the smaller towns too and are equipped to deal with international PIN numbers.

O

Opening hours

Banks: 8.30am–3pm Sunday–Thursday. Some reopen 3.30–5.30pm. Closed Friday and Saturday. During Ramadan, 9am–1 or 2pm.
Businesses: Winter (November–April) 8 or 8.30am–1 or 1.30pm, 3 or 3.30–6.30pm; summer (May–October) 4 or 4.30–7.30pm. Most businesses close Friday, some close for all or part of Saturday. A few

businesses owned by Christians in particular are often closed all or part of Sunday. Some travel agencies stay open during the lunch break. During Ramadan: 9am–3 or 6pm.
Government offices: 8am–2pm Sunday–Thursday. Closed Friday and Saturday. During Ramadan: 9.30am–2pm.
Museums: 8am–5pm, closed Friday, but times do vary.
Post offices: Winter: 7am–5pm Saturday to Thursday and 7am–1pm Friday; summer: 7am–7pm Saturday–Thursday and 7am–1pm on Fridays. During Ramadan, post offices open 8am–3pm.
Shops: 8 or 8.30am–8 or 8.30pm. A few shops close in the afternoon for about two hours any time between 1pm and 4pm. Some close Friday, except for Amman's downtown suq. During Ramadan: 9am–1pm and after the break of fast, most will reopen until 9 or 10pm.

P

Photography

Always ask permission first if taking pictures of people, or use a zoom that will allow you take pictures unobtrusively. Women in Jordan often object and you should never insist. Beware of taking photos of any military installations or anything where security is sensitive, including the airport, border crossings, bridges and similar installations.

The best time of day for taking photos in Jordan is early morning and late afternoon when the sun is much less "contrasty" – in other words, shadows are less dark and highlights are less bright.

Postal services

The postal service (www.jordanpost.com.jo) in Jordan is generally reliable. For times of opening see "Opening Hours". Most four- and five-star hotels also sell stamps.

Mail is not delivered to addresses in Jordan but to post-office boxes.

Registered or express mail sent from Jordan is relatively cheap, but parcels are expensive to mail and must be left open for inspection by customs officials.

A poste restante service is available at some post offices. Poste

restante letters are kept for only one month from the date of their arrival at the post office.

The Central Post Office (Al-markiz al-baridi al-ra'isi) in Amman is located near the bottom of Shari' al-amir muhammad on the 1st Circle, Jabal Amman.

Public holidays

Friday and Saturday are Jordan's "weekend", when government offices, banks and most offices are closed. However, some airline offices, travel agents and shops stay open at weekends also. Most businesses and banks have a half-day on Thursday, and banks take Friday, Saturday and all public holidays off, including extended holidays such as Eid al-Fitr or Eid al-Adha.

Fixed public holidays

1 January New Year's Day
30 January King Abdullah's birthday
1 May Labour Day
25 May Independence Day
9 June King Abdullah's ascension to the throne
10 June Army Day
14 November King Hussein Remembrance Day
25 December Christmas Day

Muslim holidays

Muslim holidays follow the lunar calendar, so move back each year by 11 days.

Holidays last one day unless otherwise stated.

Eid al-Fitr – A three- or four-day feast marking the end of Ramadan.
Eid al-Adha – A four-day feast at the end of the Hajj (month of pilgrimage to Mecca). It commemorates Abraham's offering of his son for sacrifice. Families who can afford to sacrifice a lamb share the meat with their poorer Muslim neighbours.
First of Muharram – Islamic New Year
The Birthday of the Prophet Mohammed
Ramadan – Although Ramadan is not a good time to come to Jordan for business, it is a great time to experience at first hand Islam's most important feast and to experience the community atmosphere that the shared hardship of fasting creates among Muslims.

Bear in mind that town restaurants and cafés close during Ramadan during the day. If looking for somewhere to have breakfast, lunch or an early dinner, head for the large hotels that usually keeps at least one restaurant open during the day and sometimes a café, and even a bar too. Avoid eating, drinking or smoking in public during the hours of daylight, which could be construed as disrespectful and insensitive.

At sundown, Jordanian Muslims break the fast with a special iftar meal and celebrate long into the evening. Huge amounts of pre-prepared food are shared and devoured after dark. As a result most people look exhausted at work the next day. Ramadan is sometimes used by public – and private – sectors workers to provide a much reduced service. Just before dawn, Muslims rise to eat the last meal to sustain them through the next day's fasting.

Christian holidays

Easter in Jordan is celebrated by the local Protestant and Catholic churches at approximately the same time as the local Greek Orthodox Churches. Three out of every four years the timing will vary by a week, but in the other year by a whole month. Eastern (Orthodox) Christians regard Easter as a more significant feast than Christmas.

Despite the fact that Jordan is a predominantly Muslim country, Christmas and the New Year are celebrated in some splendour, thanks to Western commercialism, the local Christian population and Western expats.

R

Religious services

Churches and monasteries of various denominations are found in Amman and in towns in other parts of the country, including Ma'daba and particularly Bithani-beyond-the-Jordan, the site of Jesus' baptism by John the Baptist. Amman has Greek Orthodox, Anglican, Roman Catholic, Evangelical Lutheran, German-speaking Evangelical, Armenian Catholic and Orthodox, Coptic, Syrian Orthodox and interdenominational churches. Churches and their telephone numbers are advertised daily in the *Jordan Times* (call for

times of services), as are the times of Muslim prayers.

S

Shopping

Jordan offers an excellent and entertaining range of shopping experiences, ranging from atmospheric and pungent suqs and artisan craft shops, to state-of-the-art shopping malls, which offer a similarly wide range of goods and crafts.

Though bartering is generally found only in the suqs (where it's usually expected), most shops usually allow for some negotiation even on apparently fixed prices.

If you have a complaint against a shop, you can report it to the police, but take your receipt as evidence of payment.

The suq

A trip to a traditional suq is a must when in Jordan. The colour, bustle and atmosphere of shopping here are unrivalled. Usually located in the heart of the downtown, a suq is the traditional Middle Eastern market, where in theory you can buy almost anything. Nowadays, as modern shops and in particular the modern suq, the shopping mall, have developed, traditional suqs are more the reserve of the fruit, vegetables, spice and household goods vendors. A trip to the pungent and myriad-coloured stalls of the spice sellers is unforgettable. If you're lucky, the stall owners may explain the traditional use of some of the herbs and spices. Traditional medicine is very much alive and kicking in Jordan, even in the cities.

Souvenirs

If you are souvenir hunting, shops and stalls can be found throughout the country, but in particular in the large hotels and in the main tourist sites such as Petra. Some of the museums also have excellent gift shops stocked by Zara, a company that produces high-quality arts and crafts.

Arts and crafts

A number of charitable projects have grown up in recent years that produce high-quality traditional Jordanian arts and crafts while

Exporting purchases

There are no export restrictions except for items over 100 years old. Shopkeepers can post purchases to your home country, but make sure you have a receipt of all purchases and make a note of the shopkeeper's name and the shop's address.

providing employment and income to local communities, particularly disadvantaged women. Two of the original projects, the **Noor Al Hussein Foundation** (near Safeway, Amman; tel: 06-560 7460; www.nooralhussein foundation.org) and the **Jordan River Foundation** (tel: 06-461 2169; www.jordanriver.jo; in Jabal al Luwaybda, Amman), produce an excellent range of beautiful and high-quality crafts hand-made by local women. Prices are fixed.

Shopping areas in Amman

As Amman has grown, so has its shopping options, with new shopping areas now catering to individual neighbourhoods. These range from Downtown's **Emir Mohammed Street** (which runs from the 3rd Circle to the city centre), to **Abu Bakr As Siddeeq Street** (known as Rainbow Street), **Wasfi Tell Street**, known as Gardens Street (from Safeway to Al Waha Circle) and the upmarket areas of **Swayfiyah** and **Shumaysani**.

All the rage in Amman, as elsewhere in the Middle East (especially the Gulf), is a new commercial and social phenomenon: the glitzy shopping mall.

Student travellers

Unless studying in Jordan, foreign students are not eligible for concessions including at museums or on public transport in Jordan. However, all airlines, including Royal Jordanian, offer discounts on airfares. Royal Jordanian gives discounts of 45–60 percent of the full fare to holders of an international student card. Discounts are also available to students under 31 years old for routes in Europe, to students under 26 for Europe and the Middle East and to students under 25 for Europe, the Middle East and the United States. Young people between 12 and 24 years old qualify for discounts of around 45 percent of the full fare. Jordan has no travel agents specialising in youth/student travel. It is recommended to check the most current policy on concessions as it may change any time.

T

Telephones

Jordan's telephone system is generally efficient. Public phone offices and booths have largely been replaced by mobile phone use, which also provide the best service for travellers. The best option is to buy a cheap local handset (or use your home handset if it can pick up local signals) and purchase a local SIM card. Both handset and SIM card as well as pay-as-you-go top-up cards can be bought at the numerous and ubiquitous telecommunications shops around the country. Fastlink (www.jo.zain.com), Orange/Mobilecom (www.orange.jo) and Umniah (www.umniah.com) are the three biggest phone companies; all three have outlets in every town in Jordan.

Additionally, some of the phone companies offer special "extras", such as offering customers big discounts on calls to, say, three "favourite numbers" (including international landline and mobile numbers). Ask for advice on the best deals currently being offered. Even without discounts, calling internationally on the Jordanian mobile networks is not unreasonable; calling locally is very inexpensive.

All landlines have a two-digit code plus a seven-digit number. Mobile phone numbers start with 07 and then have eight digits. Toll-free numbers are prefixed 0800.

The international network access code is 00. If you want to call a number outside Jordan, you must dial 00 + country code + local code + number.

Directory enquiries: 1212 or 464 0444 for Amman numbers, and 1213 for international numbers.

Local codes

02 Irbid, Umm qays, the North, Jarash, 'Ajlun, Al-mafraq
03 Wadi musa region (Al-'aqabah, Petra, Ma'an, Al-karak)
05 Al-salt, Jordan Valley, Dead Sea, Azraq, Ma'daba, Al-zarqa'
06 Amman

Time zone

Jordan is two hours ahead of Greenwich Mean Time and seven hours ahead of US Eastern Standard Time from the beginning of October to the end of March. It is three hours ahead of GMT from April until the end of September.

Tipping

In a country which doesn't enjoy the benefits of a social welfare system, where unemployment is historically high and where salaries are low and the cost of living high, tips can be an essential means of survival. Though you won't be solicited for them as much as in countries such as Egypt, it will be expected if a service has been provided. The more upmarket hotels and restaurants may add 10–12 percent service charge to your bill but waiters do not always get this. Other establishments expect you to leave a tip for all staff or give something to those that worked for you the most. Taxi drivers are generally not tipped but it is customary to round up the price on the meter. Anywhere else, tip according to will and level of service but don't feel obliged to if the service has been bad. Also, try to avoid over-tipping, which can lead to raising expectations unfairly. If service has been good and you tip accordingly, it will be much appreciated.

One place where you may be pressed very hard to tip is Petra, particularly if you rent a horse. You need not tip more than 10 percent of the price you paid for the horse. If you are seriously harassed or abused, you can complain to the Tourist Police at the Markaz al-zuwwar.

Toilets

You'll find "Western-style" toilets in most hotels and restaurants, apart from those in the lower budget bracket. The hole-in-the-floor-and-squat style toilet might take a bit of getting used to at the beginning, but you will soon get the hang of it. The level of cleanliness of public toilets is very variable. If there is a caretaker, they may provide you with toilet paper. Don't put paper down the toilet (which leads to blockage); that's what the little baskets are for. It can be useful to carry your own supply of toilet paper. Alternatively, adopt the local habit of using water.

Tourist information

The Jordan Tourism Board (JTB), partly private and partly linked to the Ministry of Tourism, is charged with promoting Jordan overseas. It has offices or agents in the countries listed below, who can supply information, helpful, often themed brochures and bookings and contacts for the country.

Inside Jordan itself, tourist information centres or "Markaz al-zuwwars" can now be found at many tourist sites and some towns. Where they are lacking, the local office of the Department of Antiquities stands in as an informal source of local information, and in their absence, the town council, but they do not keep brochures.

JTB offices

Jordanian Tourism Board (Head Office)
P.O Box 830668
Amman, Jordan 11183
Tel: +962 6 5678444
www.visitjordan.com
Email: info@visitjordan.com
The office occupies the ground floor of the Ministry of Tourism & Antiquities building in Jabal Amman in Jordan's capital.
The Jordan Tourism Board UK
3 floor Terminal House, 52 Grosvenor Gardens
London SW1W 0AU
Tel: +44 (0)20 7326 9880
www.visitjordan.com
Jordan Tourism Board North America
1420 Beverly Rd., Suite 203
Mclean, VA 22101
Tel: +1 (0)1 703 243 7404/5
Toll free: 1-877-seejordan (733-5673)
www.na2.visitjordan.com
Email: contactus@visitjordan.com

Other tourism websites

www.tourism.jo
Ministry of Tourism and Antiquities
www.johotels.org
Jordan Hotel Association
www.tourguides.com.jo
Jordanian Tour Guides Association
www.jordanrestaurant.com

Jordan Restaurant Association
www.ammancity.gov.jo
The city of Amman's website
www.ammantoday.com
What's on in Amman
www.aqabah.jo
Al-'aqabah's website of the town, its surrounding area and things to do. Updated quite regularly
www.wadirum.jo
Wadi Rum
www.rscn.org.jo
Royal Society for the Conservation of Nature
www.mota.govdoa.jo
Department of Tourism and Antiquities
www.kingabdullah.jo
The King's official site, with detailed articles on Jordanian history, the royal family politics and tourism
www.queenrania.jo
The Queen's official site
www.kinghussein.gov.jo
The late King Hussein, biography, history and tributes
www.yellowpages.com.jo
Jordan's yellow pages

Tour operators

Tour operators in Amman and Al-'aqabah organise an excellent variety of independent tours, ranging from camel caravan trips to desert racing, scuba diving and staying with a Bedouin family in the desert. The following is a small selection of agencies. Though expensive for individuals, independent travellers might consider trying to form a small group.

Adventure Jordan
Tel: 0795 641911
www.adventurejordan.com
One-man outfit run by licensed trekking/tour guide Yam'an Safady, who leads walks and weekend adventures of all kinds around Jordan.

Desert Guides
Tel in France: +33.4.50.54.70.98
Tel in Wadi Rum: 777471960
www.desertguides.net
French company, partly based in Jordan, running wilderness expeditions and horse-riding holidays near Rum and Al-'aqabah.

Discovery
Tel: 06-569 7998
www.discovery1.com
One of the best eco-friendly Amman tour companies, able to put together any itinerary at short notice.

International Traders
Tel: 06-560 7014

www.traders.com.jo
Email: guest@traders.com.jo
Jordan's best-known and longest-established tour company.

La Beduina
Tel: 06-554 1631-2
www.labeduinatours.com
Excellent, full-service tour company based in Petra, and able to get you off the beaten track in comfort.

Petra Moon
Tel: 0- 796 170 666
www.petramoon.com
One of Jordan's top adventure tour operators, based in Petra.

W

Weights and measures

Jordan employs the metric system: length is measured in metres, distances in kilometres, weight in kilograms and volume in litres.
1 inch = 2.54 centimetres (cm)
1 foot = 0.30 metres (m)
1 yard = 0.91 metres (m)
1 mile = 1.61 kilometres (km)
1 acre = 0.40 hectares (ha)
1 ounce = 28.35 grams (g)
1 pound = 0.45 kilograms (kg)
1 British ton = 1016 kilograms
1 American ton = 907 kilograms
1 imperial gallon = 4.55 litres (l)
1 American gallon = 3.79 litres (l)

Women travellers

Rates of sexual crime against women are very low in the Middle East, including Jordan, and far lower than they are in the West. Nonetheless, harassment of female travellers does happen and reports of hassle have sharply increased in recent years.

A combination of factors is probably responsible: the strict segregation of the sexes, which can lead to frustration among young, unmarried men; a skewed view of Western women fuelled by trashy television and easily accessed web porn (which usually features Western women); cultural misunderstandings (Jordanian women never go out unaccompanied, and lone travellers are viewed as inviting overtures); opportunism (such as single females roaming lonely sites); lack of recrimination (the strict moral code enforced by closely knit communities does not operate here), and

last but not least, precedent: as one Jordanian male put it: "For every 14 tourists I ask, one will say yes!", and word spreads fast.

Though harassment usually doesn't go beyond hard stares and mutterings, it can be more serious. Women travellers have been solicited, groped or even assaulted in ruins when wandering alone or apart from a group. If travelling as a lone female, the best thing is to pair up with others especially if travelling to less visited sites. Ideally, at least one male should be included in the group, who should make it clear if necessary that approaches are not welcome. If you do run into problems and are groped, assaulted or experience other serious sexual harassment, call the police (tel: 191).

Reports have also been received of locals trying to take advantage of female tourists overnighting in budget hotels (peep holes are also a problem in some), as well as Bedouin camps in Wadi Rum. Stick with the recommended campsites and ensure other travellers overnight with you.

Beware of accepting any invitations from groups of young men and avoid drinking alcohol with anyone you don't know, even in a group. Things can rapidly turn nasty, particularly if expectations aren't met. Don't forget the basic rule of female safety: tell your hotel where you are going if you go out at night or accept an invitation.

Other tips include avoiding eye contact with men you don't know, sitting next to women in buses, cafés and restaurants (as the locals do), choosing the back seat of taxis, and wearing a wedding ring even if you are not married. Most important of all if you want to avoid attracting attention is to dress conservatively (see page 295). Body language is also important. Local women avoid eye contact, smiling and conversation with men they do not know; smiling and laughing is seen as flirtatious.

Though most women experience some degree of (generally) mild harassment, the incidents of extraordinary kindness, generosity and unforgettable Jordanian hospitality usually far outweigh them; don't let a few individuals mar your impressions of one of the most beautiful and hospitable nations in the world.

Though officially Jordan's second language is English and it is widely taught in schools, levels of fluency vary considerably. Though fluent speakers are rarely found outside the tourist hotels and sites, most people can usually muster enough to help with directions and other enquiries. Outside the educated classes and in rural areas in particular, English fluency is much less common. For this reason, it's well worth learning some basic words and phrases. An effort is hugely appreciated by Jordanians and it will be repaid a thousand times in terms of the welcome, help and services that often follows.

As in any Muslim country, God is frequently invoked in conversation, especially when there is a degree of chance involved. You will frequently hear phrases such as *Inshá allá* (God willing) and *Al hamdu-li-llá* (thanks be to God), which is even added when something bad happens – the logic being that it could have been worse and it is all God's will anyway.

GREETINGS

Hello *Márhaba, ahlan*
(reply) *Marhabtáyn, áhlayn*
Greetings *As salám aláykum* (peace be with you)
(reply) *Waláykum as salám* (and to you peace)
Welcome *Áhlan wasáhlan*
(reply) *áhlan fíkum*
Good morning *Sabáh al kháyr* (morning is goodness)
(reply) *Sabáh an-núr* (a morning of light)/*Sabáh al wurd* (a morning of the smell of flowers)
Good evening *Masá al kháyr*
(reply) *Masá an núr*
Good night *Tisbáh al kháyr* (wake up well)

(reply) *Wa ínta min áhlu* (and you are from His people)
Goodbye *Máa Saláma* (with peace)/*alla Máák* (God be with you)/*Ya'atik aláfia* (may God give you health)
How are you?
Káyf hálak? (to a man)
Káyf hálik? (to a woman)
well, fine
mabsút or *mneeh* (for a man)
mabsúta or *mneeha* (for a woman)
please
min fádlak (to a man)
min fádlik (to a woman)
After you
Tafáddal (to a man)
Tafáddali (to a woman)
Afáddalu (to more than one)
Excuse me
Samáhli or *Idha láwu samánt* (to a man)
Samáhili or *Idha láwu samánti* (to a woman)
Sorry *Áfwan* or *mutaásif* or *ásif* (for a man)/*Áfwan* or *mutaásifa* or *ásifa* (for a woman)
Thank you (very much) *Shúkran* (*jazilan*)
Thank you, I am grateful *Mamnúnak* (to a man)
Mamnúnik (to a woman)
Thanks be to God *Al hámdu li-llá*
God willing (hopefully) *Inshá allá*
Yes *Náam* or *áiwa*
No *La*
Congratulations! *Mabrúck!*
(reply) *Alláh yubárak fik* (Allah bless you back)

USEFUL PHRASES

What is your name?
Shú ismak? (to a man)
Shú ismik? (to a woman)
My name is... *Ismi...*
Where are you from?
Min wáyn inta? (for a man)
Min wáyn inti? (for a woman)
I am from... *Ána min...*
... England *... Ingíltra*

... Germany *... Almánia*
... the United States *... Amérika*
... Australia *... Ustrália*
Do you speak English? *Btíhki inglízi?*
I speak... *Bíhki...*
... English *... inglízi*
... German *... Almámi*
... French *... Fransáwi*
I do not speak Arabic *Ma bíhki árabi*
I do not understand *Ma báfham*
What does this mean? *Ya'áni esh?*
Repeat, once more *Kamán márra*
Do you have...? *Ándkum...?*
Is there any...? *Fí...?*
There isn't any... *Ma fí...*
Never mind *Ma'alésh*
It is forbidden *Mamnú'a*
Is it allowed? *Masmúh?*
What is this? *Shú hádha?*
I want *Bídi*
I do not want *Ma bídi*
Wait *Istánn* (to a man), *Istánni* (to a woman)
Hurry up *Yalla* or *bi súra'a*
Slow down *Shwáyya*
Finished *Khalás*
Go away! *Imshi!*
What time is it? *Adáysh as sáa?*/*kam as sáa?*
How long, how many hours? *Kam sáa?*

VOCABULARY

General

embassy *sifára*
post office *máktab al baríd*
stamps *tawábi'a*
bank *bank*
hotel *otél, fúnduq*
museum *máthaf*
ticket *tádhkara*
ruins *athár*
passport *jiwáz as sáfar*
good *kuwáys*
not good, bad *mish kuways*
open *maftúh*
closed *musákkar, múghlik*

Jordanian mosaic.

today *al yáum*
tonight *hadhi-l-láyl*
tomorrow *búkra*

Eating/drinking out

restaurant *máta'am*
food *ákl*
fish *sámak*
meat *láhma*
milk *halíb*
bread *khúbz*
salad *saláta*
delicious *záki*
coffee *áhwa*
tea *shái*
cup *finján*
with sugar *bi súkkar*
without sugar *bidún súkkar*
wine *nibíd*
beer *bíra*
mineral water *mái as saha*
glass *kubbaiya*
bottle *ázaja*
I am a vegetarian
Ána nabbáti (for a man)
Ána nabbátiya (for a woman)
the bill *al hisáb*

Getting around

Where...? *Wáyn...?*
downtown *wást al bálad*
street *shária*
Amir Mohammed Street *Shária al amir Mohammed*

car *sayára*
taxi *táxi*
shared taxi *servís*
bus *bas*
aeroplane *tayára*
airport *matár*
station *mahátta*
to *íla*
from *min*
right *yamín*
left *shimál*
straight *dúghri*
behind *wára*
near *aríb*
far away *ba'id*
petrol, super *benzín, benzín khas*

Days of the week

Monday *(yáum) al itnín*
Tuesday *at taláta*
Wednesday *al árba'a*
Thursday *al khamís*
Friday *al júma'a*
Saturday *as sábt*
Sunday *al áhad*

Numbers

zero *sifir*
one *wáhad*
two *itnín*
three *taláta*
four *árba'a*
five *khámsa*
six *sítta*

seven *sába'a*
eight *tamánia*
nine *tísa'a*
ten *áshara*

Shopping

market *súq*
shop *dukkán*
money *fulús*
cheap *rakhís*
expensive (very) *gháli (jídan)*
receipt, invoice *fatúra, wásl*
How much does it cost? *Adáysh?/ bi-kam?*
What would you like? *Shú bidak?* (to a man)/*Shú bidik?* (to a woman)/*Shú bidkum?* (to more than one)
I like this *Buhíbb hádha*
I do not like this *Ma buhíbb hádha*
Can I see this? *Mumkin ashúf hádha?*
Give me *A'atíni*
How many? *Kam?*

Looking for a room

a free room *ghúrfa fádia*
single room *ghúrfa munfárida*
double room *ghúrfa muzdáwija*
hot water *mái súkhna*
bathroom, toilet *hammám, tuwalét*
shower *dúsh*
towel *bashkír*
How much does the room cost per night? *Adáysh al ghúrfa al láyl?*

GENERAL

A History of the Arab Peoples, by Albert Hourani. A landmark history of the Arabs by the 20th-century doyen of Middle Eastern studies. It spent several months on the US bestseller list.

Heart-Beguiling Araby – The English Romance with Arabia, by Kathryn Tidrick. A fascinating account of orientalist obsession in the 19th century.

Jordan: A Hashemite Legacy, by Beverly Milton-Edwards, Peter Hinchcliffe. An informative introduction and analysis of Jordan for the non-specialist reader.

Jordan: Living in the Crossfire, by Alan George. A look at daily life in Jordan, based on interviews with a wide range of Jordanians.

Jordan: Federal Research Study and Country Profile with comprehensive information, history and analysis (2017), by the U.S. Government, Library of Congress.

ART AND ARCHAEOLOGY

Al Kutba Jordan Guide Series, in English and French on: Petra, Wadi Rum and Al-'aqabah; and in English only on Jarash, the Desert Castles, Amman, Umm qays, Pella, Um al-jimal, Ma'daba and Jabal nibu, Al-karak and Shawbak, and the King's Highway. Written by experts but in an engaging and easy style.

The Antiquities Of Jordan, by G. Lankester Harding.

The Art of Jordan – Treasures from an Ancient Land, by Piotr Bienkowski (ed.)

Gerasa and the Decapolis: A "Virtual Island" in Northwest Jordan, by David Kennedy.

Jarash and the Decapolis, by Ian Browning.

Petra and the Lost Kingdom of the Nabateans, by Jane Taylor. Coffee-table book outlining the history of Petra, illustrated with lovely photographs.

ARTS AND CRAFTS

The Art of Jordan: Treasures from an Ancient Land, by Piotr Bienkowski (ed). An historical overview of Jordan's main art forms from pottery and mosaic-making to traditional costume and jewellery-making.

The Crafts of Jordan, by Meg Abu Hamdan.

Palestinian Costume, by Jehan Rajab. A look at the fashions of townsfolk, villagers and nomads since 1900.

Palestinian Embroidery, by Shelagh Weir and Serene Shahid.

Traditional Palestinian Embroidery and Jewellery, by Abed Al Samih Abu Omar. In a mixture of Arabic and English, this definitive work is illustrated with pictures of the different ensembles actually being worn.

BIOGRAPHY AND AUTOBIOGRAPHY

Glubb Pasha: A Biography, by James Lunt. A sympathetic account of the life of the British commander of the Arab Legion, by one of the officers who served under him.

Glubb Pasha: The Life and Times of Sir John Bagot Glubb, by Trevor Royle. An engaging and entertaining read.

Hussein of Jordan: A Political Biography, by James Lunt. Biography of the King. Sympathetic and very readable.

King Abdullah, Britain and the Making of Jordan, by Mary C. Wilson. A scholarly book covering the period from the founding of the Emirate to the assassination of King Abdullah. Wilson's book looks more closely at the controversy surrounding King Hussein's grandfather than does Kamal Salibi.

Lawrence of Arabia: The Authorised Biography of T. E. Lawrence, by Jeremy Wilson. The definitive account of Lawrence's life.

Leap of Faith: Memoirs of an Unexpected Life, by Queen Noor. Readable and inspiring account of Noor's extraordinary life, from her American origins as Lisa Halaby to her long-lasting marriage to the late King Hussein.

Memoirs of King Abdullah of Transjordan, by H.M. King Abdullah of Jordan. The Emir's (and later King's) account of Jordan's very early days.

A Soldier with the Arabs, by Sir John Bagot Glubb. Autobiography of the British commander. A good read which gives Glubb's perspective on Jordan.

Story of a City: A Childhood in Amman, by Abd al-Rahman Munif. Tales of life in Amman in the 1940s, as the city progressed from a placid backwater to a modern metropolis at the eye of the Arab-Israeli conflict.

Uneasy Lies the Head: An Auto-biography, by King Hussein. Particularly interesting about the King's early life. The King also wrote his account of the run-up to the 1967 war in *My War with Israel*.

For French-readers, a later autobiography is *Mon Métier de Roi*, published in 1975, in which the King brings the story up to and beyond Black September. Surprisingly, this book is not currently available in English.

CULTURE/SOCIOLOGY

Bedouin: Nomads of the Desert, by Alan Keohane. Though covering Bedouin from across the Middle East, the book is a fascinating, well-researched and well-illustrated insight into the Bedu people.

Nine Parts of Desire: The Hidden World of Islamic Women, by Geraldine Brooks. Meticulously researched book on the lives of Middle Eastern women in all walks of life, by an American journalist.

Voices: The Pioneering Spirit of Women in Jordan, by Jacky Sawalha. A collection of interviews (recounted in the third person) from a wide range of "pioneering" Jordanian women from a tribal sheikh and cabinet minister, to dental surgeon and headmistress.

FICTION

Arab Folktales, by Inea Bushnaq. A delightful insight into popular Arab wisdom.

Blood Brothers, by Elias Chacour. The effort of a Palestinian in Israel to bring about reconciliation between Arabs and Jews.

Nisanit, by Fadia Faqir. The harrowing story of a young Palestinian refugee woman living in Jordan who falls in love with a Palestinian guerrilla in the West Bank. Running parallel to the story is that of her boyfriend and his experiences at the hands of an Israeli torturer.

Pillars of Salt, by Fadia Faqir. The unsettling twin tales of Maha, a Bedouin woman, and Um Sa'd, an Ammani woman, who meet in Fuhays Mental Hospital after being labelled "insane" by the intransigent, patriarchal and often abusive societies they have grown up in.

Sweetest Night, by Mounis al Razzaz. A leading figure in Jordan's literary scene until his death in 2002, this was Mounis' last (and satirical) take on his homeland.

HISTORY

The Crusades Through Arab Eyes, by Amin Maalouf. Another modern historical classic and a fascinating and revealing insight into the story of the Crusades – told as it should be.

A History of Jordan, by Philip Robins. An excellent recent history, which also covers the initial reign of King Abdullah II.

The History of the Middle East, by Peter Mansfield. Another classic, though much more readable than most and a useful introduction for the lay person.

Jordan in Transition: From Hussein to Abdullah, by Curtis R. Ryan. A concise and insightful analysis of Jordan's recent past and the challenges posed by continual change.

The Modern History of Jordan, by Kamal Salibi. The best history of Jordan, by one of the most eminent historians in the Middle East. Very readable and informative. Cheaper in Jordan.

The Nabataeans: Builders of Petra, by Dan Gibson. An excellent and comprehensive (if slightly academically in tone) introduction to these fascinating ancient people. A great guide to Petra.

Nomads and Settlers in Syria and Jordan, 1800–1980, by Norman Lewis. A fascinating look at the land and people of the area. Scholarly, but also a good read by the man who introduced the concept of a "frontier of settlement" to describe the region.

MIDDLE EASTERN COOKING

The Complete Middle Eastern Cookbook, by Tess Mallos. Illustrated and divided into country/regional sections.

A New Book of Middle Eastern Food, by Claudia Roden. Unique for its culinary history of the region.

RELIGIOUS

A Brief Guide to Islam: History, Faith and Politics: The Complete Introduction, by Paul Grieve. Though not particularly brief, the book is comprehensive, informative and engaging. **The Dead Sea Scrolls Deception**, by Michael Baigent and Richard Leigh. A fascinating account of the controversy surrounding the ancient scrolls discovered in caves by the Dead Sea in the late 1940s. **Who was Jesus? Conspiracy in Jerusalem**, by Kamal Salibi. Thought-provoking look at the mysteries surrounding Jesus' life.

⊙ Send Us Your Thoughts

We do our best to ensure the information in our books is as accurate and up-to-date as possible. The books are updated on a regular basis using local contacts, who painstakingly add, amend and correct as required. However, some details (such as telephone numbers and opening times) are liable to change, and we are ultimately reliant on our readers to put us in the picture.

We welcome your feedback, especially your experience of using the book "on the road". Maybe we recommended a hotel that you liked (or another that you didn't), or you came across a great bar or new attraction we missed.

We will acknowledge all contributions, and we'll offer an Insight Guide to the best letters received.

Please write to us at:
Insight Guides
PO Box 7910
London SE1 1WE
Or email us at:
hello@insightguides.com

TRAVEL LITERATURE

Dead Sea And the Jordan, by Henry Tristram. Historic book by 19th-century clergyman and Darwinist about his discoveries in Jordan.

Famous Travellers to the Holy Land, by Linda Osband. Ranges from William Makepeace Thackeray to Gertrude Bell and Mark Twain.

Married to a Bedouin, by Marguerite van Geldermalsen. A Dutch traveller's account of her life with a man from the Bduul tribe who she fell in love with on a visit to Jordan.

Live from Jordan: letters home from my journey through the Middle East, by Benjamin Orbach. Pittsburgh native Benjamin Orbach travels to the Middle East on the eve of the US invasion of Iraq.

Seven Pillars of Wisdom, by T. E. Lawrence. The controversial but epic, gripping and lyrically written account of Laurence's two years spent with Arabs fighters during the Arab Revolt in 1916.

Travels in Syria and the Holy Land, by J. L. Burckhardt. Another classic describing the journeys of the 19th-century Swiss traveller who famously rediscovered Petra.

WILDLIFE AND NATURE

The Birds of the Hashemite Kingdom of Jordan, by Ian J. Andrews. Comprehensive summary of all 374 bird species recorded in Jordan.

The Camel, by Robert Irwin. A well-researched and delightful new history of the camel and the roles it has played in society right up to the present.

Field Guide to Jordan, by Jarir M'ani. Though currently only available in Jordan, this excellent fieldguide is well worth seeking out. The RSCN shops and many large hotels stock it.

Jordan (Wadi Rum) Climbs and Treks, by Tony Howard. A must-read for any travellers keen on serious hiking, trekking or climbing. Further books by the same author and Di Taylor include "Walks, Treks, Caves, Climbs and Canyons in Al Ayoun Jordan".

CREDITS

INSIGHT GUIDE CREDITS

Distribution
UK, Ireland and Europe
Apa Publications (UK) Ltd;
sales@insightguides.com
United States and Canada
Ingram Publisher Services;
ips@ingramcontent.com
Australia and New Zealand
Woodslane; info@woodslane.com.au
Southeast Asia
Apa Publications (SN) Pte;
singaporeoffice@insightguides.com
Worldwide
Apa Publications (UK) Ltd;
sales@insightguides.com
Special Sales, Content Licensing and CoPublishing
Insight Guides can be purchased in bulk quantities at discounted prices. We can create special editions, personalised jackets and corporate imprints tailored to your needs.
sales@insightguides.com
www.insightguides.biz

Printed in China by CTPS

Editor: Helen Fanthorpe
Authors: Frances Linzee Gordon and Rowlinson Carter
Updater: Jaroslaw Anczewski
Head of Production: Rebeka Davies
Update Production: Apa Digital
Picture Editor: Tom Smyth
Cartography: original cartography Berndtson & Berndtson, updated by Carte

First Edition 1994
Seventh Edition 2018

CONTRIBUTORS

This new edition of *Insight Guide Jordan* was commissioned by **Helen Fanthorpe**, and copyedited by her and **Sîan Marsh**. It was updated by **Jaroslaw Anczewski**. The book builds on the success of earlier editions, the last of which was overhauled by **Frances Linzee Gordon**. Smitten with travel since winning a scholarship to Venice aged 17, Frances writes and photographs for magazines, newspapers and guidebooks, presents and consults for TV and radio and lectures on travel and countries.

The text of writers who contributed to previous editions include **Rowlinson Carter** who wrote the majority of the history chapters, **Paul Lalor**, **Rami Khouri**, **Jane Taylo**, **Alison McQuitty** and **Mariam Shahin**. Also **Chris Bradley**, **Amy Henderson**, **Floresca Karanasou**, **Rebecca Salti**, **Peter Vine**, **Roger Williams** and **Ian Andrews**.

This book was proofread by **Darren Longley** and indexed by **Penny Phenix**.

ABOUT INSIGHT GUIDES

Insight Guides have more than 45 years' experience of publishing high-quality, visual travel guides. We produce 400 full-colour titles, in both print and digital form, covering more than 200 destinations across the globe, in a variety of formats to meet your different needs.

Insight Guides are written by local authors, whose expertise is evident in the extensive historical and cultural background features. Each destination is carefully researched by regional experts to ensure our guides provide the very latest information. All the reviews in **Insight Guides** are independent; we strive to maintain an impartial view. Our reviews are carefully selected to guide you to the best places to eat, go out and shop, so you can be confident that when we say a place is special, we really mean it.

INDEX

MAIN REFERENCES ARE IN BOLD TYPE

INSIGHT ● GUIDES

OFF THE SHELF

Since 1970, INSIGHT GUIDES has provided a unique perspective on the world's best travel destinations by using specially commissioned photography and illuminating text written by local authors.

Whether you're planning a city break, a walking tour or the journey of a lifetime, our superb range of guidebooks and phrasebooks will inspire you to discover more about your chosen destination.

INSIGHT GUIDES

offer a unique combination of stunning photos, absorbing narrative and detailed maps, providing all the inspiration and information you need.

PHRASEBOOKS & DICTIONARIES

help users to feel at home, when away. Pocket-sized with a free app to download, they go where you do.

CITY GUIDES

pack hundreds of great photos into a smaller format with detailed practical information, so you can navigate the world's top cities with confidence.

EXPLORE GUIDES

feature easy-to-follow walks and itineraries in the world's most exciting destinations, with our choice of the best places to eat and drink along the way.

POCKET GUIDES

combine concise information on where to go and what to do in a handy compact format, ideal on the ground. Includes a full-colour, fold-out map.

EXPERIENCE GUIDES

feature offbeat perspectives and secret gems for experienced travellers, with a collection of over 100 ideas for a memorable stay in a city.

www.insightguides.com